It was the best of times, it was the worst of times, it was the age of wisdom, it was the age of foolishness, it was the epoch of belief, it was the epoch of incredulity, it was the season of Light, it was the season of Darkness, it was the spring of hope, it was the winter of despair, we had everything before us, we had nothing before us, . . . Charles Dickens — A Tale of Two Cities

LUDWIG BEMELMANS

the best of times

AN ACCOUNT OF EUROPE REVISITED, WITH 50 COLOR
AND 110 BLACK ILLUSTRATIONS BY THE AUTHOR

SIMON AND SCHUSTER ~ NEW YORK

I wish to say "thank you" to the editors of Holiday Magazine, without whose generosity of mind and pocket this book would not have been possible.

After the most casual arrangements and without writing anything down on a contract form or even the back of a menu, I left, virtually from the table of the restaurant at which Ted Patrick suggested the voyage. I traveled wherever I would have gone had I been on my own holiday. I stayed everywhere as long as I liked. I wrote of and made pictures of what I thought would interest the people back home, who found travel just now impossible or inconvenient. The co-operation of the magazine with the publishers of this book has helped to make these surely the very best of times.

All in all, no one could have asked for greater considerations. I have endeavored to hand the freedom given me over to the pages that follow.

HÔTEL FRANCE ET CHOISEUL   L. B.
PARIS

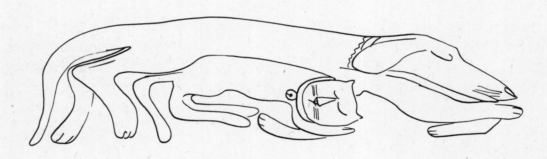

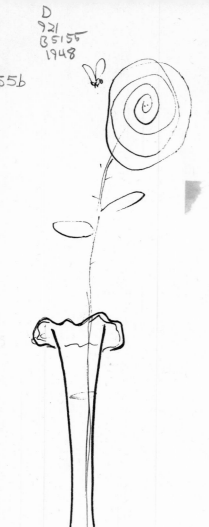

Foreword

I SET OUT *to write a happy book. The mood was somber, then as it is now, but I disagreed with the opinion that was screamed at us from the radio and the front pages, that this was "the last chance of civilization."*

I had, and have, too much faith in people to lean in that direction. I don't believe there is such a thing as a "bad people." There are in my opinion only misguided people and rotten governments. The average citizen of any country—and that includes the Russians and the Germans—is a decent person and wants a decent life for himself and for his children. My faith is in the plain people, in what is badly called the "little man," the small bourgeoisie. I am convinced at the end of this voyage that I am right.

I wanted to go then and report the patient's recovery—of which I was, and am, certain. I wanted to stop wherever the flame of hope burned, and write of it, and even wherever the smallest flower of happiness grew, bend down to it, and carefully note its design and color.

However, outside the crystal-lit salons of palace hotels, and a few choice fun places to which the various travel agencies and tourist offices pointed with eager fingers, and here and there an out-of-the-way place that was untouched, there was little gaiety. One would have had to travel blindfolded in the dark stretches that lay between. The original plan, then, was changed, and the reader must be warned that in spite of its gay pictures this did not turn out to be an altogether happy book. Most of the little flowers that I found barely held their heads above water, and the flame was frequently only a flicker in the window of a building whose foundations trembled. Man had fallen into the zeros, and he was at the mercy of politicians and bureaucrats, of whom his world is deadly sick.

One of them has said: "People don't completely collapse, they go on living anyway."

And that is as true as it is terrifying. You see them, those that don't completely collapse, in every place, and every one of them has a face just like yours and mine. He drags himself along with the same hopes and thoughts. He shelters, under his tattered cloak, the stump of a candle whose wick is still a hope for light. But for that fact, and if it were not for men like Marshall, one might join in the philosophy of the two benevolent, motherly ladies who played in Arsenic and Old Lace, *and help to hurry them on to that most democratic institution, in which room is reserved for all of us.*

PARIS 1948   L. B.

Table of Contents

Color Illustrations

Würzburger
Boxbeutel

Come fly with me

THE ORDERLY TRAVELER who presents himself at train gates, piers and airfields in good time is always the drab citizen who arrives in haste and with the expression of worry that properly belongs to the late-comer. The elegant voyager is the last to arrive and always calm.

At the marine terminal, at the end of La Guardia Field from which the planes for Paris take off, a group of the early-bird category of passengers left the doors of their taxis open in the rush of arrival. They were there an hour ahead of time as the airline had requested of them. They disarranged their clothing as they frisked themselves, searching for passports and tickets, and when they had located the papers they dutifully handed them to a uniformed, athletic young man who had held out his hand in bored and silent expectancy and checked their names against a typewritten list which was attached to a small board on the counter before him.

He handed the papers back to them and then busied himself with weighing the baggage. The travelers calmed down and wiped their faces and the more curious among them examined a gigantic WPA-type mural which fringes the rotunda of the

terminal and shows the history of man's flight. Under that part of this work of art, in which the over-life-size figure of Icarus takes to wings, stood a jovial fat man who announced that the plane for Paris would not leave on time. He pointed at the door over which PARIS was lettered; the fog beyond this door was so thick that it seemed as if bolts of gray and brown flannel were being unrolled out on the field.

The Constellation, said the man, might take off around noon, if the sun broke through. The beast of time stretches itself nowhere with slower motions than at an airport. The early passengers kept looking hopefully through the windows. The soup outside stirred occasionally and it lit up briefly as if strong white lamps were played on it, but with hopeless regularity the light went away and it turned gray and brown again.

The fat man and the uniformed youth mopped their lips with paper napkins and put down their coffee cups a while later, and the echoes of the gay laughter of the hostess, who had served them at a counter under the scene at Kittyhawk, changed to the gay high notes of Frenchwomen's voices. Two

busloads of the Sisters of Charity of St. Vincent de Paul, in bulging, sky-blue skirts and on solid, clattering shoes, moved across the floor and their wide starched hats seemed like the wings of seagulls flying toward the door to Paris.

The fat man took up his post again under the spread-eagle figure of Icarus and waited until his companion had checked the papers and tickets of two Mothers Superior of the charitable order who were flying home to France. Keeping his right hand in the coat pocket of his pale blue pin-striped suit, in a position of elaborate nonchalance, the master of ceremonies pointed to the befogged door again and made the second of the many announcements he had to make that day.

He spoke melodiously and in well-prepared public-relations phrases, lifting the end of each sentence with a small laugh. He said his piece with that peculiar mixture of authority and jest with which Robert Benchley entertained his audience. After the announcement of the delay and after the nuns had looked through the door at the fog he pointed to the coffee counter and said that, until the Constellation would take off, refreshments were served, and with suavity and the Benchley smile he added, "*Avec les compliments de* TWA." The wings of their hats turned and fluttered to the coffee counter, the nuns smiled, while the fat man wiped his face and turned to make the next announcement to the largest group of passengers, who had arrived aboard one of the long, funereal limousines with which the airlines take their clients to and from the airfields.

A while after this contingent had been processed, a minute ahead of the scheduled take-off, but calm and collected, there arrived the last group, with smart, efficient luggage, dressed in the most costly travel simplicity and rich with mink, sable coats and a chinchilla cape.

The world air terminal is designed for quick dispatch and there is no proper waiting room. Seating is limited to a set of marble-and-wood benches, decoratively spaced and arranged in a circle. The rest of the passengers stood about and only the nuns had gone out and sat in their two buses. Around noontime the master of ceremonies lifted both his hands and, when everybody stood before him, he announced that the passengers would be served luncheon over at the regular airport restaurant. After luncheon there was again an announcement, this time to the effect that we would all be taken to Newark and depart from there, because in Jersey there was a higher ceiling and the conditions were more favorable for the Constellation. The young man checked everyone into cars, and the nuns in their buses followed the cavalcade over the Fifty-ninth Street bridge and through the Lincoln Tunnel to the Newark airport, which was visible at a distance of five hundred yards. Our friend and announcer in the blue suit was there again. Around five he collected his group and, leading them across the high-

way, invited them to another meal, *avec les compliments de* TWA, and right after that, he promised, we would take off for Paris.

Opposite the air terminal, in the center of an expanse of blackish parking gravel that smelled of crude oil in the oppressive heat of the Jersey meadows, stands a small tavern with a banging door, a juke box and booths with metal chairs and plastic table tops.

The daily menu is mimeographed in violet ink on half a sheet of paper which is stapled to a grease-stained, orange-colored folder on which the specialties of the house appear in print. The food was on the company, but as a drink was ordered the waiter said, "All right, give me the fifty-five cents and I'll take care of it." Seated in a booth to one side, six of the Sisters of Charity stared through the lenses of their gold-rimmed glasses silently down at their hands as the juke-box voices sang "Prisoner of Love," "They Say It's Wonderful" and "Doing What Comes Naturally." The younger of the nuns had wisely been left outside, sitting in a bus.

After the coffee, half of which was in the saucers, the passengers walked up and down on the gravel and then wandered to the airport. The jovial master of ceremonies waved his arms again and said with relief that we were about to go aboard the plane.

It was a little before seven. There was the last formality of filling out baggage declarations and as everybody did, so the two Sisters of Charity certified on printed forms that their ancient and bulging black valises did not contain more than three firearms or five hundred rounds of ammunition.

The long, sleek silver bird stood waiting on the field. The passengers passed the young man who checked them off on his list, and walked up the ramp and into the Constellation's cabin. The fat man wiped his face and smiled with relief as the ship slowly turned on its vertical axis. One of the nuns filmed the farewell scene and the others waved until the blast of the four propellers tore into the white wings on their hats.

After that very brief, exciting moment at the take-off—that is as if a vibrator were pressed to the base of the skull—after the motor's thunder lifted the ship from the earth, this polished, racy instrument soared up through the layer of heavy clouds smoother and faster than I have ever experienced it.

One of the nuns filmed the farewell scene

The Constellation was in the blue sky, her cabin filled with bright, early afternoon light for which it had seemed much too late a few minutes ago; the cabin was filled with cool air and everything was as neat and efficient as it had been slow and muddled below. Leaning back in a seat as comfortable as a hammock, the passenger could contemplate that, while he can fly at fabulous speeds, it has taken him three months to get a passport, two weeks to get a visa, and ten hours to get from Queens to Newark.

The man in the seat next to me should have been made to pay excess baggage for his stomach. He introduced himself as a Swiss citizen, an aeronautical engineer and a consultant on international air traffic. He started most of his phrases with the words "I would recommend."

"I would recommend," he said somewhere over Connecticut, "to a young man, to marry one of these." He nodded in the direction of the plane's hostess. "In fact," he continued, "if I would not be already married, that is the kind I would marry, that is the only kind of American woman I would

marry." He smiled at the passing hostess and told her that he felt a draft on his feet. "Watch," he said, "immediately she will bring a blanket and tuck me in. Also a pillow if I want one. She will later on carry forty-and-some trays of food, giving one each to a passenger and later collect them again, all without any fuss. She will bring you magazines, chewing gum, anything you want and with a smile. She will always have a polite answer, never argue; she's besides a trained nurse, besides not bad-looking."

The hostess did everything the Swiss consultant said she would do, and occasionally found time to kneel on one knee in the aisle and talk to a passenger. She also stopped at my neighbor's chair. He leaned down and told her a joke and she laughed. "Besides a sense of humor," he said, "very rare with American women."

Smoothly as she had taken off, the Constellation landed at Gander, Newfoundland, taxied up to the terminal, and was grounded there, because that afternoon a sister ship had crashed in flames, killing five of her crew.

The flying public is a game and loyal crowd. Every one of the passengers aboard this ship wanted to continue in her despite the disaster, and deplored the order of the authorities.

One of the Mothers Superior asked whether the captain could not proceed on his own authority if all the passengers agreed to go on. But the plane sat there in the icy night. It shone like a newly peeled onion, and the passengers looked at her sadly as they were carted in a worn-out, unheated bus to the airlines hotel.

The establishment that feeds transient passengers, as well as those who are delayed by unfavorable weather and such mishaps as befell the Constellation, is a barracks of wooden construction that was, until recently, dedicated to the entertainment of troops stationed there. The décor of the restaurant consists of faded green window curtains, the size of a bartender's apron, tied back with package string, and of thirty-four artificial roses, one of which leans out of a water glass in the center of each table.

The menu is about the same as was offered at the Newark Airport; the service is rendered with great willingness by very young and friendly girls with the complexion of children who come running into a warm room after having thrown snowballs outside. Next to the restaurant are the washrooms.

The toilet facilities are those of the military, this spirit being supported by signs on the wall. To hang up your clothes there is a row of sixpenny nails hammered into the side of a partition. At times these quarters were so crowded that three men stood, one in back of the other, trying to shave at the same time within the frames of four small mirrors nailed to the wall.

Connected by a corridor with the dining room is a second hall of the same character as the restaurant. In one corner of this a bearded Maharajah had that night barricaded himself, his sad-eyed, bespectacled small daughter, a companion and a nurse, behind great amounts of airplane luggage. At the opposite end of the room, on half a dozen stained and disemboweled couches whose dirty cotton stuffing sagged through cuts and torn arms, civilians and soldiers lay sleeping face down to shut out the glaring light. On a bar that served rum and coke and also a mediocre gin, leaned a few fair-faced air-force boys listening to the stories which a Negro fighter told of his white manager, who lay collapsed and open-mouthed on two chairs. There were three parsons, a rabbi and his assistant, some home-coming sailors, and our two Mothers Superior, who were joined by two nuns of the same order who, returning to America, had also been grounded in their plane.

Overtired children cried, and some slept, leaning

on their mothers. Again there were not enough seats. Everybody sat or leaned against the walls of this hall, because it was the only warm refuge in Gander. The place of our master of ceremonies at La Guardia had been taken by a harassed local youth with wild black hair that stood off to one side of his head as if he were wearing a dry sponge on his head. He did his best, but he seemed to be hiding and afraid of his passengers. He lifted the padded shoulders of his poorly fitting old suit when he was cornered, he had no information, and there were soon rumors to the effect that army planes would come and take us back to New York; that we would be delayed in Gander several days; and frequently another to the effect that the grounding order was lifted and that we would be on our way to Paris in half an hour. A notice was finally tacked to a bulletin board, but it read:

REWARD

For very valuable ring, lost by passing Archbishop who returned from canonization of Mother Cabrini in Rome.

In the corner opposite the one occupied by the Maharajah and his group, under an extract of the fishing and game laws of Newfoundland framed and attached to the wall, there is a stack of free literature that proclaims the attractions of this part of the world and is published by Imperial Oil, Limited. In this corner is also a draft, sharp like a cut inflicted by a thin-bladed knife, from the bottom of a window.

A wooden armchair, of such massive construction that no one can move it to a warmer place in the room, stands there unoccupied. In this I sat down and the confinement became more and more breezy as I read that here is the home of the hardy Newfoundland dog, that the rivers are packed with salmon which can be taken from May first to September first, and that in the short months of summer the natives dry cod on the roofs of their houses, except on rainy days, when they collect same and carry them inside their habitations. Not far away is Labrador, with whaling waters and the even more hardy Labrador retriever. I was reading about icebergs when the passengers were called together and informed that, as soon as houses were heated for them, they could go to bed.

An hour later, two of the Sisters of Charity—enveloped, by the kindness of the elegant passengers, in a sable coat and a chinchilla cape—were led by the backward-walking guide to a shack on which was still lettered STRICTLY OFF LIMITS FOR ALL MALE PERSONNEL. The young man returned with the coats to ferry the other two nuns to their barracks. The sky was green, the stars shone like rhinestones in a theater, the land beyond was visible for miles and looked like the waters of the ocean. The guide's sponge hair, the fir trees, and every blade of grass were leaning under the weight of the wind and the young man's ears were as red as the crimson patches on his Mackinaw. The only comfortable creatures in this scene were a mother Newfound-

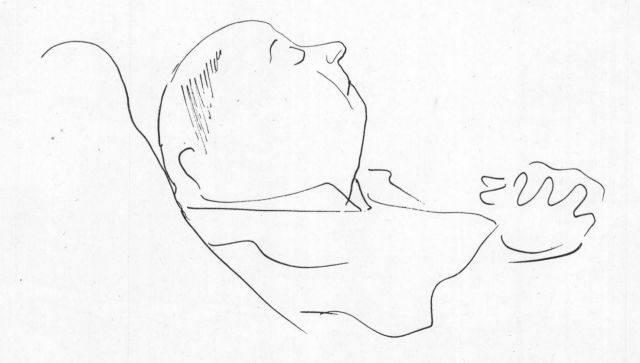

GANDER
New foundland

land dog and her pup. They stood in the street and looked like the models for a Thurber drawing.

The Swiss consultant occupied the lower of a double tier of army bunks, and after I had used the chair that was the only other piece of furniture in the room to climb into the upper, a fellow passenger from a chairless room came in and borrowed it to climb into his own bed.

Toward four in the morning of the second night spent in these accommodations, the light was turned on and the frightened, tired young man announced a plane was ready on the field and would take off in half an hour for Paris.

As at La Guardia Field, the drab passengers were again the first in the dining room. The elegant ones were tired and only the nuns neat and fresh, enjoying the advantage of their costume. The ruddy girls had been replaced on that shift by pale night waiters, the orange juice was canned, but the bacon and eggs, the rolls and hot coffee were excellent. The voyagers were warm inside and cold outside in the bus that took them back to the plane, and then warm and comfortable all over in the seats of the new plane, which was somewhat slower than the Constellation.

The Swiss, seated again at my side, asked for a pillow, and a hostess of precisely the same allure and efficiency as the first brought it for him. After the take-off into the dawn, the passengers all fell asleep until they felt the touch of a hand and, sitting up, found a plastic tray with various recesses placed on their laps. There was a dish containing an Irish stew, a saucer on which reposed a yellow cling peach, several small radishes, sugar in an envelope and coffee in a tubular container, also plastic.

The Swiss ate and then he said, "I recommend to throw out the tray, and throw out the pantry. This," he said, "is like for an invalid, and who cares about the free meal—the people who travel by air can buy themselves a meal." He took out an envelope and made designs. "Throw out the pantry and make a lounge—a bar—where people can talk and forget time," he said, "and a place where people can stand up and look at the view. We are," he continued, "still pioneering, and before the luxury liner gets back into service, I would recommend some changes.

"We want a plane faster than the Constellation, we want a quick flight in any weather to a place like Gander, only with a first-class restaurant and a bar there; and then a quick flight across and the next meal in Paris. I would recommend bigger windows, and to do something for the man with the seat on the aisle. Why does everybody have to face forward and look for the whole trip at the back of the man's head in front of him, or at the ceiling? When the boats are back we will be up against the pleasure of the midnight sailing, the comfortable room and bath, the morning walk around the deck, the floating night club, the swimming pool, and the unrestricted amount of luggage you can take along, besides the dog you can take along. Besides, coffee from a plastic cup on your lap doesn't taste like coffee."

The stewardess collected the forty trays and the Swiss folded his hands over his stomach. He dozed into a guttural nightmare, and I reached for the gadget which provides ventilation and turned it so that it blew cold air in his face until he turned his head out toward the aisle. He slept until the small Irish fields of varicolored green slid under the wing and the plane landed in Shannon.

In the lounge of the airport restaurant sat a complete cast of Irish characters. The Isle's neutrality was still fiercely proclaimed by an interpreter on whose jacket was embroidered *Ich spreche Deutsch*. A good meal was served and afterward, on the last lap of the journey, the people who occupied the seats on the aisle leaned over those at the windows and strained their necks to look at the scenes below.

The flight ended in darkness, the sky over Paris disturbed by frequent lightning, but there was no discomfort. The plane landed at Orly without any sagging or wobbling motion. In a most courteous passport examination, a personable agent of the po-

lice asked people to fill out information desired by the French Government. With his hands folded in back of him, he walked about like a professor in his schoolroom and, looking over people's shoulders, he helped, or corrected the papers, or just said, "Oh, how nicely you are doing that!" A well-timed bolt of lightning and downpour of rain put out the lights in the customs shed at the moment I opened the bag that contained all the contraband, and it passed without high duty.

There was no trace of war damage as the bus went from Orly into Paris. Miraculously preserved from fury, the silver and golden roofs glowed; the majestic perspectives of velvety black and gray stone, the horizon framed in old trees, the arches, fountains, and the lampposts with their peculiar green

27

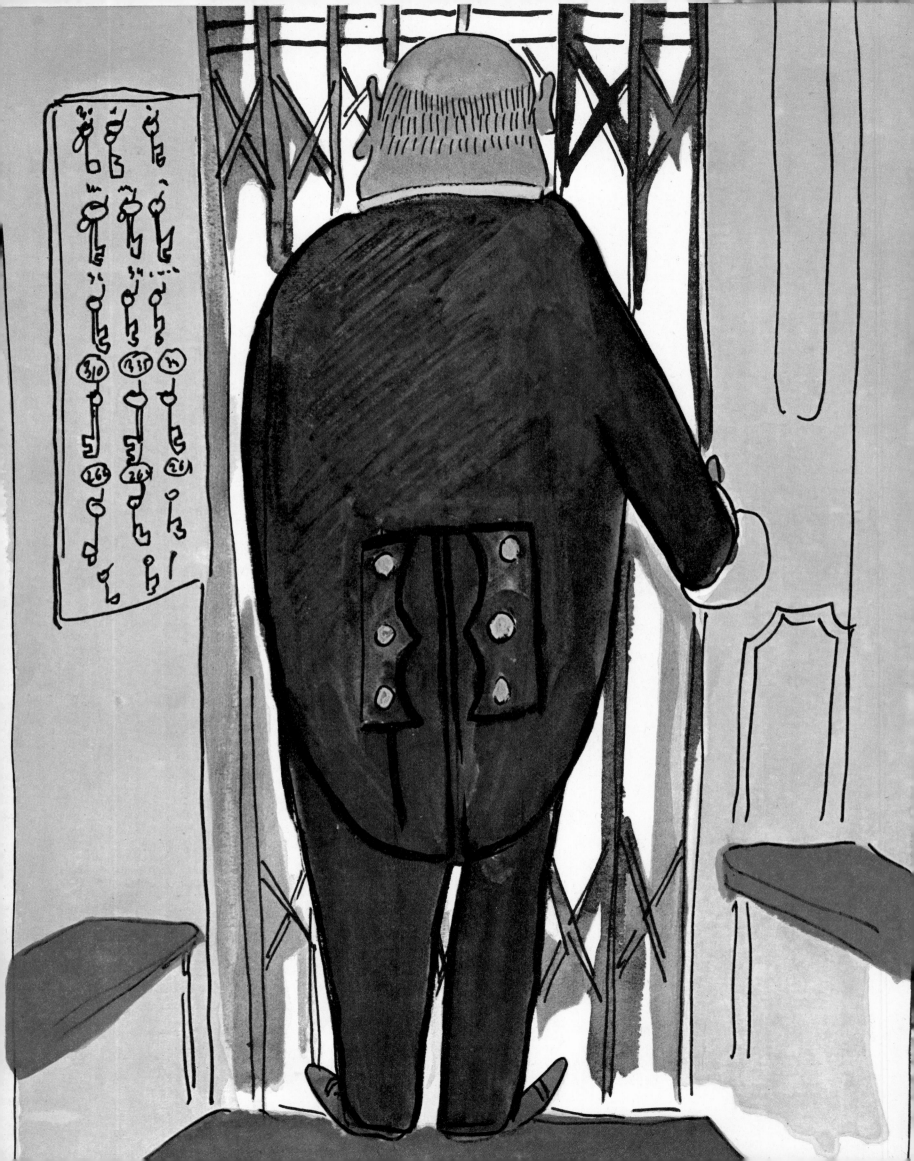

light, all welcome you back. The nuns pressed their faces to the windows as the bus swung through the Place de la Concorde, which was deserted but for one policeman and a bicyclist.

The first fact that came to my attention the next day was that, of all people, the proprietors of luxury hotels, of the best restaurants and night clubs, weathered the war and political upheaval better than anyone else. Their faces are the least lined; they and their headwaiters and wine butlers are of the same weight, humor, and philosophy as they were before.

The pleasures they dispense render these high priests of the good life and friends of the stomach immune to the persecution and the disasters that befall the ordinary citizen.

One of the most esteemed clients of the Paris Ritz before the war was Miss Barbara Hutton. She left to make room for Herr General von Brauchitsch, who appreciated a well-laid table also, celebrated his conquest with goose-liver paste and truffles, and discussed wines in the language of the fancier and expert. After he packed, the silver was polished again, the same pans went over the fire and the corks popped once more, now in celebration of the departure of the Herr General. And when the broken glass and the confetti of that glorious fiesta were swept up and the barracks air cleared from the rooms, the old suite

was made ready again for Miss Hutton. *Bonjour, mademoiselle*. *Guten Tag*, Herr General Brauchitsch. Welcome, General Eisenhower. *Bonjour, mademoiselle*.

In a white-and-gold, small temple of gastronomy whose blue-ribbon chef is also its proprietor, and who now carves his black-market hams and fine meats with his old skill, I was shown the table where Göring munched his caviar and smiled down at the quail and the other game of which he was so fond. "He sat over there," said the famous cook, pointing with his carving knife. "He brought his own provisions; we had everything we wanted. He made the iceboxes burst with Persian caviar, Polish geese, wild boar, Westphalian hams — everything he brought along. Enough to feed a whole battalion."

I asked him whether the Field Marshal ever became interested in his views or political opinions, or what he thought about the Wehrmacht and the Third Reich. "*Ah, non, alors*," said the cook, who is as portly still as Göring was in his Paris days. "*Ah, non, monsieur*, he was not so crazy as all that! Here in my restaurant he sat where I placed him, he spoke low, and the conversation was limited to praise of the cooking. And when he left he thanked me nicely."

Later on he said, "Now I remember—one of them touched on the subject, once. One of them, a Gen-

eral, once asked me what I thought of their efficiency, because, a few hours after they had marched in, the truck with provisions was at the back door of my establishment and also an adjutant at the front door who made the reservations and discussed the preferences of the High Command and arranged the menu.

"I told the General that I found it remarkable. Nothing wrong in that. I did not give praise, I only called it *remarquable*.

"The General said that in the last few months they had taken several capitals and everything had gone like clockwork. His aide-de-camp always reported to him an hour or so ahead of time, and he would say:

" 'Excellency, we are occupying So-and-so, according to plan, at exactly ten minutes past eleven,' or whatever time they had arranged to occupy the place. The aide would continue, 'We shall enter the city through this or that avenue, and over this route, and Your Excellency's quarters are rooms number so-and-so at the Hotel So-and-so.'

"The General said, 'When we got there, not a minute late, I always found the rooms ready and my luggage there.' The General laughed then, and turning to another officer, he said smiling, 'You know what I am afraid of? I have a nightmarish fear that one day we shall take another capital, and my aide will come and tell me at what hotel I am staying and the numbers of my rooms, and when we get there the rooms will not be ready. And that, my friend, will be the disastrous moment after which the entire magnificent and minute organization of the Reichswehr will collapse.'

"They clicked their glasses then and laughed," said the cook, who was stirring the sauce for a lobster in a little pan over an alcohol lamp. "But you know, that is almost the way it happened," he continued. "They failed to reserve rooms at the Savoy in London, the Metropole in Moscow, and the Waldorf-Astoria in New York."

The first thing the American who comes back to Paris has to get used to again is the service. The guest is always addressed in the third person, food is served as in a religious ceremony, and of the man who runs the elevator at the Ritz I have only seen the back view. He must see me long before I see him, and most probably in a set of obliquely arranged mirrors. He precedes me into the cage of the lift. The top of his head is salmon-colored and fringed with neatly brushed hair, like a friar's. Each strand of the hair seems to have been sewn into his scalp carefully spaced from the next. The back of his collar is spotless, the shoulders of his plum-colored tunic free of dandruff or dust. He works the controls standing at attention, and as the elevator rises he reaches for the room key which hangs on a board attached to the left wall of the cage. He knows the guest's name and the room number and he knows on what hook the key is. He doesn't have to turn to look, and after he stops on your floor he hands the key to you, bowing deeply and whispering:

"*Merci, monsieur.*"

He remains in the position of the humble servitor as you pass down the corridor, whispering, "*Bonsoir, monsieur.*"

Sometime I hope to see his face.

No. 13 Rue St. Augustin

MY ONCE FRAGILE and nervous Paris underworld friend Georges thrived on the Germans while they occupied his city.

He says loudly, and with pride, that by operating alone and unofficially, he dispatched more of them to hospitals than he could possibly have put there had France allowed him to put on a uniform and shoulder a musket.

He has become respectable. The once thorny individual and hard hunter, who walked fast, on thin soles, constantly looking in back of him, who watched the reflection of the street in the shop windows that darkness turned into mirrors, now saunters along with a cane and in the center of the street.

The decay is evident also in the loudness of his talk, the steady look in his eye, in his genuine pearl stickpin, and the general air of martial bourgeoisie that he exhibits in his clothes.

"The house is Number Thirteen, Rue St. Augustin"

There are others now, who freeze and sweat on his behalf, and move along the walls of the houses, looking back. You find them along the Faubourg St. Honoré, the Rues Royale and Castiglioni, and two of them share in the business of the Place Vendôme.

The contacts they make are ushered into a floating office that is located today in this bistro and tomorrow in that. The grand advantage of this arrangement is that there is no office rent and that it complicates matters for the gendarmes. For in the back room of the bistro the dollar is exchanged at a rate more realistic than that officially paid.

This service is supplemented by a kind of traveler's aid. The amateur, newly arrived in Paris and looking for amusements, is not left to his own helpless fumbling, but is taken by the hand and properly guided.

An ever-widening circle of grateful and steady clients testifies to the reputation of the enterprise and the sound principles on which it is run.

Georges has come by his eminence after a slow, grim battle, up from sleeping in caves with *clochards* and under bridges, up from the narrow cots of the mean and hungry girls of the Boulevard Sébastopol, and from horse steak and the hard plotting of complicated games of confidence.

"It won't be grand and noble company," he said to me on a Thursday afternoon, holding his hand over the mouthpiece of the telephone.

"I warn you that one will stay long at table, and the food will be so-so, because they are not *eingerichtet* for that kind of entertaining." Georges had learned German during the war and occasionally used words like "*eingerichtet*," which means furnished, or equipped.

"The wine I can vouch for," he continued. "But

there will be *heulen und Zähneknirschen,* which means howling and gnashing of teeth, because this is the sad day on which this establishment, which is one of the oldest and most reputable in Paris, will be closed by law. I must explain to you what happened," said Georges. "For the first time in history the women of France vote, and their deputy is one Marthe Richard. The first proposition she offered was a vote on the abolition of establishments such as Numéro Treize, and every woman in France, except the keepers of such houses and the inmates thereof, voted to close them. The women voted one hundred per cent, naturally. I can promise you that it will be interesting."

He took his hand away from the mouthpiece and asked Mademoiselle Geneviève if he could bring a friend, and with metallic sharpness her voice recorded through the room as from a trumpet: "*Mais venez donc, avec votre ami, mais ça nous fait treize à table.*"

"I hope you attach no importance to numbers," said Georges. "The house is Number Thirteen, Rue St. Augustin, and there will be thirteen at the table. You may, however, if this upsets you, stop trembling, because we are invited to this little family celebration by Mademoiselle Geneviève, and her patron

saint, Ste. Geneviève, is, as you perhaps know, the protector of Paris."

After a very short ride from the Hôtel de France et Choiseul, the taxi stopped, not in an obscure and somber alley or in a hypocritically genteel location. but in the center of a busy thoroughfare lined by respectable shops and businesses, all located in solid houses. There was no hidden entrance: the door of Number Thirteen, with the number boldly lettered on it, was heavy and oaken, carved, and had immense polished brass knobs for handles. It was still light, and the street was filled with people. Part of Number Thirteen was occupied by a firm that sold filing equipment, and the brunette young women in black who stood there waiting for customers looked at us without any kind of expression on their faces other than that with which people look out into a street in which nothing of particular interest happens. While we waited for the bell to be answered, there were also women who came out of a grocery store, and children who seemed to belong in the street. While it is a curious feeling to stand and wait outside an establishment of the reputation of Numéro Treize and wait a long while to be let in, it seemed to bother nobody. We were not even taken notice of.

No. 13 Rue St. Augustin

The foyer was furnished with a blue Oriental rug, stained-window background, and a table on which stood an artificial palm. There was a seascape, two matching Japanese silk screens, and at the foot of the stairs, looking upward and holding a cluster of light fixtures above her head, was a more than life-size marble statue of a nude woman of the degree of artistry and voluptuousness of the one that stands in a similar place and pose at the exclusive Travellers' Club on the Avenue des Champs Elysées. This latter statue, however, has been worn away in places by the hold the older members take on her as they support themselves mounting to the upper rooms.

"We wait here for the signal to go up," said Georges. While waiting I opened the stained-glass door beyond which there was the usual Parisian courtyard, with light like that in a good studio. Two of the walls in this yard were lined with six rows of empty champagne bottles stacked eight feet high, the longer wall made up of quart bottles, the side wall of pint sizes—all of the Veuve Clicquot. Opposite the pint bottles was a curious French toilet. There hung dozens of towels to dry and bed linen, and from a window even with the ground came the warm vapor smell of a laundry. Warm soap-water smell is rare now in Paris.

"Here is where you formerly left your hat and coat," said Georges, indicating a small *garde-robe*, when I had returned from my inspection of the courtyard.

"And you waited for the signal to go up. I don't see the need for that any more," he said. So we climbed the stairs to the first floor, where in a second foyer, as elaborate as a Fifth Avenue shoe salon, we were received by the Gouvernante of the house. I did not hear her name as I was being introduced because her face and person accosted me with an old and shocking familiarity, and later, all the while I was being presented to several other ladies, I sought to place the Gouvernante.

The ladies present on that evening seemed to have been singled out for this honor by the length of their service and their loyalty to the house. The Gouvernante, as she is called, who wore the same costume as the rest, is comparable to the sergeant of an infantry company in her closeness to her charges and absolute authority over them. The dresses they wore were of the kind of couture in which the ladies' or-chestra indulge—cloth cut from the same bolt of old-rose satin with a pattern like that of hardwood paneling woven into it. It was somewhat faded and soiled. From much undoing and putting on, the hooks and eyes were strained along the opening under the arm down to the waist, where the dresses were especially stained and worn, as in the case of the ladies' orchestra, where the costumes are stain-streaked on the side of the violinist's fiddling arm, and ravaged also at the knees where the instrument is gripped by the cellist.

With a gracious smile, and holding a welty arm and pudgy, rosy hand in the direction of a small salon, the Gouvernante asked me to enter and, with a lion tamer's look, turned to the ladies, who thereupon turned around and made excuses, saying that they would busy themselves with the last preparations for the dinner.

The Gouvernante, sitting on the edge of a tufted satin chair, under an obscene painting, started a polite conversation with me. She sat erect and directly opposite me, and looked down on the carpet while arranging some ribbons that were embedded in the yellow lace on her collar. Her body was a puffy sack that seemed filled with small objects of rounded and oval shapes. She had pulled up the wide skirt showing two upside-down-bottle-shaped legs crossed, and broad feet in discolored satin slippers modestly half-hidden in the tassels that hung from the bottom of the chair. She later brought her hands down from the lace and placed them one above the other, palms up in her lap, and kept on talking and sweetly smiling. The wrist watch which she wore on a black, silken cordlike strap was like a string tied about a sausage, and the whole arrangement, with the exception of the painting in back of her, closely resembled a pose in the atelier of a photographer thirty years ago.

As I looked at this scene a bizarre emotion came suddenly upon me, a condition of the mind that rides

As the bus swung through the Place de la Concorde

along with fevers and gives you a reverse clairvoyance which you lack when well—you see sharply as into a long black box, back into your life; and as if on the most marvelous and clearest stereopticon slides, forgotten scenes appear and live afresh, while at the same time the person you look at, the table before you, and the chair on which you sit, are only half there.

The scene that had come back and lit up was from my childhood in Regensburg. Among the people I knew then was a distant relative, a Fräulein Käthchen, who visited us every week, and sat often in our

garden, mostly in a blue satin dress, with snow-white lace on her sleeves and throat, or white ribbons tied in a bow on an institutional collar. She looked like Renoir's paintings of sweet young women. She walked through the city with upraised head, and would smile at me. I was happy when she visited us and spent an evening embroidering or playing the piano.

Sweet Käthchen worked as a receptionist and retoucher for a photographer, an artistic individual who wore a beard and Bohème cravat, and embossed all the portraits he took with the golden coats of

36

arms of the King of Bavaria and the Duke of Thurn and Taxis, whom he had also photographed, and was therefore privileged to add the word "Hofphotograph" to the shield of his firm on his visiting cards and letterheads. It was hoped in Regensburg that he would marry Käthchen and make her the Frau Hofphotográphin. He was the city's best photographer, and Käthchen was envied until the day it was discovered that the Hofphotograph had taken pictures of women in the nude. Although he swore that he had done his evil posing on Sundays, behind locked doors, and that he had never taken any pictures of Käthchen, that she had never retouched any of the Sunday pictures and had no idea of their existence, it was all over. The ribbons and white lace and the beauty of her face were of no avail. Poor Käthchen was dropped by the ladies of Regensburg—no one asked her any more to eat napoleons and drink chocolate with whipped cream at the Schürnbrandt Konditorei on the Neupfarrplatz, which is the Café de la Paix of Regensburg. Poor Käthchen soon disappeared.

After this excursion into the past my mind came back to the room in which I sat opposite the Gouvernante of Numéro Treize. The only meaning I got from the last of many words that she had spoken while I was away was that it was about the closing of the house, and I observed that her French was weighted down with German inflection and mispronunciation.

I answered, "*Ja, es ist schrecklich.*" I was certain by then that before me, as the Gouvernante of Numéro Treize in soiled lace and satin, sat poor Käthchen. She looked past me to another obscene still life and said, "*Ja, furchtbar ist es—*" and with the expression of one recently bereaved, she added, "*Entschuldigen sie bitte,*" and ran out of the room to greet a new arrival. She stood out there, surrounded by the ladies of the house, who were wiping their hands on the towels they had tied around themselves to protect their satin costumes, and smiled down the stairs. It was all exactly the same in shape, color, and light as Toulouse-Lautrec has painted it—vile, warm, and sad. I have always thought that to partake of the offerings in such places is to do the most painful and desperate act of charity there is. "Only the Senator is missing," said the Gouvernante, "and then we will sit down."

I walked out into the stair hall. The bell rang after a while, and there was below again a scene as in a photographer's studio. The man who was referred to as the "Senator" arrived. He was in black with a high stiff collar, a very flat derby, the thin ends of long white mustaches sticking out left and right beyond his cheeks. He had very long legs which he employed in the fashion of a crab, lifting them extraordinarily high as if they were feelers. He put his arm around the waist of the nude and began to mount the steps, after for a moment having held his cane and hat in vain in the direction of the small room at the foot of the stairs where he usually was relieved of them. He entered the salon with that expression of the acceptance of the unavoidable which was already on everybody's face.

The soup was on the table in a room to which two maids had opened the mirrored doors. It was decorated in the monotonous aphrodisiac school of the rest of the house. My mood was further bent when Georges, after bringing Käthchen's pudgy hand to his lips, said that after endless apprenticeship and ardent devotion in this and other establishments, by application and hard work Käthchen had risen to her present position of importance, and that he, for one, would see to it that she would not suffer by the

change of things. The Gouvernante thanked him and put her hands around Georges. She motioned to the door and said that Mademoiselle Geneviève wanted everyone to sit down and not let the soup get cold, and that she would be with us presently.

I reached for the chair that was indicated to me and stood between the places of the Patronne of the house, Mademoiselle Geneviève, and that of the Gouvernante. The Senator had the place of honor at the head of the table.

"To put at ease any who suffer from superstition," said Käthchen, "the thirteenth we have invited will not come—it is Marthe Richard."

A voice rich in contempt, of low register and carrying through the corridor into the dining room, repeated the name "Marthe Richard," and a second after as the guests arose, Mademoiselle Geneviève entered the room, circled the table, and then sat down.

Mademoiselle Geneviève tilted her head and attached an enormous pendant of antique design to her left perforated earlobe. She then unfolded her napkin and looked serenely and with authority over the table.

A servant poured Bâtard Montrachet from a magnum bottle, the conversation was fit for the ears of the Pope, and the manners and small pleasantries of handing around the bread and smiling across the table were as frequent as are only those of the small bourgeoisie when invited out.

I forgot how good or bad the Poulet Grandmère was on that evening: there was too much to observe. I was brought back when, with a push of her arm and a nod, because her mouth was full and she could not speak, Käthchen offered me the use of the small extra plate on which she was depositing her bones.

After the chocolate soufflé and the coffee, Napoleon inhalers were half filled with brandy. The Senator dipped one end of his napkin carefully into the crystal bowl that held the flowers, and then wiped his mustache and that part of his beard that was under his lips. He slapped himself on the chest and stood up, glass in hand, facing Mademoiselle Geneviève.

He lifted his glass and started to speak. He reviewed the history of the house, and also that of France and mankind. He went back to Paradise and Adam and Eve, and returned to the world at the time of the end of the First World War. His speech was too long to report in full but passages from it deserve to be rescued:

"We French," he said, "are the only nation who have had the courage to recognize life and deal with it without hypocrisy and to the benefit of everyone.

"We are ridiculed for our humanity, and our own government now bows its head to political expedience and rewards those who have paid heavy taxes with expropriation—and such as our beloved Mademoiselle Geneviève, who have served it well and beyond the call of duty, are rewarded with threats of imprisonment.

"Does anyone in the government remember, for example, Mademoiselle Geneviève came to the aid of the Republic after the last war, when on the occasion of the glorious visit of the distinguished foreign statesmen, she took upon herself the delicate task of arranging some quiet diversions for those men who were so beloved and honored!"

"*Oh, ils étaient charmants!*" said Käthchen.

"*Des vrais amis de la France—*" broke in one of the ladies.

"*C'était épatant,*" said Mademoiselle Geneviève.

"That, of course, is something the world has forgotten about—just as they have forgotten what you did for the Allies in this war, Geneviève," said the Senator, looking at Mademoiselle.

"I did not do it with any thought of reward," said that one, and looked sadly into the flowers.

He came to the end after that, saying, "While everything sank all about us in scenes of infinite desolation, *cette fée merveilleuse*"— he lifted his glass and everybody stood up—"made it possible for

us to find in this sequestered retreat some consolation, and lifted from us, for golden hours, the dreadful burden that life had become.

"Marthe Richard, who is responsible for this—Marthe Richard, opportunist, swindler, collaborator, and a woman so conveniently forgetful of her own beginnings—what does she hope to accomplish in her small time? *Révolutionner le monde?* Bah—!"

Amidst violent headshaking and murmuring from the people seated at the table, the Senator sat down and waited for the applause to end. Then he got up once more and recited:

Dans le gazon d'Avril où nous irons courir,
Est-ce que les oiseaux se cachent pour mourir?

Mademoiselle Geneviève looked at me with interest while she kept turning one of the three rings on the ring finger of her left hand, exactly as my mother did before she asked someone an important question or said something of great consequence.

She said finally, "*Non,* they won't hide, neither will they die, nor will the ladies who have consecrated themselves to this *affaire* enter into a convent. It has been orderly up to now and properly regulated, and, as the Senator said, everyone has been benefited thereby. We had a philosophy about it. But from now on everyone will suffer. It can easily become vicious."

A maid passed a box of exquisite long cigars from which Mademoiselle Geneviève took one and lit it, holding it away from herself, watching the flame while slowly turning the cigar.

"I take the distant view," said Mademoiselle Geneviève, and asked me about America. "You had a problem somewhat like this one in America—you had *La Prohibition* for a while?"

"Yes, it lasted several years."

"Did it work?"

"No, it did not work."

"It never works to forbid pleasure to people. And is it not true that many Americans who did not drink

before Prohibition started to drink just because it was forbidden, and that the cost of drinking doubled?"

"That is right."

"*Alors,*" she said, looking through the smoke of the cigar, with half-closed eyes. "*Alors,* it is then perhaps not the catastrophe we think it is. We are now stunned and lying helpless on our backs like flies that have been swatted, but that will change—it all may be for the best—it may turn into a really big thing—if intelligently done."

The Senator took Mademoiselle Geneviève by the arm and made her comfortable in the small salon under the obscene painting. There was a tour of the *maison* under the guidance of poor Käthchen.

"How strange to find all the doors, otherwise tightly shut, open," said Georges in the corridor. Inside the rooms the beds had been dismantled; here and there a mattress, worn as the dresses of the ensemble, was leaning against a wall sagging like someone hard hit in the stomach.

"The excuse for taking even our house from us," said Käthchen, "is that people need homes. *Alors,* this is going to make a fine nursery, *par exemple!*" she said, pointing into a room that was decorated with a frieze showing the intimate acrobatics of satyrs and wood nymphs. This décor was repeated with Egyptian, Moorish, and Parisian personnel in the other apartments. There was always a large mirror on the ceiling, and some of the de-luxe suites had mosaic decorations in the baths, and one—the most ornate—offered a miniature swimming pool and Roman couch between its pillars.

On the first floor there was a small theater. The salon in which we had eaten was where the ladies of the house were usually presented to the clients. This was equipped, for those who were considerate, bashful, or had a desire for anonymity, with a single-view, plate-glass pane, the size of a shop window, which was mirrorlike on the side of the ladies, in which they could see themselves pose, while the buyer sat on the other side, nodding his approval, pointing at this or that one, or saying "Thank you."

Protected by this device, which is usually employed to observe the behavior of babies and children in various institutions dedicated to research, the selection was made in the comfort of deeply upholstered *fauteuils*, with champagne and without embarrassment to either the ladies of the house or to the client.

"This mirrored glass pane, whose name is Argus, which was made in America, has cost us a fortune. We shall take it with us," said Käthchen, after she had turned off all the various trick lighting effects that were controlled from behind the marvelous mirror. We examined a mild kind of torture chamber and a lacy, virginal bedroom.

"You have seen it all," said the Gouvernante.

The Senator was out on the staircase, as we came down, with his hat, cane, and coat.

"But you're not going?" said Käthchen.

"Ah, no—" he said, and went downstairs followed by one of the maids. He left the house—and a second later as everybody upstairs watched, he rang the bell outside and came in the door again. He handed his things to the maid, who now stood in the *garde-robe*, and he waited for the signal.

"*On peut monter?*" piped the maid, and falling immediately into her role, Käthchen upstairs sang out, "*Le passage est libre—on peut monter,*" meaning "The passage is free, one may come up." That is the way people are asked to come upstairs, so that their identity remains protected.

To this trumpet call and signal to advance, the old carcass below trembled, and the bug legs took the steps two at a time.

The ladies, who had been honored with attending this last night, received the Senator with tears and led him into the salon. Their soiled costumes shone in the amber light, there was laughter and dancing.

Mademoiselle Geneviève stood with a handkerchief pressed to her eyes.

"*Ah, les enfants préfèrent toujours le jeu à l'étude,*" she said. "Children always prefer play to study."

A few weeks later after a long ride in a sleigh, I was back in Tyrol and sat with my back against the big oven in my mother's three-hundred-year-old house.

She smoked her after-dinner cigar, and I thought it was a good moment to ask her. I said—"Mother, whatever became of poor Käthchen?"

My mother turned the center one of the three rings she wore on the ring finger of her left hand slowly, and then looked at the white ash of the Ramon Allones I had brought her from America. She held it away from herself and blew the smoke toward the paneled ceiling into which the former pious owners of the house had set an azure medallion showing the Holy Ghost. She half closed her eyes, and said,

"Poor Käthchen! After that terrible scandal she left Regensburg, and she married another photographer, who also turned out to be no good. She moved to Dresden, and now she lives in what is left of it in the Russian Zone."

"She couldn't possibly be in Paris?" I asked.

"Oh, no, somebody heard from her only a week ago. You must send her a little fat when you get back to America."

Back again in Paris

As I walked quietly down the Rue Royale on my first day in Paris, a New York fashion photographer let out one of those enthusiastic screams with which women of her group recognize people in foreign cities. Before she had spoken a word to me, she abruptly turned to her assistant, a man who proclaimed his total indifference to fashion in his own costume, and was loaded down with cameras, bags, and paraphernalia like a glacier tourist.

In bad French, but with great efforts at pronunciation and accents, she sent him ahead, saying, "Auguste, run along and set up the camera. We're going to do the Empire nightie in summer gold first and then the school-girl navy-velours coat."

The slave turned without emotion and slunk away, and she blew the little veil from her nose and arranged it on top of a square bowler. She waved a box-coat sleeve the color of mountain fir out toward the Place de la Concorde. "Oh," she said, "to be back in Paris. Isn't it wonderful? Isn't it just too divine? I don't know what everybody is screaming about. I'm having such a gay time. And, you know, everybody is here, and it's just as it was, only much nicer. And the French—don't you love them? Just think of it, Monsieur *et* Madame Lamourplaye——"

Again she took pains with the name as if she were in school. "Monsieur *et* Madame Lamourplaye, who

took care of my little flat all during the war, were standing there waiting with tears in their eyes, welcoming me, just as if they had stood there since I left. Now who in hell would do that for you in America? Of course, they all have stories. Oh, what stories they have! Everybody has a story, and that gets a little tiresome after a while. And then there is a small extra charge for this and that, but you can't blame the poor darlings, after what they've been through. And then they talk of nothing but the black market where they have to go to buy anything they really want. Well, good-by."

She was gone with an energetic wave of the hand, marching in a straight line toward her destination.

I met a man whom I knew from New York in the hotel lobby later. This one said, "Let me out of here. I can't wait to get back to the States. They're washed up in Europe. They're thieves, and they hate us and the English, too, and they're a bunch of communists besides. Wherever you go, you're overcharged, everybody holds out their hand. I had some cigars sent to me, registered mail, to my hotel—never arrived. In Switzerland I gave my passport to the French for a visa and they lost it for three days. You have to stand there and hold it in your hand, like so. I've had enough, they're finished. This time they'll never

get back on their feet. Everything is black market. By the way, if you want to eat well, go to So-and-so, near the Madeleine, it's the only place."

He went up to his room to pack.

The line between good and bad is thinner and more wobbly in France than anywhere else in the world, and hard to follow. Consider this set of circumstances as they unrolled the next day when, near the Arc de Triomphe, I remembered the address of the black-market restaurant and looked for a taxi.

The taxi, a small maroon-colored Renault, stood alone in the center of the avenue where taxis wait. I walked over, and before I got in the driver turned and said gruffly, "One moment—in what direction are you going?"

I told him.

"Oh, no," he said, "I cannot take you. That is not my direction. I am about to turn in. I have very little gas left. If you were going the other way, that is, in my direction, I would gladly take you."

I said, "I will give you a good tip."

"*Ah, alors,*" he said. "What do you consider a good tip?"

I said, "Double the fare."

He climbed out of his cab. He was an old and corpulent man, and he said, "Well, then, we must first see, we shall examine the tank to find out how much *essence* we actually have."

He pulled a dirty wooden ruler from under the seat and walked to the back of the car and stuck it down into the tank, and as he pulled it out again he said, with feigned surprise, "I am almost certain that we shall arrive at our destination, monsieur. Please to enter the car."

He drove at a furious speed to the restaurant and there thanked me in several elegant phrases. The fare for the considerable distance was half of what it would have been in New York and quite in line with the prices of other things.

The black market operates openly. The prices are published in newspapers along with those of the controlled market, and outside the black market restaurant, whose door is wide open, stands a smiling doorman who waves you in. From the street you can see the people eating and through the door you can enjoy the view of a buffet spread with delicacies. The one that is near the Madeleine is crowded for lunch and dinner, and usually you have to wait a little while for a table even if you reserve it. A girl takes your hat and disappears down a stairway to the basement, where the washrooms are.

I don't know what nationality they were; I can tell most languages by the sound, but the "good-by" that the two men whose table I got shouted to a friend seated farther back went, "Shgib, Shgib, Goomy." If either of them had come from my Balkan tailor in New York to call for a suit, I would have gone through the pockets once more before handing it to him.

"From the peace conference," said the headwaiter as he seated me, meaning the two departing delegates.

LE FOUQUET'S

A bottle of
Pouilly
Frcs. 250

Homard à l'Americaine Frcs 283.—

There is no bill of fare. The headwaiter recites the menu to you, first the various things to start with, like smoked salmon, caviar, goose-liver paste and things in oil and vinegar. Then he makes a pause and tells you about the soups, the fish and the lobsters and langoustes. Then he puts that down on his block and asks you about the next course, the meats, the game, the chicken, duck, or goose, and when he has the order—and he will not be happy if you just take one dish—he calls the wine steward, who rattles off his beautiful litany of vintages with half-closed eyes. Then you sit back, and butter is brought, and bread, and a napkin unfolded in your lap, and you can look around.

There was that day a woman at the table opposite me, a treasured and spoiled client to whose table the headwaiter regularly returned like a mother bird to the nest of its young. You have seen her before. You have been pushed by her in an elevator at Saks Fifth Avenue. You've seen her in Buenos Aires or Palm Beach, and listened to her complaints about the service in the best restaurants of New York or Beverly Hills.

She's ancient, formidable, and grim, but she knows the good life and never stops chewing like a rabbit. You try to guess at her nationality but you can't decide. She's international and eternal. An assistant headwaiter was carving a chicken for her then, while she still munched whatever she had had before, and the wine waiter half filled her glass, watching her face, and then smiled as she nodded under the big hat which wobbled in assent. She tapped the glass with a fingernail as a signal to pour more wine into it. She had eaten the breast of the bird after it had simmered over an alcohol lamp in a sauce for a while. She worked with a knife and fork, and then took the wing joints in her fingers and nibbled at them, and as a concession to elegance she stuck the two little fingers away from her hands as she chewed. She wiped the grease from her mouth after that and sat still again, and, after the headwaiter had bowed down to her and she had ordered the dessert, a box in which six peaches lay bedded in soft cotton was brought. While the assistant headwaiter, who had carved her chicken, was busy cutting up my duck, a younger man occupied himself with the peaches. The process was as adroit as the work of a precision machinist. He speared the fruit

The wine waiter half-filled her glass, watching her face

with a slim fork and with a sharp knife he made a small incision in the skin, then quickly he ran the knife around the peach, and neatly placed the skin on a serving plate. She was the while picking her teeth and watching the two processes, alternating from the peach to the mirror of her compact, which she held up with her other hand to look at her teeth.

"Where have you been, Sebastian?" she inquired after looking up at the man.

He put the peach on her plate, and rubbing his hands he said, "I was in Dortmund; I worked for the Boches in an armament factory." He spread out his fingers. "They·are a little rough yet, madame," he said, "but I take care of them and they are rapidly improving." He rubbed his hands nervously again.

She looked up at him the way a fish looks out of the window of an aquarium. For a moment she was afraid he would tell her more of his story. She asked next for a grape, and I said to myself, "What can you do with a grape?"

Sebastian brought a vaselike glass standing in a silver base. It was half filled with water. Then he

45

brought the basket of fruit, and with special silver prongs he lifted a grape and dipped it into the water and slowly moved it up and down, and then placed it on her plate. She had coffee and brandy and eventually left with two purple patches on her cheeks, after the headwaiter had run outside to wake up her chauffeur.

The restaurant was empty. The proprietor and his wife were eating in a corner the same large midday menu as the guests. They were cutting into their filets mignons when at the door there appeared a frail, limping, poorly dressed old woman who carried two plants in her arms. One was a long-stemmed

carnation, the other that plant which seems artificial and is made up of leaves only, with a silvery and green sheen, a dark red border and stubby, silvery hair all over the leaves and stems. She walked to the headwaiter, who said he was sorry. "Look, madame," he explained, pointing to the buffet, which was topped by a bush of large gladioli, "we have all the flowers we need."

She ignored him and walked past him back to the table where the proprietor and his wife sat and ate, and she said, "You know how to live, *hein!* Your table bends under the weight of your elbows. But what about me? I have to live too. Look at me!"

The proprietor's wife stared at the dour visitor and told her to go away, and then she called for the headwaiter, but the proprietor turned his fat face toward her and told her to be quiet. Then he said to the headwaiter, "Buy them, the two pots—one for the house and one for the restaurant."

The little woman left, and then came the man who had the privilege of collecting the cigarette and cigar butts under the tables of the restaurant and, after he had crept around, the coat-room girl came up out of the basement and said, "Can I let them in now?" The proprietor said, "Yes, let them in."

Up the stairs came two small children, their faces gaunt like those of seahorses, and they ran past my table through the restaurant into the kitchen.

"I hope, monsieur," said the headwaiter to me, "that this doesn't disarrange your good mood. These children belong to the extra dishwashing woman whom we had to employ on account of all the new business that came with the peace conference, and these children come here every day. They are not used to it yet, and we keep them downstairs out of the way until the restaurant empties. They are feeding out there now like two small tigers. Only their ears are out of the soup. For them, at least, the conference has been of benefit."

I asked him when he thought that things would return to normal.

"It will be much better," he said, "every year from now on, and if nothing goes wrong, I should say 1950 would be normal."

He said that they would also rather run a normal restaurant. "While one charges high prices, one pays them out, too, and not only to the butcher."

The luncheon was no more than it would be in

any of the good restaurants in New York, say at "21," where soft-shell crabs are three dollars a portion. No bill is presented here. The headwaiter tells you confidentially what you owe.

Parisian restaurants are classified and the menu and the prices are shown on a card that is placed in the window under the letter *A, B, C,* or *D.* There is at the top a restaurant whose designation is "Restaurant of Exceptional Category," and under this heading go places like Fouquet's, the restaurant of the Ritz, the Tour-d'Argent, and others famous before the war. These places one might call gray-market restaurants, for with or without the consent of the government they allow themselves some leeway.

For example, the waiter will ask for your food tickets and not even wait for the answer if your expression shows that you haven't got them. He simply starts to get the bread and butter. The butter in these places is pressed into quarter-sized wafer-thin pats; the price on the menu, 127 francs. Below the table-d'hôte menu is a list of supplementary dishes of which each client is supposed to have but one, but they will serve you the whole list, and here the headwaiter will be unhappy if you order the 127-franc menu. Below are better things, goose-liver paste, and on every menu, every day, lobster *à l'américaine,* superbly cooked in every place, and 250 francs the portion. There are also chicken and duck, but here you get only a quarter of the chicken and a slice of the duck. A fair bottle of wine is 400 francs.

"Headwaiter, tell me, this wine is all right, but what has happened to the famous vintages?"

"Monsieur, that is a sad story. It is sold for export to get the money to pay the loan to the Américains back. What folly! Who ever pays a loan back to the Américains? I cannot get a single bottle of good wine, of kirsch, or Cointreau, all on account of the Américains."

In these places, if you ordered a glass of port or sherry or a Martini made with French gin, which is not bad (Dubonnet is also sent to the "Américains" and not available, nor is Pernod), and after that a melon, a quarter chicken with one vegetable and potatoes, some salad and cheese, or the small forest strawberries without cream, and coffee with one gray piece of sugar ("Do you wish the real coffee, monsieur, or the 'national'?"), and with that a bottle of very drinkable wine, the bill with tax and tip

will come to approximately 850 francs per person.

If you buy the franc at the official rate of exchange, your dollar at present brings you one hundred and twenty. But if you follow the little man who falls in step with you at all the main thoroughfares, the way the sellers of dirty post cards did before the war, and go with him to a near-by bistro, you get two hundred to two hundred and thirty. He takes your money or hands you a fountain pen so that you can countersign your traveler's checks, and at that rate your luncheon at a legal restaurant has cost about four dollars, and that is about as it should be.

In the restaurant of category D, where the tables are without covering, the high music of the French language protects the desperate efforts of the chef. You see placarded in the window, written on a slip of paper:

MENU
Potage Germiny
Sauté de Veau à l'Ancienne
Compote de Pommes

There are no supplementary dishes, the wine is ordinary red or white, the beer thin, and the price of the meal is fifty francs.

Here the owner's problems are simpler. He has a more optimistic outlook.

"Next year, monsieur," he says, "everything will be back to normal. We will have white bread, we will have butter, we will have cream, we will cook again."

This café is on a square and faces the old church of St. Germain

You see an occasional French family with children, of the bourgeois class, meditate over the menu of the restaurant below the class "*Exceptionnelle,*" and the height of their enjoyment is the langouste, which corresponds to our crayfish, but here has less of the taste of iodine than you find in the California and Florida variety. Papa and Mamma get one each, and the children, who have more nourishing things, get the thin tubular legs which in America are thrown away. They break and suck on them with delight.

There are other pleasures in Paris, and the best of them, for me, is the street scene. A good place to watch it is from the small tables of the sidewalk café that is called the Deux Magots. This café is on a square and faces the old church of St. Germain and two rows of old houses. The traffic conditions are very bad in Paris now on account of the lack of automobiles, which allows every driver to go as fast as his machine will go. This causes frequent accidents which, by the grace of God, never seem to call for an ambulance or undertaker but result in great arguments and exhibitions of temper, addresses to bystanders, and back talk to the police. The gendarmes throw back their short blue capes and after licking the points of pencil stubs write essays of several pages on what happened. Expressions such as "Sunday chauffeur" or "head of veal" cut the air, as the participants in this sport point at bicycle wheels bent into the shapes of pretzels and at scratched fenders. The slightest accident holds up all traffic, as nobody pulls over to the side, and the whole thing is enacted exactly in the middle of the street or square where the collision took place. At the end, the policemen, who now are all young, stow their books away, go back to their beats, and resume saluting the citizen who asks for directions, and saluting him again after he has received them, which is a nice habit of the police of Paris.

Here you can also prove that the belief that the Parisienne is elegant and beautiful is as untrue as the idea that the French are especially immoral.

The Parisians have always been good at producing beauty and elegance for others, but they have never done much for themselves. The average Frenchwoman is and always has been drab and comfortable. She disdains the discipline demanded to combat the loss of curves. She has, besides, no time for such exercises as are recommended this month for tired eyes: "Use a strengthening eye lotion, night and morning, preceded by alternate baths of warm and cold water. On waking, let the eyes follow an imaginary fly from corner to corner of ceiling, keeping the head still. Blink, change focus, lay palms over closed eyes and see 'black'." (Advice in a women's magazine bought in a newspaper kiosk.)

The elegant Parisiennes, the ultrasmart group of women who have the great income, the long legs, and the inclination to spend their time following the flight of imaginary flies on the ceilings, or to worry in the shops of dressmakers, were never more than enough to fill the boxes of the Opéra, and today you can place them in one black-market restaurant and have half the tables left for the Americans and English of the same persuasion.

You see people kissing everywhere with the casualness with which women smile at men in other lands and with which the English lift their hats to ladies. It is nice kissing, not the vulgar, pneumatic, and endless embraces projected on the screen. It is a signal of affection rather than the peddling of desire. The man kisses the woman tenderly and lightly on the temples, on the forehead, on the wings of the nose, or with humor on the tip of the nose itself and on the throat. He looks at her afterward with care, and kisses her again, or she returns his declaration. You see couples sitting together at the side of a monument or in the park, holding hands, and while she speaks, he will bend to her shoulder, or she will press her lips to his hand as he talks.

The simplest girls then begin to shine in the rich, proud garment of the loved, and you feel better seeing that this greatest of all gifts is available to women, be they ever so far from the set and brutal pattern of perfection. They walk hand in hand through the park, and the one who would follow them hoping for sly sequestering in a shady grove, or for mischievous poses in an alley, will be disappointed because in all likelihood they will end up at the window of a store, where, sighing, they will look at unattainable household goods and furniture.

The women you see in the street are stocky and most of them have bad legs. The legs are minipiano legs, legs like planks without any modeling, legs with a dumpling of a muscle attached below the knee, and perhaps once an hour a well-turned one passes. Most women wear a black, glossy kind of overall dress; others have combinations of skirts and sweaters that they seem to have taken from the store counters with closed eyes.

It has always been that way. There is an occasional beautiful girl, but she makes nothing of it and doesn't parade her charms, and there are others who have a wild and amorous quality, and parade it without knowing it.

That this hasn't changed is attested by the paintings of Rousseau, Monet, and other Frenchmen. If you judge by the regularity of features that has become the American ideal you will sit unrewarded. But as in the paintings, there is quiet magic in the scene if you look at it with a slow eye and have a desire to like what you see.

There is character and individuality in every human being that passes. The men of France are in general better looking than the women; they have a better life. They lean on girls and kiss them in the middle of the street.

Here and there you meet a man who has been through the worst, and his look is as if he were throwing stones at you.

You see little girls here walking home with a stick of bread in one hand, a small metal container of milk in the other. On them, the legs are thin and long, and they have large dark eyes in pale faces and look like the children of genius.

Misery also appears again in the man who comes to get the cigarette butts under the sidewalk tables. The one at the Deux Magots has a little stick with which he reaches under the cast-iron bases of the tables where the shifting foot of the client may have placed the butt, which today is just long enough not to burn the lips.

That, too, is nothing new. I knew a place in back of Notre Dame before the war where every morning the collectors of stubs opened newspaper packages

It looked like a canvas by Matisse

They fought valiantly with the hose

filled with stubs, and assorted them neatly, and then got the quotations of the day for the various qualities and sizes. They traded then mostly in cigar butts, which now are a great rarity.

One of the happy pictures in the square is the bicycle excursionists. Before the war they went out into the country for their "pique-niques." Now they go for food and a little extra money for their own black market by bringing back an extra pound of butter or some cheese. The baby is in a basket in front of the mother's bike, and the dog is riding along behind the father.

In a small and cozy hotel on the Left Bank where the rooms are one hundred and twenty francs a day, the proprietor told me that he was brightening his hotel for the return of the tourists. He had bought a new carpet on the black market, and he was about to have it placed on the stairs. The carpet consisted of small remnants of the carpets of a very good hotel; the patches were just large enough to cover one step each, and as they were put down, each step had a different color which made the whole very gay.

It looked like a canvas by Matisse, who likes to paint into his pictures violent carpet and wallpaper patterns. The artist that is in all Frenchmen entered into the long tirades between the carpet man, his assistant, and the owner of the hotel, concerning the arrangement of the patterns. Had nobody cared about the effects of the various colors, the work would have taken half as long.

For a while I lived in this hotel, and one day the maid, an otherwise disagreeable woman with the promise of a beard on her chin, brought a small, smelly sack along, and put it on my table as she got ready to clean up. The sack, which was tightly closed at the neck with a piece of rope, she explained, contained her black market, which consisted of forty garlic bulbs, which she had come by after much trouble and a lot of running around.

The bulbs, she said, while cleaning the room, were destined for the child of a widow on the floor above. The maid had many long stories, and I had trained myself to nod and say an occasional *"oui"* or just make a sound, as if I were listening, as she never stopped talking, but the forty garlic bulbs and the little girl were outside her usual recitals, and I listened to what she said that morning.

"What for, so much garlic for a little child?" I asked.

"For the worms," said the maid and proceeded to give me a thorough account of the little threadlike worms with which the child was afflicted.

She talked about the habits of the worms and their size and tenacity. She also said that the mother had tried every doctor and medicine, and that the child had taken pills and treatments of all kinds and still had worms. She put her broom down and came so close that I saw that she also had a mustache, and she said, "All children have worms, and I know, because I had six of them, and this is the only remedy that works. The peasants used it ever since time began and it is very simple.

"Also it is absolute and it causes no discomfort." She started to open the bag and continued, "This is all you do. You boil fifteen of these bulbs of garlic for fifteen minutes in just enough water to give the child, when the bulbs have cooled off sufficiently, an enema. You take another five bulbs of garlic and these you boil also for fifteen minutes. With this second brew you use less water, so that it is good and strong, and you ask the child to swallow four times a day, each time a teaspoonful of it. You do this one

day, then give the child a day's rest, and then repeat the treatment on the third day. You may not want to be too near the child during this time, but, I promise, neither will the worms. They go and they don't come back again." She opened the window and dusted the furniture, and then she took the bag with the treasure of forty bulbs of garlic, and climbed up to the next floor.

The maid later introduced me on the stairs to the afflicted child and her mother, and said that I knew about the treatment and was the father of a child in America who was plagued by worms also.

The garlic bulbs now formed a bond of mutual concern and interest, and the cure was told to me again in detail while the little girl hopped on one foot from the pink piece of carpet of the first step to the blue of the third. The treatment, madame said, was completed and the worms liquidated. It was a great success. It is the frankness with which the French discuss such phenomena and the ills as well as the pleasures of the body which gives them their reputation for immorality.

Another fallacy is the rooted belief that Paris is a woman's town. It is, but again only for the women of the visitors. Frenchwomen work continuously—you see them on their knees scrubbing stone floors with

"For an aesthete," he said, "for an artist, the perfect retreat"

brush and bucket, you see them carrying loads, and pushing or pulling at wagons. They work with the needle and sit long hours in their little shops. I have never seen a woman among the fishermen, who sit all day along the banks of the Seine; and of the comfort stations that are crowded along every thoroughfare, on not one appears a sign saying LADIES.

On one of my walks along the Quai des Grands-Augustins I stopped and took out a piece of paper and sketched one of these curious cast-iron fixtures that are as much a part of the Paris scene as the Eiffel Tower is.

A voice in back of me said, "Ah, monsieur is an artist, and obviously a foreigner, and perhaps interested in a studio to rent, no?"

Since it is as hard to get a place here as it is in New York, I said that I was interested. The man who had spoken took me a few steps down the quay and

walked ahead into an old house. The stairs of this building went upwards in such narrow spirals that going up seemed like standing in place marking time, and gradually losing breath and making five turnabouts, I arrived eventually in a typical Paris garret.

The room was red and the scenery outside also. The sun was low and the place looked as if the late Doctor Petiot had done his butchery on its carpet. The ceiling was so low that the proprietor stood bent over.

"For an aesthete," he said, "for an artist, the perfect retreat, and look at the inspiring view." He pointed out the one window.

"It looks like nothing now, but I have connections, and if we come to an agreement, monsieur, then I shall furnish this studio to your satisfaction. I will build you a little bath there and a small pantry with

53

icebox. The building is being reconditioned, as I have acquired it only three months ago, and therefore the rental laws do not apply."

He mentioned a fantastic rental and set the cost of construction of pantry and bathroom and the furniture at roughly two hundred thousand francs.

Before getting mad about this I thought about a place in New York where, two months before, I had inspected an apartment. This place was also a reconversion job, and there were bricklayers tearing down partitions and installing bathrooms and kitchenette units. The agent of this building offered a two-and-a-half-room apartment with a kitchen unit in one room for $350 a month, and he said that there was furniture which I must buy for $1500 and which I could do with as I wanted. Also he said no children were allowed. The Paris landlord objected to nothing.

Farther up on the bank of the Seine past several other bridges is the ornate Alexander Bridge, and there the next day between the Grand Palais in which the Automobile Show is housed and the Petit Palais in which sculpture and painting are exhibited, the wide avenue was roped off.

A band and many policemen with folded arms stood about. On the terrace of the building at the right, carpets had been placed and, on these, three rows of about fifty chairs each—the front row upholstered in red velvet and with red arm rests. The others, just plain chairs, were gradually filling with government officials and their ladies and children.

There were magnificent uniforms, straw hats with flowers, and top hats, bearded dignitaries and an occasional mumbling in the audience when this or that celebrity arrived. Opposite this tribune and on the sidewalk, also at the roped-off ends of the street, stood a crowd of several thousand Parisians. In the roped-off arena appeared firemen in golden helmets, and the band of the Paris fire fighters began to play. The sun was shining, and the women in the crowd were in light dresses. There were British and American soldiers, French sailors, and the more agile spectators climbed on trees and lampposts, the ledges and window sills of the two palaces, and seated themselves on various stone ornaments and statuary.

The occasion was a competition of various fire departments from communities outside Paris. They had arranged their apparatus along the Seine and, at the signal of a trumpeter, from a given starting point raced into the arena with the peculiar signal of the French fire engines, which is a deep "poohpah, poohpah, poopah," much easier on the ears than our sirens and bells, and as effective.

As each team started, an impartial fire chief of the Department of the Seine, which puts out Parisian fires, and who stood on a small, decorated platform,

announced in ringing tones, "The Company of Sapeurs Pompiers of Orly," or whatever place they came from. The small fire engine then rushed in, the men jumped from it, upon command, assembled in line, properly spacing themselves by bending out one elbow and turning the head to the right until the line was correct. Upon another command they faced forward at attention and saluted the tribune from which they were saluted in turn. Upon still another command they fell into wild activity with their hoses, unrolling them, running this way and that, attaching the hose to the hydrant, and finally, to the applause of the crowd, squirting a thin stream of water into the air.

Back again in Paris

The equipment would have been inadequate for a fire in the metropolis, but it was sufficient protection for the one-story houses of the towns from which the fire fighters had come. The smaller the crew and the car the more enthusiastic was the crowd, which supported every entry with applause and with sympathetic "Ohs" and "Ahs" when the entrants fumbled, ran into each other, or dropped their hose. At the end of each performance when the

hoses were rolled up and stowed away and the fire engine was ready to roll out, the crew assembled again, and with proper commands came to attention, saluted once more, and were saluted in turn by the Parisian fire chief and the burgomaster. After the time they had taken to function was announced, and the next crew had driven into the avenue, they left. There was a great stir and shouts of admiration as the last entry, a shining new vehicle larger than all the others, rolled in. The letters on it read Sa-peurs Pompiers de Versailles.

The firemen jumped from their seats and, after the saluting, attached to the hydrant a new, bright red hose of large circumference. They worked quicker and with smoother action than all the

others. The pump inside the wagon became active. Two men jumped on top of the engine and began moving upward on an automatic extension ladder. Halfway up, one stopped while the other was raised to a height of forty feet.

The crowd applauded, and after the chief of these firemen had given the command, there were several hollow burping sounds, then a liquid explosion at the end of the nozzle, and after that all dignitaries below were soaking wet. Great tumult and name calling followed. The man at the halfway mark of the ladder ran up to help his fellow fireman, with the result that, after a while, they succeeded in directing the stream on the crowd at the other side of the street. They fought valiantly with the hose, and it played by turns on dignitaries and the people until somebody thought of turning off the water. Only the firemen of Versailles were chagrined, wildly gesturing, stamping their feet, and almost crying. They let down their ladder, folded their hoses, and, without assembling in line or being saluted, drove off in shame and disgrace.

The officials shook the water out of their hats and clothes, wiped their faces and beards, the mothers dried the children, and everybody was gay. The crowd had taken over the open space and several girls and boys took each other by the hand and danced.

A girl who walked in the high, wooden platform shoes that are the fashion now, with a hair-do that extended her silhouette to the height of the G. I. she was with, held the little jacket of her dress and wrung the water out of it, and another girl said to her, "Oh, *chérie*, how you worked to make that—and you love blue so much!"

"Doesn't matter," said the other, laughing, and hung it on a bush to dry, and all sat down on the stairs of the palace to wait for the sun to dry their hair and their clothes.

It was that brief while a happy place and the misery forgotten, and if politicians can clean up the messes they have made and are making, then Paris will be the old place again, not only for the tourist whose dreary routine is the Folies Bergère and Chez Florence, but, what is more important, for the French, who haven't much reason to laugh and who detest nobody just now as much as they do themselves.

This is Monsieur Albert of Maxim's in Paris—

The maître of maîtres d'hôtel—

and the unquestioned first Headwaiter of France and perhaps of the world.

He seats the guest of his restaurant with a regard for protocol and politics as stiff as that of the Pope's Chamberlain.

He places a Balkan pretender no higher or lower than his present chances merit, he bows deeply to the Duchess of Windsor and puts Elsa Maxwell where he thinks she belongs, and he remembers those of the French aristocracy who have in the past remembered him.

Imprisoned both by the Germans and by the French, he was always returned quickly to the door of his establishment and in the hazardous years gained seventy pounds. He stared Göring into acquiescence, and today many a gourmet who goes to Maxim's, when offered the card, says: "Why a menu, when Albert is here to order for us?"

Albert has a share of the profits of Maxim's, which is owned by a British syndicate.

Unless you are a confidence man of great resource, a Maharajah, a multimillionaire, or, like the gentleman in this picture, an old and esteemed habitué of the place, it is better to keep away altogether from the chi-chi restaurants of the category marked *Exceptionnelle* just for now, for they are tough on the average citizen even in normal times. First of all, you will most probably commit the cardinal fault of arriving too early, and Monsieur Louis, Luigi, Albert Joseph, Ambrose, or whatever the name of the maître d'hôtel of such an establishment as the *Folie de Grandeur*, which is pictured here, will hold that against you. And although he bows and smiles, his debonair greeting—*"Bonsoir, m'sieur-dame"*— translated properly would be: "Oh, dear—two deadheads."

He will take you for a long walk, on a tour through the whole place, and pilot you to the most remote section, where the few tables that are not decorated with the sign that reads RÉSERVÉ are there at the last outposts of civilization; you are left to contemplate the candlestick, the glasses, and the designs on the ceiling. While you are yet denied the pleasure that is reading a menu, you can smell the cooking through the kitchen door.

You can also fold your hands and listen to the interesting conversations of the waiters who congregate here and discuss De Gaulle, the black market, the Marshall Plan, and the latest scandals. Since their tables are in the good part of the restaurant, none of them see your distress signals, and they don't hear your *psst, garçon,* or any other sounds you make.

When at last the maître d'hôtel decides to come to your table, he will suggest the menu—the food will be good, the portions ample.

The sommelier, or wine waiter, approaches next. He takes care of the drinks. Don't order a Martini anywhere in Paris—they are awful, including at Maxim's.

The champagne costs about seventeen dollars a bottle, and don't look startled if the wine waiter, after having rolled it in ice and with ceremony opened it, pours himself a glass; he is only tasting to see if it is the proper temperature and not corked, or flat.

No matter how addicted you are to nicotine, don't ask for a cigar, even in the very best places. The humidor is in the back pocket of the trousers of the doorman, who has this concession. He will slip you a

Perfecto wrapped in cellophane, with a band around it on which you read "El Triumpho," "Victory," "Clementine," or "Manuel Garcias." It is a weed dry as dust, and it will scrape your throat. In America, if at all, it would sell two for a nickel; here it costs $2.50—straight.

In the other pants pocket he has cigarettes; those you can buy at a dollar and a half for a pack.

is a 15 per cent tip put on the bill, all the hands will expect additional proof of generosity. You hand out then, say, a thousand to the maître d'hôtel, a five hundred to the wine waiter, another five hundred to the waiter, and a thousand to the gypsy fiddler. There is also the girl with the hat, and the old lady with the towel and the soap, and a youth who salutes you as he opens the door, and out-side is one who calls a car, and another who opens the door of it.

You have eaten, and the plates of your dessert are cleared away. All this time the restaurant has slowly filled, there is conversation, and the brandy and wine have done their work. You are comfortable in your corner and contented, you don't hear the slamming of the service door any more, and gradually the lights go down. At your table appears the leader of the orchestra, who asks you for your favorite tune and plays it with virtuosity. He also likes champagne, and the wine waiter puts down an extra glass for him. As the lights go on again, you see that the first bottle is empty and stands upturned in the bucket, but a second one is on the ice. With his hands on the wire that holds the cork, the wine waiter looks into your eyes, and of course you nod. That adds another seventeen bucks.

At last you utter that fatal French word "*l'addi-tion.*" When it comes, you try to focus on the total. At this moment you face a pitiless battery of eyes, which follow every motion of your hand, as you reach for your wallet and bring it to the table, and extract the beautifully printed, easily expendable, pale blue pieces of tissue which the French use for money. Perhaps you have a command of the language and the courage to ask, "*Le service est-il compris?*" which means, "Is the tip included?" to which you get the answer, "Certainly." But although there

At this stage you may not have enough left to pay for the ride to your little hotel (you have been told that it is impossible to get a taxi at this hour, and that this is a special car "of the house" and that the tariff is five dollars), but walking in Paris at night is as nice as in the daytime, and as you pass the little old woman who searches the Place Vendôme for cigarette butts and hear the singing in low bistros, and while you haunt the desk of the American Express Office, waiting for a new remittance, you will discover that all over Paris are simpler restaurants, with good cooking, considerable service, and prices that you can afford.

The result is that with the exception of a very few, in most of the chi-chi places the waiters stand around talking to themselves and each other all night, and it will be that way until sanity returns. There aren't enough silken sheep to shear just now.

It must be said, also, that the organized thievery and mischief inflicted on the customer is not confined to restaurants in Paris—you will find it all over the world in various forms. It is an international game that proprietors and maîtres d'hôtel play with gusto in New York, Hollywood, Rio, Rome, and all over the rest of the world.

Switzerland

There is red and white wine of the most ordinary kind

Switzerland

T HE WANDERLUSTING TOURIST who is refused a passport to Europe by the State Department should be grateful for the time being, not disgruntled. Accommodations in the best classes of European train travel are still grim, and yesterday's pleasure-swaddled traveler today will find himself cold and bruised, rocking over loose rails on uncertain schedules. Only a man recently out of a concentration camp would have described my recent trip on the Arlberg-Orient Express as comfortable. Nevertheless, reading in the Paris papers that the Orient Express had resumed its runs was uplifting to the spirit.

Mention of its magic name recalled a string of shining cars, a fascinating passenger list, and a perfect train crew. Now, the Orient Express is tired and reminds one of a rescued bauble of an old countess. Its only remnants of elegance are the brass letters on the dining car that spell out COMPAGNIE DES WAGONS-LITS ET EXPRESS EUROPÉENS. The letters are green with neglect; the train needs varnish and new round wheels, a new engine, and, for that matter, a new roadbed. That it runs at all is amazing; that it gets as far as Vienna is remarkable testimony to the Frenchman's ability for making broken things work and to his eternal optimism.

To get aboard this train at all you must be lucky, resourceful, patient, and equipped with many papers. To reserve a berth in less than ten days you must be prepared to hand five thousand francs to the *portier* of a de-luxe hotel, or an equally influential official who has a friend at the Gare de l'Est from which, if you are still lucky, the Arlberg-Orient Express leaves daily at 8:50 P.M.

As the spaces between the houses widen and the fields outside Paris appear, you hear the tinkle of a silver bell as the brown-uniformed steward runs through the train announcing dinner. He tears from a pad a small paper with a number on it, and this entitles you to a seat in the dining car for the first or the second sitting.

In the dining car a sheet of paper like newsprint covers the table, and on your plate is a paper napkin of the poorest grade. Service begins only when everybody is seated. A piece of gravel-textured bread is hurriedly put before each passenger, and with it thin soup in a thick, chipped cup which is coated with dishwater film. The plates on which the next course is served, from a large platter, are as filmed as the soup cups. This course is the main dish and consists of a loaflike mass of anonymous meat, reddish in color, tasteless, and fried inside a jacket of tough dough; the whole is lukewarm. With it are mixed flageolets and peas, ladled from a dripping platter which the assistant steward heaves hastily between the diners of the first sitting in his hurry to get to the dessert, which is a pear for each person. There is red and white wine of the most ordinary kind, bad coffee, but tolerable brandy. The charge for the meal is low, and while you drink your brandy, the soup cups for the next sitting are put down in front of you on the paper tablecloths, which are unchanged.

The floors and corridors of all the first-class cars are covered with brown linoleum worn through, here and there, like the sole of an old shoe. Some of these holes are covered with patches nailed down and projecting at the edges so that you frequently trip and tear up a patch with the toe of your shoe.

There is one lesson our railroad people could learn from this train, and that concerns passing from one car to another. I have often struggled with the dual steel doors separating cars on the Twentieth Century Limited and other good American trains. Your arm is limp by the time you get to the dining car, from opening the doors for yourself and holding them for women and children who can't handle them at all. After dinner you get the same exercise going back. On the Orient Express the concertinalike passageways between cars are open, the doors folded back, and you can walk through the whole train with your hands free to steady yourself.

The bedrooms on the train are as limited in space as the boxes in the Paris Opéra, and upholstered in the same material. As you pass them you see the occupants framed, like Byzantine icons, in oppressive colors. There is a beaten little pad of mattress, rough linen, and a hard pillow, and in the corner a washbowl that almost flows over when a man puts both hands in it at the same time. The water runs cold from both faucets, and a little gray towel completes the equipment. The one toilet for both sexes is at the end of the car and is lighted and decorated by an oval, leaded, stained-glass window. It is cold and drafty and badly in need of paint. There is neither soap, towel, nor paper in it. Anywhere in the end of the car on which this compartment is located it is difficult to breathe.

After you have climbed into your bed the train will not let you sleep. It jolts you, throws you against

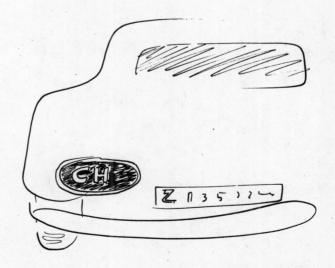

The Arlberg-Orient Express

ST. Moritz
1856 M.ü.d.M.

A battalion of porters, dressed in all styles and colors

the wall, and then rolls you to the edge of the berth. It knocks in one tempo on level ground, changes the beat on upgrades and curves, and all night it is noisy otherwise with activity in the corridor outside your room. You may drop off from exhaustion in the early morning only to be awakened at 5:35 as the train, if it is on time, rolls into Basel, where the Swiss customs examination takes place.

The Swiss are proper and polite, and after going through the train permit it to leave at 6:56. You hear the tinkling of the silver bell of the steward again and go for breakfast to the dining car. There is new good bread on the table and the aroma of fine coffee, for you are now, of course, in Switzerland, where food is more plentiful; but as you sit down, the steward asks you, before taking your order, whether you have Swiss money. I said that I had American traveler's checks and showed them to him, but he shook his head. I told him that I had American dollars and English pounds. He said he was sorry but could not accept them. I told him I would exchange them at any rate he offered. He shook his head again and said he was very sorry; the regulations forbade it.

Unless you have provided yourself with Swiss

francs you get up and go back to your car. Hungry, cold, and in one of the worst moods that bad traveling can provoke, you sit on an unmade bed on a dirty train and look out at the Swiss scenery.

The train rides on smooth rails now, and several of the noises have fallen away. The pretty cows, clean and chewing, look at you; the houses, too, are meticulously clean and so are the citizens. In this landscape there is a lot of electricity humming through the wires stretched over fields and forests, wires suspended from steel-and-concrete towers. All the equipment is solid and costly and better than anywhere else. Trains swish by, going in the opposite direction, or sometimes ride alongside for a while, and then you see occupants from another world, people with contented faces such as you have not seen for years. The clocks on the church steeples and on the many small railroad stations you fly past all tell the correct time.

At 8:25 the train arrived at Zürich-Enge, where I got off. I found a taxi driver who agreed to tip the porter in Swiss francs, and then to drive me to Schweizer Vereinsbank so I could change some money. Next, he drove me to the Hotel Baur-au-Lac,

63

A curious assemblage of people have congregated on this mountain, and you meet them over and over again. You see them as they pass through the village looking at jewelry and wrist watches in shop windows. You meet them on walks in the woods and around the lakes.

The finest specimens are in the halls of the Palace Hotel. They promenade from the great salon, through mirrored doors that are opened by two pages, down into the dining room, where they eat to the music of a four-piece ensemble, and then stagger up again to the salon for coffee and more music. The descent and ascent of the dining-room stairs is the only exercise most of them take.

When the dining room is full you have all the characters needed for musical-comedy plots. At a table next to a window overlooking the entire lake below the hotel sits the young King of Yugoslavia, who looks like a freshman from N.Y.U. and frequently probes his nose. He walks ahead of his Queen as they leave for their coffee table up in the lobby. Near them sits a rich Turk with eyebrows like two furry caterpillars, coffee-colored eyes, and a skin like the hide of a rhinoceros. He wears his overcoat as if it were a bathrobe, and with him are two very exotic oriental beauties. To the left of him is a noted gland doctor. Persons who see him wonder if he has been able to do anything for himself, as he looks like the late Conrad Veidt playing Methuselah. He enters like a sandwich man about to proclaim his wares; parading ahead of him is his wife, bursting with youth and hormones. There is also the former wife of Fritz Thyssen. With her is a man who speaks German with a heavy Russian accent, is registered as an American citizen, and at whose approach the orchestra always plays the French Communist song, "Ma Plaine, Ma Plaine." In a corner, always close together, are a man and wife whom I have seen sitting just so in hotels, restaurants, and on ships all over the world. They are delicate, perfectly matched, weighing about a hundred and ten pounds each, and seem to have stayed the same age for the last twenty years. They are known as the Lovebirds. Wherever they are, they are always together, always quiet, always frequently looking at each other, and always smiling. Mostly they sit in long silences of apparently complete understanding; one, birdlike, surveys the field to the right, and the other, birdlike,

where the clerks said that they would have a room in two weeks. The same was said at the Dolder Grand Hotel, and all the others I drove to. The hotels of Switzerland are as crowded as those of the rest of the world, and the only room vacant that night, found for me by a friend, was at the Palace Hotel in Saint-Moritz, about six hours from Zürich. But Saint-Moritz is reached by excellent trains that arrive and depart on the second hand of the most accurate Swiss chronometers.

A battalion of porters dressed in all styles and colors, from the smart, variously colored uniformed envoys of palatial hotels to the invariably green-aproned porters of informal inns, await the train and relieve you of your luggage worries. Saint-Moritz is the ultimate in thoughtful service to travelers demanding luxury and comfort. Its walks are carefully laid out, the distance to each point of interest noted on tablets. Access to the tennis courts is by an elevator hewn into the rock. The same convenience takes you to the skating rink. Most of the ski runs are so carefully laid out that only an epileptic can come to grief on them. But for the expert there are terrains on which speeds of sixty miles an hour can be made. There are, of course, also the best bone-setters among the resident doctors. Whether you are on deep-piled carpets or skating on the ice, a servant is always at your elbow. The chamber-maid speaks four languages.

surveys the scene at the left; when one sees something interesting, that one moves closer, just like a lovebird on his perch, and whispers, and then both faces turn in the direction of the new discovery. In this golden cage there is much for them to observe.

The kitchens of Saint-Moritz hotels of this class are fine, the sauces made to please the French, the roast beef rare enough for the English. There is a bow in the direction of every national appetite; good bortsch for the Russian with the American passport, rice in the Greek fashion for the Queen of Yugoslavia, and excellent *Hasenpfeffer mit Kartoffelklösse* for the Germans who were foresighted enough to rescue themselves and sufficient capital for first-class refuge. From the American viewpoint the prices are extremely reasonable, the charges for room and three meals at the very best hotel in Saint-Moritz coming to about ten dollars a day; and the same can be had for two dollars at a clean, well-run inn.

Saint-Moritz is as spotless as any other place in Switzerland; you could walk through its streets in white socks without soiling them. Here the postal and telegraph service is unequaled; here every bench on every neat promenade is newly painted, and the distances on all traffic signs are correct. If you were the housekeeper of the gigantic hotel that Switzerland is, and you ran inspecting from roof to cellar, and through the halls and the garages and the gardens, you would finish with a smile on your face, because everything is in the best possible condition, and there is nothing at all that you could do to improve it.

In the shaded beer garden of the Restaurant Strohhof

Up the mountains run compact, trim trains with electric motors, and down the mountains runs the water that is the white coal of Switzerland. The water agitates the machinery that lights and heats the nation, and moves its trains. When those little trains coast down the mountain, their motors act as dynamos, returning to the powerhouses most of the energy they have borrowed for the climb. It is all measured, nothing is wasted, and money here is a far holier and more treasured thing than it ever was in America.

Among the books in the library of the Palace Hotel is Thomas Mann's *The Magic Mountain*, and here is a good place to reread it, because a few mountains away is the magic one, and near its summit the sanatorium which is the scene of Mann's book. I have read it often and it has always remained new and exciting for me, and the English translation is as good as the original German. I promised myself on coming to Switzerland that I would make a pilgrimage to the Magic Mountain.

In the cool and orderly fashion in which they solve the rest of their problems, the Swiss deal humanely—but also profitably—with the ills of mankind, and they have come to the aid of sufferers from pulmonary diseases by isolating them at Davos.

A narrow-gauge railroad with the smallest of all dining cars, its plate-glass windows washed and polished, takes you up the mountain. At tables covered with fine and spotless linen and so close together that without leaning over you can reach the salt and pepper on the next table, an excellent meal is served. The wine card is filled with agreeable names.

As the train started off in the valley, there came into the dining car a Hindu of indigo hue, with horn-rimmed glasses. He carried a morocco jewel case, a long sable coat with dolman sleeves, a jacket of gray fur, and a miniature camera. He put the jewel case on the table opposite mine and looked expectantly toward the door. There appeared a young woman who seemed to be stepping out of the stage door of the Ziegfeld Theater. She was platinum-blond and shapely. In the few steps it took her to reach the table, however, she aged disastrously. The jewels that once, apparently, were in the Indian's case hung on her arms and throat. She wore a mink coat and, with the aid of the Indian, settled herself among the furs he had brought. She brushed a hand

over the bracelets on one arm, arranging a fruit salad of emeralds, rubies, and topazes. She touched her ears for reassurance that the large pearls were still there, and then unpacked a diamond-studded cigarette case, a ruby-strewn compact, an ebony-and-ivory cigarette holder, and a solid-gold lighter with initials in emeralds.

This performance was watched by all the passengers in the car, and most intently by a German-type Swiss, the back of whose shaven head was peppered

with small red pimples, and whose neck ran in a straight line from the widest part of his skull into his stiff collar. This traveler, who drank three bottles of beer on the way up, turned his massive head several times and then, so that he could observe the phenomenon in comfort, got up and exchanged seats with his wife. The glamour lady had by then twisted a cigarette into the holder, and the Indian had lit it with his own lighter. The train tilted upward, and the waiters, going downhill to the kitchen, walked fast. Coming back into the car to serve, they labored uphill.

The people in the car looked like slate-colored cutouts, rendered opaque by the brilliant sunshine and scenery outside. They assumed color only when the windows became mirrors as the car entered the darkness of a tunnel.

Switzerland

The platinum-blond passenger to the Magic Mountain had a loud voice, as hard as the stones she wore. She looked into the window, stroked her hair, then pulled down her small mouth in a grimace of annoyance. As she started to talk, the world seemed to contract. It was as if the train, instead of passing through a tunnel, stood in a Madison Avenue cocktail lounge, where Eddy Duchin played the old favorite melodies of the '20's.

"So, I was very good all summer," she announced,

and the pimply Swiss tilted his head. "I lived in New York at the Savoy-Plaza, and like a good girl I never went out. But here I am again going back. Once you've been here you always come back. Oh, the so-and-so's in Washington who hand out passports made a fuss and wouldn't let me go. They said, why didn't I go to Saranac? So I had to invent a romance. I said I wanted to marry a South American in Saint-Moritz. 'All right,' they said in Washington, 'but we want an affidavit to that effect.' So I said, 'My God, that's going to ruin the whole thing, because South Americans are very romantic and I can't ask a romantic guy to make out an affidavit; and besides, Europe is full of idle and eager girls and absence does things to South Americans.' Well, that was something they didn't understand at all, and I was in a big fat hurry to get over here.

"So I went to my lawyer who takes care of my investments, but he's the kind you can't tell the truth to, and I had to tell him that an Argentine wanted to marry me. 'Well, then,' he said, 'it's easy. We'll just get him to put it on paper.' So I was back where I started. So, luckily, at El Morocco a couple of nights later I met an Argentine. They live at El Morocco— all Argentines live at El Morocco, it's their embassy in New York—and this guy had a brother in Paris and he said, 'Sure, I'll call him up,' and so he telephoned him at four A.M. and we tracked him down and he filled out a form. So that's how I finally got here."

She pulled out an immense powder puff and washed her face with it. Then after she had traced the outline of her lips with a small brush, she pressed the lower lip under the upper to smear the rouge evenly.

During this operation she noticed that the thick-necked Swiss was staring and that he was busily nudging his wife, who slowly turned and also stared at her.

She looked at them and then at the Hindu, and said in an unnecessarily loud voice, "You know what my maid said to me—well, she said, 'The Swiss, they won't like you. They don't like women who make up. No Swiss would ever marry you; they only marry women nobody else looks at.'

" 'Well,' I said to my maid, 'they certainly have them.' "

The Swiss gave her a long look of disapproval, which she countered by announcing, "And have you ever noticed how these yokels stare at you!"

The Hindu must have mumbled something about taking a picture. He lowered the protective leather flap from the front of his camera and began winding the instrument. The blonde was looking out the window, now a gray silhouette in the high, bright light. The Hindu said, "Magnificent scenery——"

"Not when you have to look at it from a balcony for a year at a time," said the blonde. A little later she added, "I'm colder than a little wolf," and wound the furs about her. On her cheeks were purple patches.

"I had one of those," she said, touching the camera with a long crimson nail, "given to me by a friend. It was one just like this one—not that I ever was able to take a picture with it. But it had a lot of

Zurich, Strehl Gasse, St. Peter

memories attached to it. A guy I knew, his name was Alexis, spent a lot of time trying to show me how it worked—it was too complicated for me. Well, anyway, I became fond of it and I took it to New York with me and carried it everywhere. You know, I was in love—but then it was all over after a while. Still, I didn't want to sell it and I didn't want to give it away. . . . Well, there was that branch bank near the Savoy-Plaza. It was like a club, they even got theater tickets for you, and when you were overdrawn they just wrote you a nice fatherly letter. And there was a little man working there, one of those good, responsible little men who takes care of his little family, and he often looked at the camera when I came into the bank. Sometimes he held it in his hands and looked lovingly through the finder. Well, I knew that good little man could never afford a camera like that in all his life, so I decided to give it to him. I went down to the camera shop and told them to clean it and get all the gadgets for it and a new case, and to wrap it nicely and send it to the little man at the branch bank. Well, a few days later I went to the bank and there was a different man at the window. He came over right away and told me the package had arrived that very morning. He said, 'You should have been here to see it. He unpacked it right there on his desk and spread all the attachments around it—oh, how his face lit up! Then he took the rest of the day off. You've never seen anybody happier. He's going to fix up a darkroom and develop his own pictures.' Well, on the way back to my hotel I cried. And since then the little man sends me a letter every week. He knows what interests me—he gets the No News from El Morocco and the news from the Stork Club, and he clips the New York gossip columns for me, and all the items about Alexis— and, of course, whenever I answer him, I tell him about the people and the scenery wherever I am—he's crazy about traveling. His letters, I must say, are quite dull. And the prints too, poor little man."

The conductor announced Davos; the Hindu paid the bill, and picked up the jewel case and the furs.

"Look," the blonde said, pointing out of the window, "look at the lovely window boxes and the flowers in them—that's the famous one-way railroad station."

In the sunlight Davos looks like a wall of bricks showing through white paint, and every one of the bricks is the balcony of a sanatorium. The people you see walking about appear excessively healthy. The purpose of the place comes upon you suddenly and grimly as you think of a large establishment on which is lettered: Laundry, Dry Cleaning, and Disinfection. You are reminded again as you pass the crematory, a churchlike building that has a chimney instead of a steeple; and again in the cemetery, a pine grove where the polyglot dead lie next to each other in peace. As out of a novel are the names you read on the tombstones: Dirk Hagenbeek Tandarts, 1909-1940. Remigio Giuseppe Rivellini, 1928-1940. In Loving Memory of Olga Irene Pidwell, 1927-1939. In Memoria de Ruy Soares Macieira, Lisboa, who also died young. The only ornate tombstone in the lot is dedicated to the memory of a Hungarian woman.

The wind sweeps the branches of the pines and presses the pale blossoms of the crocuses into the short grass, and the brassy clatter of cowbells peals over the strumming sound of bumblebees. The smoke from the disinfecting plant drifts up the side of a hill, and this Grand Hotel fashion of luxurious dying away from home is sadder than any other I have seen. The graves here lie in greater and more aching lonesomeness than soldiers' graves in foreign lands.

As efficient as the Swiss are, there is one problem they have been unable to solve: they too have to die. They depart from the world, however, after fulfilling life expectancies that satisfy any insurance company. Demise by violence is rare, industrial accidents are at a minimum, and the safety record of their power-driven vehicles is admirable. A benevolent climate, moderation in all things, and a lack of passion in the average individual further encourage longevity. The Swiss national of small means, when ill and in need of cure, has at his service the best

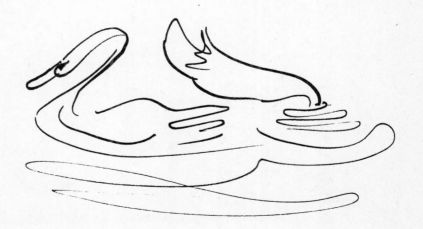

specialists and nurses. The cubic feet of hospital space given to the poorest bed exceeds anything we have, and the detailed attention given to the patient's comfort is extraordinary. When taken through the wards of the magnificent Citizens' Hospital I was shown that every patient has a key to the drawer of his night table, and another to a private closet. He hangs the keys on a string around his neck as he is taken to the operating room. "Knowing that his small belongings are safe," explained my guide, "the Swiss patient is able to relax completely. He smiles confidently at the anesthetist and sinks away happily, holding the two small keys on the string around his neck."

The unhappy aspect of the picture is that life, shielded and coddled in this benevolent republic which lies among the torn landscapes of Europe like a national park for the salvation of human beings, is static. "*Ja*, in many directions we are sterile, and have been for some time," said a publisher. When I asked what was being painted in Switzerland, an art dealer said, "*Ja*, painters we have, quite good ones. Some of the best work they do has been taken at times for that of the great Frenchmen."

While the culture of a people and civilization may lie in its literature and art, the quality of government to me is most evident in what the common man has—how he eats and sleeps, and how much he enjoys his free time. In this regard the Swiss set an example for the world. The only man who seems to be idle in Switzerland is the Minister in Charge of the Unemployed.

Even third-class accommodations on trains are good; comfortable autobuses supplement the trains at low fares; houses of the workers are attractive and individual in design; and everywhere are restaurants, beer gardens, inns, and pastry shops in which the offerings and the service, even for the small pocketbook, are as good as at the Palace Hotel.

There are singing societies on the German pattern, theatrical clubs, groups of nature lovers, bowling societies. This old-time harmony is especially evident in the historic parts of Zürich, where one feels it in the façades of houses and in the clanging of the church bells. The traveler who loved the *Gemütlichkeit* of places like Munich, now destroyed, will find it here, kept under glass as in a museum of the good old time. It resides in the beautiful shops along the Bahnhof-strasse, in the country's good hotels, and particularly in the railroad station. One of the world's best hotels is the Baur-au-Lac, which strives successfully for that rarest of accomplishments in innkeeping—a comfortable and homelike hospice with perfect service and cuisine. In the garden of this admirable house is an umbrella sixty feet high operated by electricity. It is opened during the frequent rain squalls that ride in from the lake, and shelters the clientele that assembles there for lunch, or to eat pastry and drink coffee or chocolate, and dance to an American-type band. Pastry eating is an important item in the Swiss afternoon and early evening living, and there are a great number of patisseries with small tables on which cakes and pies, ices, chocolate and coffee are served. For the English, there is tea. These pastry shops are the counterparts of American drugstores, and are important in the love-making of the Swiss. They are called "*Konditoreien*."

In the plain establishments, taverns, low-priced inns, restaurants, and *Konditoreien*, girls wait on table. To dignify this profession, they are called *Saaltochter*, which is best translated as "dining-

room daughters" rather than "waitresses." They are a group of very sturdy, able, quick, and wholesome girls.

In the shaded beer garden of the Restaurant Strohhof in the old part of the city of Zürich, as the clock on the near-by steeple of St. Peter's struck off noon, there gathered a group of men all dressed in black, all wearing top hats. They were a singing society, and they stood facing a man, apparently their president, mounted on a box. He was presently joined by another who looked sad, as all the others did, and who held up his right hand for silence, and then started conducting. The group sang a requiem in the beer garden. It lasted long enough for every one of those solid citizens to go to a table and take a deep draught of dark and musty beer. Those with mustaches licked the foam from them, and the others wiped their mouths with the backs of their hands. After a while they formed a half circle, once more facing the president. The flag was tilted forward, and the president said: "The heart of a true singer has stopped beating. . . ." The sorrowing group nodded. "Last Monday an honorable member of our society, a singer of the ancient, blessed male-chorus time, a dependable first tenor equipped with an indestructible voice, a veteran of every rehearsal and performance for the sixty-seven years that he was a member of our society, has gone. Honor to his memory."

There was another song, this time a happier one, then the members stood about emptying their beer mugs and slowly moving out of the garden. The rest of the diners started to leave, and when the two-o'clock bongs of the clock sounded through the beer garden only one person was eating—one of the dining-room daughters. She ate slowly, the long heavy jaw that you see on most Swiss women moving slowly as she pondered some problem. She took away her own dishes and returned to the table with writing paper and ink, and from under her apron she brought forth *A Letterwriter for Those in Love* (*Briefsteller für Verliebte*), published in Zürich, and from page thirty-five of that volume, I learned later, she copied the following:

Dear Martin:

I am deeply depressed to have to inform you today that for considerable time, and from various, highly dependable sources, I have been warned that the statements you have made concerning your position, your income, and your fortune, which you have made to me and to my parents, are not true. I am particularly told that your income is much less than five hundred francs a month and that your financial position otherwise is anything but sound. You know, dear Martin, that I have believed you always, although I have had opportunity to observe that you take things lightly. But again and again I gave you the benefit of the doubt, and believed that the reports about you were exaggerated. Yesterday, however, I was told again, from a most trustworthy and serious person, that I must demand of you an immediate, written declaration, in which you will clear yourself once and for all of these accusations. I must ask you for that, dear Martin, in respect to my parents, but also in view of our happiness and later life, and lastly, but not least, on account of my good reputation.

Before I have your written answer in hand, we will not see each other, and our weekly meeting at the *Konditorei* must be discontinued.

Looking forward to hearing from you soon, I remain your ——

For this intelligence I am indebted to the president of the singing society, and to the wind. The singer came back looking for a *portefeuille* containing something of value to him, and the dining-room daughter was obliged to leave her writing to help him look for it, both inside the building and out. The letter was weighted down with the inkstand, but the wind shifted the *Letterwriter for Those in Love* and I saved it from falling into the gravel. I noticed that its back had been opened to page thirty-five. Later, I bought this interesting volume in a bookstall at the Zürich railroad station. It is filled with advice

and sample letters covering all the contingencies, happy and sad, that befall people who regularly meet in a beer garden or *Konditorei* and plan to spend the rest of their lives together. The word "love," however, appears only in the title.

Ringed by many swans busy arranging their plumage, in front of the Hotel Baur-au-Lac, float broad, paddle-wheel steamers that ply over the lake to such idyllic places as Küsnacht, Rüschlikon, and other bathing areas and small-boat harbors. The charges are minimum, and an orchestra plays on board. Music also is played by a very good band in a park alongside the Limmat.

I arrived at this park toward the end of a Sunday-morning concert and saw on a tree near the band-stand a tablet with the program printed on it. Behind the conductor hung a white card bearing the number "six," which referred to the concluding selection. It was called "Rienzi," and the orchestra was in the middle of it. I know the music of "Rienzi" by heart, because the people who lived next door to a thin-walled apartment I once occupied had a player piano. Their favorite roll was "Rienzi."

A man with a coin machine attached to his belt leaned against one of the trees. Facing the band-stand were several rows of chairs which were rented at thirty-five centimes each for the duration of the concert. These chairs were the concession of the man with the coin machine, and upon them he kept close watch. The man had a cane, and I observed after a moment that he had, also, a stiff leg. There was one vacant chair in the last row, the fourth one in from the aisle. The narrow passage to this chair was obstructed by two umbrellas and a cane, all extending beyond the knees of the people sitting in the first three chairs.

I calculated every handicap, carefully estimating the distance from the man at the tree to the vacant chair, taking into account his game leg. I checked once more to make certain that "Rienzi" was the last piece on the program, waited a little longer, watched the conductor, and listened carefully. And then, when I thought I had an even break, I made a silent bet with myself, stepped over the two umbrellas and the cane, and sat down on the vacant chair. I regret to state that I lost the bet. The Swiss was there before the last note of "Rienzi" and collected his thirty-five centimes.

In front of a shop window along the Bahnhof-strasse was conflict. Open-mouthed with admiration, a Swiss Hausfrau looked at a pressure cooker that was among a shining display of electric mixers, irons, iceboxes, and deep freezers. She pointed at the pressure cooker. Her husband pulled on her arm, saying, "Mamma—that's much too complicated for us." They strolled along, comfortably, and came to a window which interested him. He pointed. Inside the window of a wineshop was an exhibition of various popularly priced Swiss vintages; the red on the right, the white on the left. But they were in a new kind of bottle. The new-type bottles held more, slightly, than a pint but less than a quart. "For two," said a sign, "a pint is often too little, and a quart, too much." The new bottle was economical, but besides it was revolutionary; it was practical. A second sign showed a woman holding the bottle, the end of which was pinched for the grip of a small hand.

"This especially designed family-size bottle," screamed the third and largest sign, in red letters, "allows the Hausfrau to pour the wine with the right hand, leaving the left free for other tasks."

The man in front of the window immediately saw the logic of that and as he walked away pointed back at the window. He must have seriously considered a purchase sometime in the future, because he returned to the window, to further fix the details and the prices of the various wines in his mind.

In a third window was the easel on which Winston Churchill painted while he was in Geneva. In this store art materials and papers are sold. Great happiness awaits the lover of paper in this republic. Its money is printed on beautiful paper. There is every shade, weight, texture, and size of exquisite charcoal and water-color paper.

The Swiss make air-mail paper so fine that it rises upward in the wake of a slight move of your hand, wrapping paper that two men cannot tear, envelopes, memoranda blocks, and labels that invite you to write. They manufacture paper napkins that feel and fold like heavy linen and paper tablecloths that fall with the grace of damask. The newspapers and magazines are printed on solid, good papers.

The type is arranged exquisitely. The pages are examples of orderly layout. The police reporting is civilized. The few cases of theft, murder, and homicide that occur are listed under "Unglücksfälle," which means "Misfortunes or Accidents." The names of the criminals are not given, in protection of the innocent members of their families and also to discourage crime for notoriety.

In a meticulous tavern in the old city, where a good meal comes to a dollar and excellent beer is served, I overheard the following dialogue in New York English:

Young Man: "What have you for dessert, Miss?"

Saaltochter: "We have Profiterolles."

Young Man: "What are Profiterolles?"

Saaltochter: "Oh, very good, small pastry, round, stuffed with vanilla ice cream, and hot chocolate sauce poured over."

Man to Young Wife: "How about that?"

Young Wife: "Oh, God, I can't eat any more—not Profiterolles—no thank you."

Young Man: "Thank you. Two demitasses and the bill, please."

Saaltochter: "Ja—bitte schön."

(He looks at newly acquired wrist watch.)

She: "Anyway, Joe—let's get out of this land of wrist watches and vast richness, before I lose what's left of my figure."

Young Man: "But, sweetie, think of the money we save—do you know we've been living here like millionaires for next to nothing!"

This happy couple lived like many others on the curious exchange regulations of Switzerland. It works this way. The government allows the tourist to spend a thousand dollars a month, and it pays him Swiss francs at the rate of 4.50 to the dollar. You can buy the dollar everywhere openly for francs 3.50, at the time of writing.

You change your thousand dollars for forty-five hundred francs, live comfortably on a thousand francs, and at the end of the month buy back your original thousand dollars with the thirty-five hundred francs you have left. The transaction entails no black market or illegal transaction.

In taverns such as the one where I sat that night, you eat at large tables, and people next to you say "Good evening," and order. They start a conversation with you, or you with them, or else you read, or they walk to a stand and take one of the many newspapers that hang there attached to a wooden holder.

"We can't take much advantage of this exchange," said a plain Englishman who had seated himself opposite me. "They only allow us seventy pounds for the trip and all, and that doesn't go far." He was a very kind man, and without being drunk or having any affliction, his smiling, lean face was in constant motion; he wobbled with his head as if agreeing wholly with something that was said, and smiled between bites and drinks.

He told me that he had come to study the latest advances in watch making. Later he said that he had seen Mr. Churchill's easel. "He is a great leader," he said later, "and I am sorry to say that I didn't vote for Mr. Churchill, and I am sorry to say that I'm not going to vote for him in the next election. You in America won't understand that, after all he's done for England. But the war's over and he's a Tory. You in America—you can get ahead, and make something of yourself, but in England a man can't. He stays where he is, and so do his children. I mean the average man—not the bright fellow or the politician or the pusher. I mean a man who just works all his

life and is a good honest fellow, saves his money, and looks after his family. We're kept down. They had their chance to make things better for us, but they didn't. Look at the coal mines—do you know that in twenty years, the original owners got back their investment three times? That's why we had to nationalize them. Don't get it mixed up with communism —it isn't the same thing at all.

"The Tories, they won't change—if they get in again it'll be the same thing—there won't be a change, and then maybe you'd have communism. The King, of course, he's got less to say than I have, and I wouldn't want his job. The King's a nice man. If he weren't nice we'd vote him out of existence— we could do that, you know. I can tell you honestly," he said smilingly, and his face wobbled more than it had before, "that the people of England, people like me, have the greatest affection for the Americans, they really like them. Of course they'll complain about this and that, but in general they like them. You know—the king business and the people still in power in England today keep us from having a total pooling of interests and of friendship with America. If we were a democracy like you, we'd just make the whole thing one—there's enough English blood in America for that. Now mind you, I'm not a communist, I'm a practical man. I say nothing against the King, he's a good man. It's the idea of the Crown, that's what's in the way. We can't afford it any more —it's not too costly—it's in the way."

The service on Swissair planes is pleasant and there is the same plane, same interior, the same type of upholstery, set of sounds, and kind of stewardess and pilot that you find in Los Angeles, Melbourne, Cairo, or Valparaiso. Aviation has the self-same pattern all over the world now.

The reader must be told that these are the observations of only a four-weeks' stay in Switzerland, and in just one corner of a country which is not the postage-stamp size it is thought to be. It must also be said that, although the Swiss are strict in their dealings with foreigners, they count pennies among themselves too; and that their prices are stable and fair. All the time they are estimating so much for this and so much for that, they are putting aside a sizable piece of money for charities and other worthy causes both within and beyond their borders.

When I left Switzerland, I discovered the Orient Express to have improved by several degrees. The golden letters on the dining car and the coat of arms were polished, and part of the *Wagons-Lits* sign was freshly painted. In two cars were new floors. The toilet in the sleeping car had paper towels, but as yet no soap.

The feeling on crossing the Swiss border, outward into the other world, is somewhat like this: You are the father of two daughters, and have just visited the one who married well and is successful in all things; her house is in order and there is no cloud to worry her. You are glad enough that her life has turned out so nicely.

But then you go back to the other daughter, the unhappy and troubled one, and she is the one who needs you, she is the one you love.

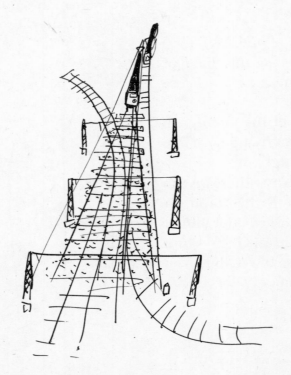

Under a Tyrolean Hat

"I wish I had brought my maid along," said a young woman with a Texas accent. She moved the nipple of a bottle to the face of an infant in her arms which impatiently kicked legs stuck in woolen socks embroidered with Alpine motifs.

A girl sitting opposite the young mother rummaged in a Swiss *bon voyage* basket and produced an orange. She pushed back her sleeves and began to peel the orange, grimacing as if already she had dripped juice on her dress. She nodded and said, "So do I, Evelyn." A moment later the baby attached itself to the bottle, made fists of its hands, and swallowed with its eyes closed.

The orange eater chewed slices of the fruit, now and then delicately catching the pulp in the hollow of her palm and placing it in a brown paper bag. She looked pensively at the village of Küsnacht and also at its inverted and chromatic reflection which

Alpine motif

the waters of the lake of Zürich presented to passengers on the Arlberg Express from three different angles as the train, leaning in a wide curve, headed toward Buchs and the tracks into Austria.

The two women occupied the window seats of a first-class compartment of the train section reserved for the military, their dependents, and civilians attached to the occupation forces. The two ladies, I learned, were members of Vienna's Dependent Colony and were the wives of a corporal and a first sergeant. They were returning from a vacation in Switzerland.

"They sure are the perfect servants," said the one named Evelyn. "Now take my Rudolf. I don't know what I'd do without him—he's our manservant, you know—and he complains all day that he hasn't enough to do, because Anna doesn't allow him in the kitchen and Hilde doesn't want him to touch the rooms. So he works in the garden and washes the car, and he takes Johnny in the park, and evenings he teaches Joe how to play the guitar and sing Viennese songs."

"Don't you love them?" said the other, whose name, it seemed, was Lilly. "They're so *gemütlich* —know what I mean, part of the family. Now you try and find anybody in the States who'd work for you twelve hours a day including Sundays, and in their free hours teach you guitar."

"You try and find anybody in the States to work for you, period," said Evelyn. "And the way they say, '*Bitte schön, gnädige Frau*' and '*Danke schön, gnädige Frau.*' "

"What does *gnädige Frau* mean?" asked Lilly, looking up slowly and smiling.

" 'Gracious lady,' " said Evelyn. "My Rudy also says, '*Küss die Hand, gnädige Frau!*' which means

'May I kiss your hand, gracious lady?' "

"Oh, they're the most charming people in the world," said Lilly. "My Ferdinand must get up around five every morning, because the house is warm at seven; and on Sunday he brings breakfast up to us, always smiling—Viennese coffee, you know—cooked with an egg in it, foamy—and *brioches* that our Fanny makes especially for us."

"Does your Ferdinand play some instrument?"

"Certainly. He plays the concertina."

The baby finished his bottle, and the ladies snuggled into their corners. The shadows of the telegraph poles flitted over their faces as the train ran out of Switzerland.

It is true that the Austrian servants get up early, are charming, and make themselves part of the family. Most of them sing as they work. And there are few maids, gardeners, or other average Austrians who do not own a musical instrument. Some are real virtuosi on the violin, the cello, the piano, or the flute. Even the less gifted Austrian is accomplished on the guitar, the zither, the accordion, or at least the concertina. With eyes closed, they play on these simple instruments the slow and melancholy ballads that praise Vienna, the Viennese, the lovely landscapes. The lyrics of some songs proclaim a homely, frugal, and good philosophy.

There is no martial note in any of those songs, no nationalism, no marching tempo; but there is a pride in being an Austrian and particularly a Viennese. Woven into these *Lieder* are the blue Danube, a green bench beside Father's grave, Grandmother, an old clock, the tower of the church of St. Stefan, girls, love, and the young, heady wine that is called "The Heurige" and is produced in the small vineyards

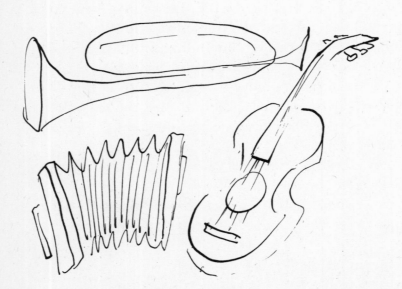

around Vienna. The words are tender and the diminutive is used always. "House," which is "*Haus*," becomes "*Häuserl*." "Alley," which is "*Gasse*," becomes "*Gasserl*"; and "Wine," which is "*Wein*," becomes "*Weinderl*." "Vienna," in German, is "*Wien*," but the sound of that is too hard for the true Viennese, and he has changed it to "*Wean*."

The true *Weaner* is able to drink unbelievable amounts of his favorite *Weinderl* and still find his way about. Testimony to this fact is found in a current popular song, which may be freely translated:

You can blindfold me and take me away;
I'll find my way back to my favorite café.

The words of another song illustrate the Austrian's plain philosophy:

Bad wine doesn't improve with the finest label,
And a small goulash doesn't grow bigger on the
best-set table.

The words of a third song hit, indicate his pride:

A genuine Viennese is a
Man who doesn't need a visa . .
Why should he ever want to go away . . .
There is no place on earth so gay.

If the bulldog is representative of the Englishman then the average Austrian is like the cocker spaniel, helplessly affectionate and sentimental. Most Austrians are happy to be what they are. Some of them, however, regret the outcome of the war and would like to be part of the Reich. Here and there you see a man who cultivates, in silent protest against his fate, the kind of mustache and forelock that Adolf Hitler affected. If I were looking for the former Führer I'd hang around Braunau, where he came from, the region in which his cast of features is common. The Führer, you will remember, was not a German, but an Austrian.

Not all Austrians, therefore, are guitar and zither players, singers of sentimental songs, or peaceful

and gay citizens who look up at the tower of St. Stefan with wine-dimmed eyes. A good many have played other tunes in the recent past. They are back now, speaking again the old soft dialect an octave below the sharp, clipped speech that was fashionable awhile ago, and they all tell you now that they had nothing to do with the Nazis. Even the director of the greatest Austrian combine, the Hermann Göring works, bleats that his office and huge salary were forced on him.

There is a peculiar rain that falls in the Alps, a slow drumming of large, glycerinlike drops that slide diagonally past the surface of the window of the train and run off hastily at the frame, the way pearls are spilled from a broken string.

The train stopped and a customs guard came in. He was wearing the gray, green-frogged uniform of Austria, and he had a face like Fritz Kreisler's. He smiled, bowed, and touched the visor of his cap with the finger tips of his right hand.

In a pleasant conversational tone he asked if anybody had Austrian currency or other contraband on his person or in his baggage. The negative shaking of all the heads in the compartment satisfied him, so he smiled again, said good-by, closed the door carefully as he backed out, and was gone. There, by the grace of God, unchanged by *Anschluss*, war, and occupation, exactly as he had always been, was the Austrian civil servant.

If good Americans go to Paris when they die, then Austria should be the Valhalla for all the world's deserving civil servants. The government functionary here is happy and held in high esteem. Austrians have a great respect for their public institutions. In them, through carefully paced stages of promotion, the best of public dignitaries march upward and come to their fullest flowering in the *fauteuils* of various ministries, with lovely titles attached to their names. There are privy councilors, ministerial

councilors, *Regierungsräte* and *Oberregierungsräte*. Even in the lower brackets there is reward in such interesting titles as that of *Spritzenschlauchschleudermeister*, an official in charge of fire hoses in the Viennese Fire Department, a subdivision of the Austrian Bureau of Public Safety, which is, in turn, attached to the Ministry of the Interior.

As dough is to the baker, as the mouse to the cat, so is the *Akt* to the Austrian official. *Der Akt* (it is masculine) is a folder containing an official document. The *portefeuille* in which *der Akt*, or *die Akten*, in case there is more than one *Akt*, are kept, is the most important piece of equipment of any Austrian official. It is called *die Aktentasche*.

"Please hand me that folder" is "*Bitte reichen Sie mir diesen Akt, Herr Kollege*," for an official always says "Herr Colleague" when addressing another official.

The Austrian civil servant is expert in the agreeable exercise of handing *Akten* from one desk to another. And these folders, stained with the fingermarks of antechamber functionaries, eventually arrive under the beards and meerschaum pipes of the privy councilors who are masters of delay and indecision disguised as deliberation. Under their care the *Akten* are carefully aged, like bottles of rare wine.

The Austrian drama is an endless succession of *Akten* that have been handed on, and of officials who have been a polite, honest, decorative, and inadequate company of men. They are like officials of most other countries, only more so, and perfected. The tragedy is that Austria hasn't been able to afford them since the Hapsburgs' glory faded.

However, they have a melancholy humor and a philosophic hindsight. A former *Ministerialrat*, who

lent his talents to the aggressor and claims that he co-operated in very sloppy fashion and thereby really hindered evil, now works as night porter in a second-class tavern in Innsbruck. He sees things clearer today, without his monocle, and sums up the catastrophe by saying, "*Ja, bitt' schön*, everything would have been all right, except that once again we licked the wrong boots." And he adds, "But then, dear sir, at the time we were given no choice—they were the only ones offered to us. The British Government will bear me out—Mr. Chamberlain was asked to lick them too." Some ex-*Ministerialräte* are chopping wood now, others are working on the railroad. Ex-privy councilors and supreme-court judges are to be found constructing buildings, or engaged in even less dignified pursuits. Walking along a road

under repair, one is not surprised to hear the laborers conversing like this:

"Please, *Herr Oberregierungsrat*, will you have the kindness to hand me that shovel?" and the Herr Colleague answers, "With the greatest of pleasure, Your Excellency."

In contrast, the soft *fauteuils* of the ministries are occupied by men whose rough voices you hear shouting the Austrian equivalent of "Hey, Joe, hand me that folder." Now in these seats, and quickly getting accustomed to them, are the former inmates of concentration camps. Now it is their turn to play cops, to put their erstwhile enemies behind the wire, to drive around on extra gas coupons. It is their turn to lean back in plush opera boxes, to promote and demote, and let the *Akten* age in the old archives.

The Arlberg Tunnel

The place of honor in the home, a bench built around an oven

A great many of the high officials who spent time in concentration camps are now repaying those who put them there. However, the general feeling is that there should be, by next Christmas, an amnesty for all ex-party members except the archcriminals; that the barbed wire should be torn down and the barracks abandoned. In one of the *Akten* is the sane proposal to punish those who were active in the party with the levy of an extra-stiff tax, but to let them return to the life of the community.

Sometimes revenge is taken with humor. There is a former Austrian Lohengrin whose first-tenor voice enchanted the Führer at Bayreuth. He belonged to a group who were not active in the Nazi movement, but who were members of the party. When answering your question concerning their former status, they love to use the phrase, "*Ich war von der Partei geduldet*," which means, "I was tolerated by the party."

This Wagnerian artist was punished by being demoted to yodeling and singing in Tyrolean hats and leather shorts, with an Alpine ensemble that tours the province of Lower Austria. On special occasions his manager allows him to sing as an encore "Ridi Pagliacci" or an aria from *Aïda* which is appreciated in taverns as it once was at the Festspielhaus in Salzburg.

Near the village of Langen, where I got off the Arlberg Express, is a prison compound. Every day a former Nazi bully was led from the wire enclosure

by his guard and marched along a brook where he had to bend and pluck forget-me-nots for the French sweetheart of the prison commandant.

The railroads of Austria are in bad shape. On sidings everywhere one sees the bombed ruins of whole trains. There is no repair work going on, and in most of the burned carriages grass is beginning to grow and birds fly through them. The locomotives are worn out and accidents happen. The brakes on one of the Arlberg locomotives failed to function, and the engine started to race down toward a village in the valley. The stationmaster there received a warning call just in time. He ran out and set the switches so that the locomotive was guided onto an idle track in flat territory, where eventually it lost momentum and came to a stop. For his quick thinking, the stationmaster was decorated and his picture appeared in the papers. Unfortunately for him, someone remembered then, on seeing his photograph, that he had been a minor functionary in the Nazi party, and the next day the stationmaster was dismissed.

The Arlberg Express is the only good train that runs in Austria today. I took it once in Salzburg, coming from Vienna. It appeared in the badly lit station at four twenty-five in the morning, its cars wet with the fogs that lie in the mountain valleys. Wrapped and half-asleep porters and conductors stumbled around the station, yawning and stamping their legs to get warm.

The corridors inside, in the first- and second-class coaches that are reserved for the military of the Allied nations and their dependents, were stacked with musette bags and valises. In the compartments the window shades were down, and the circular hoops that shade the light on the ceiling were shut. People in uncomfortable poses breathed audibly through their mouths, their bodies and limbs held down all free space, and although my ticket had the number of a seat on it, a WAC had her bags folded on this seat. I was wide awake, the air was blue and thick, so I put my bag up in the baggage net and went out into the corridor. The two last cars on the Arlberg Express were assigned to Austrians, who had to show a good reason to travel to be allowed in them.

In these quarters was the European misery on wheels. The windows were replaced by boards, the seats were hard, and the light from the one bulb was unshaded. It was like a set from the Moscow Art Theater's production of *The Lower Depths*. It was cold, and the car rattled and shook so much that no one in it was asleep. In one corner sat a man of the white-bearded Viennese scientist type, and a man in the opposite corner was discussing Vienna with him. Judging from his dialect, the speaker, in contrast to the other six occupants, came from Vorarlberg, an Austrian province bordering on Switzerland. He looked well even in the bad light, and he had a stomach. He was chewing. He said that he had found out that some of the stories that were told about the Russians in Vienna were not true. He said that he had a relative in Vienna who occupied an important post in the Government and in his high, official capacity, had frequently to do with both the American and the Russian authorities in charge of the respective zones of occupation. In some ways, he said, his cousin preferred the Russians to the Americans.

The white-bearded gentleman asked the Voralberger: "Can you tell me why?"

"But certainly," said the comfortable traveler, who had a rug over his legs, and offered everyone a slice of hard sausage. "For one thing, they have manners," he said. "They are polite." He used the word "*hoflich*." "Yes—one can call them 'courtly.'"

"Let us explain. For example, the American Captain—he comes when he feels like it, unannounced, he comes in the door, and you know what he says? He says 'Hello' as if he were on the telephone, then as if he were at home he sits down, and then—listen to this:—he puts his feet on the desk—on the desk of an Oberregierungsrat! All this time he chews or smokes. And he talks to my cousin as if they had herded pigs together. When he sends his Lieutenant, or even a noncommissioned officer, the formalities are equally loose. I don't know how they won the war with that kind of discipline."

"I know what you mean; that's the way they are,

but they're that way among themselves too. That's what they call democracy," said a voice in the dark.

"And the Russians?" said the white beard. "Tell us how they deal with the Herr Oberregierungsrat."

"Also, that is something entirely different," said the man in the opposite corner, and carefully wiping his knife, he closed the blade, and put away the end of the salami in a rucksack between his feet.

"The Russian makes an appointment, he salutes as he comes in and stands straight until he is asked to sit down. He conducts himself properly and always maintains a certain polite distance, and when he sends somebody, then that one doesn't expect to sit down at all—he takes his place along the wall, near the door, and remains there at attention, with his hands on the seams of his trousers, while my brother reads the communication. And when the proper disposition has been made, he picks up his *Aktentasche*, salutes, executes a proper about-face, and leaves the room in respectful fashion. Also, the Russians address my Herr Cousin by his proper title. Yes, I must say, the Russians are polite."

"Ah yes—polite they are," said the white-bearded man. "For example, they always say, '*Bitte schön*' and '*Danke schön*' for everything they want. They say 'Please' and 'Thank you.' Let me illustrate. I am a doctor, a heart specialist. I was summoned one day to examine one of the high officers of the Russians. The appointment was for three o'clock, and I was in the General's antechamber exactly on time. I will never forget that, because I looked at my beautiful golden watch, my last valuable possession, a chronometer with a solid gold cover that jumped open when you pressed a button, and an inscription on the inside of that cover.

"Guarding the door to the General's inner office were two soldiers. I sat on a sofa, and a moment after I had looked at my watch one of the soldiers came away from the door. He marched to where I sat, saluted, and then saying '*Bitte schön*' he held out his hand for my watch, which naturally I handed to him, together with the solid gold chain. He put it inside his tunic, and after saluting and saying '*Danke schön*' he turned, as you say, correctly, and went back to the door.

"After I had done examining the General's heart, I told him the story. I had parted with my watch and chain, certain that the General would get them back

for me. The General listened with sympathy and laughed in his deep Russian fashion as if I were telling him an anecdote, and at the end he politely showed me to the door and said, in broken German, '*Ja, ja*, Herr Professor, my soldiers—they are like little childrens; what they see they must have, and once you give it to them they don't like to part with it.' But I must say, the Russians were all very polite."

"Do you think it's wise to tell stories like that one about the Russians?" asked the man with the stomach.

The old gentleman smiled and said: "Yes, now it is because we're in the American Zone."

Before going abroad I said to myself that whenever I came upon a happy scene, whenever I found the flame of hope burning, no matter how weakly,

The foxes can easily be recognized, as they are wearing Tyrolean hats

I would do all I could to reveal it. I found it burning brightly in Tyrol, despite the winds of occupation.

What I saw of the French occupation of Tyrol impressed me as being civilized and intelligent. I would have been satisfied to find its administration proper and correct, even if dull. There is no need for me to say how it is achieved, because the good thing about it is that it works quietly, and is evident only in its results. I observed these results in Lech, a village on top of the Arlberg.

The village of Lech, like all Austrian mountain resorts, is built around the Catholic church. There are several comfortable inns along its main thoroughfare, and a turbulent mountain stream, also called the Lech, rushes noisily through the valley. Its water is a bluish, opaque color that is called "glacier milk." Halfway up the mountains that surround the village stand broad, low, peasant houses most of which are three hundred years old. Inside

them, in rooms paneled with exquisitely hand-carved wood, you find romantic-looking, bearded, and somewhat musty old peasants, who gaze out their tiny windows and prophesy the weather according to the rheumatic twitching of their toes. In the winter they are entitled to the place of honor in the home, a bench built around an oven which is wood-fired from outside and is never allowed to cool until spring. The old peasants are inquisitive, listening alertly and observing with small, wise eyes. They suck a long time at their pipes and think before they comment, uttering their words as carefully as they spend their money.

They have committed themselves to few things outside their religion, and some of them not even to that. The young are clear-eyed and pleasure-loving, and all can dance with extraordinary agility. The girls are ardent children of nature; and frequently their gaiety and the shortness of their skirts are

84

made subjects of sermons by the local priest. The men are good hunters and like to fish. Most of them are athletic, and some are reliable skiing instructors in the winter. There are also city people who have moved up to Lech and become the victims of unscrupulous architects who have built for them a dwelling known as a *Schwyzerhäusli*.

This is a cuckoo-clock-type house burdened with jigsaw balconies, and with birds and flowers painted on its shutters. The ladies who live in these cute chalets usually wear dirndls, and, it so happens, they are the only people except professional entertainers that I have ever heard yodel.

Among other residents, there are the Catholic priest, who guards the peasants' morals and also dabbles in politics, the priest's housekeeper, and a doctor who specializes in setting broken bones and who, during the winter, gets a good volume of business from the advanced skiing slopes. There is a baker, a manufacturer of cheeses, a butcher, a sawmill operator, and a smith; several shepherds, an idle gendarme, a postmistress, a letter-carrier, a combination plumber-mechanic, a tailor, and a shoemaker. In addition there are a few people who live off the tourists, such as various hotel employees, mountain guides, chauffeurs of the sight-seeing busses, teamsters and coachmen. And there is a vender of beauty creams, sunglasses, and picture post cards.

The French occupation forces in this still valley, under General Emile-Marie Bethouart when I was there, seem to be totally absent. During a month's stay I did not see one man in uniform. General Bethouart, in an effort to encourage understanding and friendship, has arranged for groups of French tourists, the members of a society called "Travail et Tourisme," to visit Tyrol.

These people were all poorly dressed and their luggage consisted of one or two worn and bursting valises of fiber or imitation leather. The shoes of the women were inadequate for the terrain, and when they read the program tacked on the wall in the lobby of the Gasthof Post, they became frightened.

In these announcements the members of the society are always referred to as the "adherents," and here is the program for their first day at Lech:

Notice

Program for Friday, the thirtieth August, 1946: Group A. Excursion to a prairie on the Valluga, the highest mountain between Vorarlberg and Tyrol. Leave Friday morning at 6:45 and return toward evening. The guide is Herr Wolf. Necessary equipment: Hobnail boots, waterproof jacket, and pullover.

The innkeepers and guides lent the adherents all the extra pairs of boots they had, but many hikers still were without appropriate shoes. So the shoemaker of Lech started a new business by renting out his entire stock of hobnail boots. From this excursion, the adherents came back almost dead. Nevertheless, another diversion awaited them for the next day. The following item was on the bulletin board:

Notice

Program for Saturday, the thirty-first August, 1946: Group A.

In the morning: A light promenade in the forests between Lech and Zurs. We leave at 9:45 and are back for lunch.

In the afternoon: A game for all groups—"La Chasse au Renard:"

In the forests around Lech there is hidden a family of foxes who for some time have disgusted the peasants of this region with their evil deeds. The adherents are requested to help us hunt these foxes. The hunt will start around two in the afternoon. The foxes can easily be recognized, as they are wearing Tyrolean hats. Those who find them and bring in the hats will receive prizes. The rules of the game will be explained before the departure for the forest. The adherents are again requested to wear the most solid shoes for this hunt.

In the evening: Hunt ball and distribution of prizes.

The morning's light promenade was a matter of walking up and down a mountain, and the adherents came back staggering.

At about one o'clock the Tyrolean guides, in their green hats, wandered up into the forest and, as I later determined, hid themselves in the most comfortable moss-carpet retreats. Protected by the coloration of their faded clothes, they slept or digested their Vienna schnitzels and plum dumplings until, just before dinnertime, they allowed themselves to be discovered by the exhausted adherents of Travail et Tourisme.

The prizes were *chapeaux Tiroliens*, pipes, and other souvenirs. Nothing makes the adherents of Travail et Tourisme happier than the chance to dress up as Austrian mountaineers, or merely to wear a Tyrolean hat.

At the end of two weeks the tourists are bronzed, know several words of German, and promenade in their rented hobnail boots with ease and not as if they were walking through a tar pit.

To terminate the vacation there is always a *soirée d'adieu*, given in the largest local hall, the Tannhof. For this event the room is decorated with pine boughs, and a four-piece orchestra plays for dancing. The villagers sit among the members of Travail et Tourisme, from which the talent for the entertainment is recruited. There is an air of great expectancy, as theater up here is rare.

The night I witnessed the farewell party a child in native costume, the daughter of the innkeeper Moosbrugger, sat on the piano and started the entertain-

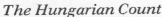

The Hungarian Count

ment by playing a Tyrolean song on a concertina. Next an old Frenchman, Professeur Honoraire Matthieu Guthex, who was the master of ceremonies and spoke the native language, walked to the center of the room wearing five hats, the topmost of which was an old lady's straw decorated with many small bright flowers. The professor waited for silence and then said:

"*Meine Damen und Herren—Mesdames et Messieurs—*" and continuing first in German, then in French, he explained that there was about to be presented a play, without words.

"First, however, we must make the scenery," he continued, and took off the topmost hat, the one with flowers. He walked to the right side of the room, bent down, and placed the hat on the floor. He picked a flower from it and said, "This is the garden." He walked to the exact center, took the rest of the hats off his head and placed them so they formed the corners of a square.

"This represents a castle," said the professor and, pointing at the first hat, he assigned to it the role of the drawbridge over the moat; the second hat was a tower, the third represented a wall, and the fourth the bedroom of a young girl.

"Now for the actors," said the professor. "We have first a true princess, beautiful, young, and devoted to her father. There is a cavalier, a young man of exceptional gallantry; and there is, of course, the old father of the princess, the duke who owns the castle."

There were no lighting effects. The princess came in wearing a long gown, her eyes downcast. Carrying a small watering can, she went to the garden, kneeled down, and busied herself with the flowers on the hat.

The old father appeared next, played by a girl wearing a beard made of flax. He stroked his beard with much contentment as he observed his daughter working in the garden, and, apparently to proclaim his age, he shuffled along in stocking feet.

Hardly had the old father crossed the drawbridge to his castle and disappeared when a young man appeared riding a horse made of a broom and a cardboard cut-out.

With the simplest means, the French mechanic who played the lover achieved elegance and authority. He strode to the girl, declared his love for her in two gestures. The happy young couple then en-

Carrying a small watering can, she went to the garden

countered the duke, who, with some difficulty because of the oversized bathrobe he wore, angrily slapped his thigh, alternately folded his hands in back of him, and then shook his fists in their faces. Finally he produced from the voluminous bathrobe one of the hotel's room keys, with which he pointed to the tower. He dragged the princess away and, pushing her into the tower, locked the door with trembling hands. Then he threatened the lover, who sadly and slowly rode away. Now inside the tower, the princess sat down and cried bitterly. And the old man, still shaking his fists in the direction of the departed lover, walked off, not noticing that the key to the tower had fallen from his hand.

After a while the princess sat up, listened, and smiled. She heard distant hoofbeats. In a short while the lover galloped across the moat. The prisoner began to ascend the imaginary circular stairs of the tower, and the lover, still on his horse, looked up at

her. This part of the pantomime was done with great feeling for theater, which was essential, because both players stood on the same level a few feet from each other, with only the Tyrolean hat reminding the audience that here was a tower.

The lover looked up and raised his arms as if he saw her some fifty feet above, looking down, and she who stood next to him, looked down smiling and reaching for him, as if he were far below. He then got off his horse, and the princess pointed from above at the key. The lover picked it up and unlocked the prison.

The princess descended then in slow circles, carefully lifting her robe lest she trip, and pointing her toes downward, while the lover leaped up the stairs of the tower. They circled each other in opposite directions for several turns, until, when they estimated each had proceeded halfway, they met and embraced. They remembered to walk down together, and once they were outside, the lover lifted the princess to his horse. Slowly and majestically they rode away, out over the drawbridge. The old man appeared with a jug of water for the prisoner, saw that she had escaped, and furiously pulled his beard. He climbed the tower and looked out over the landscape. He tottered, lost his balance and fell down into the garden to his death.

The daughter returned, looking for her father. She went up the tower, discovered his lifeless form below, and promptly fell to his side in death. The lover returned, and when he saw the tragedy he drew his sword and tried to stab himself in several places, mainly in the chest. But his weapon was too blunt and eventually he gave up in disgust and threw it away. He bent down and kissed the princess on her forehead, gently bedded her head on the flowers of the garden, folded her hands on her breast, and rode away.

At the end of the performance the players bowed, the professor came forward again and said in German to the people of Lech: "We hope that our little play has entertained you. We of France wish to tell you how happy we have been here; we wish to thank you from the bottom of our hearts for allowing us to be with you and see your beautiful country. We shall go back and tell the people of our towns how nice it has been here, how well you have treated us. We wish to thank the burgomaster, the baker, the maîtres d'hôtel of the various inns, the mountain guides, and everyone here, and I ask my compatriots to join me in a toast to friendship between our peoples."

After this there was dancing. The wood choppers and mountain guides danced with the French girls, the postman and the professor danced with the teachers, the daughter of the butcher danced with the actor who had played the lover, and the ladies in Lanz dirndls with the electrician from Saint-Mandé and the insurance man. The Hungarian Count danced with his landlady, Filomena.

This aristocrat of ancient lineage, once owner of magnificent estates, has lost everything except his elegant manners. He now lives in a single room in one of the old peasant houses which are owned by Filomena.

"Not a bad life," he says, as he sits on a bench in the sun, in Filomena's courtyard, busily darning his socks. "At last I have a longing for peace and quiet," he says. "In me you behold the only decent-living Hungarian in the whole world—I have never made love to a woman behind her husband's back. I have never played the wild Magyar, I have never had an 'affair.' I have always done it correctly."

"And how is that?"

He looked at me with surprise. "Very simple. I have fallen in love with them and married them—always."

"How often have you married?"

"About ten times, I think."

"But what did you do with the woman you were married to, when you fell in love with a new one?"

"Oh, I threw her out, of course."

Just then Filomena walked past carrying in each hand a heavy pail of slop for the pigs. Smiling, she balanced herself neatly on the slippery boards that were laid across the dung heap.

Finally, as she disappeared into the stable, the Count said, sighing in utter contentment, "Somehow, there is nothing so clean-smelling as a dung heap."

Before the adherents of Travail et Tourisme left, one of them, a passionate fisherman who had brought his equipment all the way from the Pyrenees, wanted to go and get a few of the mountain trout for which the river Lech is known. He was told that the fishing season had ended the day before he came. The proprietor of the hotel at which the fishing enthusiast stayed told him, however, that since he was a Frenchman no native would dare interfere with him, and the gendarme would look the other way. If he chose to violate the ordinance, he could go take all the fish he wanted. The cook of the hotel would prepare them for him.

The Frenchman said, "Thank you, but just because things are the way they are, I will not fish. We have to start living again *comme il faut*—and I will start by respecting the laws of your country."

Return to Munich

I saw Munich then as a place of happy people

Return to Munich

THE ELECTRIFIED TRAINS of the Mittenwaldbahn that ran from Innsbruck to Munich now stop a few miles this side of the Bavarian border. You get off the train at the last outpost of the French Gendarmerie and walk, carrying your bag, to the Bavarian border, where you are thoroughly examined and your papers carefully studied by a detachment of American Military Police.

If you have to travel in this part of Europe, take no more with you than you can carry comfortably, because the portage may be long.

The American soldiers here were as neat as if waiting to go on parade; correct and pleasant, they offered me a seat on a truck to Garmisch Partenkirchen. Along the route were signs which later I

Now there is a mountain of rubble

saw along most roads in Germany. The biggest of them say "Drive slowly, death is so permanent." Others read:

No Can Do—No Can Do—
Out of uniform—May be rough on you.
No Can Do—No Can Do—
Arm around a Fräulein.

We drove through the villages, and except for these signs and the U. S. Army truck, it might have been in the good days of peace.

The old peasants sat in front of their houses turning their heads with stiff, wooden toy motions in the direction of the approaching car. Hay was stacked in the fields, and barefoot, well-fed children came home from school, lugging their books in packs which are carried on the back like those of soldiers. In these packs are also slate tablets with wooden frames, and in these frames holes are drilled, a string is put through the hole, and at the end of it is a piece of cloth with which to clean the slate tablet. On the way to and from school this rag swings on its string outside the pack. This detail—like everything else—was exactly as it had been long ago.

We slowed down for hay wagons. The oxen and horses which pulled them were well-fed animals, the gear was polished and in order. On top of the wagons sat women with colored kerchiefs tied around their heads, and they were also as they had been, full breasted, wide hipped, with short muscular legs. The muscles on the lower part of the leg are the most celebrated part of the female anatomy in the mountains of this country. They must be thick and round, solid to the feel, and are called *Wadln*. A girl who has a fine pair of *Wadln* wears them with pride, especially on Sundays and the feasts of the many saints, when they are exhibited during a dance called the *Schuhplattler*.

In my search for signs of happiness on this trip, I found the first in Garmisch, where a troupe of *Schuhplattlers* entertained a mixed audience of American soldiers and German civilians, who enjoyed themselves equally well.

There were two men and a girl. The dance, like a ballet, has a plot. The two men are jealous of each other. First one dances with her, and then the other; the girl also dances by herself, turning like a top until her skirts are off the ground. One of the partners slaps himself on the seat of his leather shorts, then—as the *Wadln* are revealed—lets out a yowl not unlike that of cowboys in America. He jumps into the air and smacks the soles of his shoes, then toggles about like a large bird that can't get off the ground, whistles, leers, yodels, and in between kicks the girl's skirts up over her head. She is revealed in many white petticoats, and in loose, snow-white linen drawers that are tied below the knee with a ribbon. But the whole dance is arranged in celebration of the joint between the knee and ankle, and the sight of this piano-leg-like ornament sets both the partners into new convulsions—they advance the tempo in which they hit themselves, and slowly advance toward each other, starting with great skill and admirable endurance, to slap in a very intricate rhythm, first the sole of the left shoe, with the right hand, the right knee with the left hand, then jumping, with a wild yoohooo—slapping the left half of their own backside with the left hand, and at the partner's left cheek with the right hand.

This trio, composed of a girl with the most extraordinary pair of *Wadln*, and the two partners, as well as the orchestra, had a grateful audience. They sang mountain songs after, in which *Wadln* again are celebrated, and the room was filled with applause and demands for encores.

Aboard the Bavarian stretch of the Mittenwaldbahn, toward Munich, looking out of the window, I saw nothing changed; the mountains recede after an hour, the fields widen. They are cultivated, and the chickens search in the short stubble of those that have just been cut, the fine forests stand, the houses are neat, and I was surprised how well-dressed the city people looked who were getting aboard the train—especially the children, who all wore good woolen clothes and white socks. Again the only note of war was two American soldiers in the compartment with me.

It was dark when the train ran out onto the wide harplike arrangements of tracks on the approach to Munich. I have always been happy to walk through Munich's lovely streets. I have liked its people. In my childhood, I found refuge from home there, when once a year a frail, old, and sainted aunt, whose name was Tante Pegler, rescued me for several weeks and took me with her to Munich. She had a little shop in an old house, which stood where the American Consulate was later located, at Lederergasse Number 6. Her husband had left her a sound business which she carried on with two old employees. Half workroom and half shop, the place was filled with the scents of every kind of wood, of stains, strong dyes, and varnishes—and there was always a pot of glue cooking. Tante Pegler sold, manufactured, and repaired bowling equipment, billiard cues, beer faucets, wooden mallets for tapping beer barrels, pipe stems and cherrywood pipes, trapeze bars, dumbbells, and other gymnasium equipment.

There was a horse and wagon for delivery, and wherever we went there was a smiling reception. The times were good, and what we delivered on our polished wagon was expected like gifts for Christmas and opened with happy faces. Seated next to the driver, I saw Munich then as a place of happy people, as the gayest capital I can remember. That was in the years 1904, 1905, and 1906. The traffic in its streets was jammed even then, and seated next to the driver, as we slowly went through the narrow

A girl with the most extraordinary pair of Wadln

towers and out through its gates, I got to know every street. Toward evening I squinted, and the street lamps showered gold as from Roman candles over the magnificent scenery along the church of the Theatine monks, and the old Royal Residence, the classical façades that King Ludwig had brought to his home town and that somehow mixed well with the squat architecture of the old great breweries and the guarantee of well-being that is in the façades of solid private houses.

Solidity it had, beauty, and an air easy to breathe and happy-making. As the train on which I arrived from Mittenwald that evening stopped in Munich, I had my first experience with destruction in a place that I had known. Through the immense sieve that is the roof of this station came the light of the moon, and as you walk outside the ruin that the station itself is, you experience emotions that you cannot catalogue. Perhaps after an amputation, when you're not used to the loss of your limbs, and try to reach for something with hands that aren't there any more, it is like that. You stand and look. New avenues of vision are blasted. There to the left stood a set of houses, each of which you knew the color of, and the architecture; now there is a mountain of rubble. There are here a thousand plots where buildings should stand and they are not there. You always went into that no-longer-existent café and visited in a room that is now part of the dark sky.

The colossal, frightening, and sometimes very beautiful thing that ruins are slowly etches itself on your mind. I stood there experiencing this awful disaster as if it still were in flames, and I did not know that I was staring at it while smoking a cigar until a little boy said, "Good-by—pliss giff me der shtump for my Vater."

I gave him the butt of the cigar, he nodded his head in quick German fashion, said "Zank you," and ran away. He looked neat and clean—and his white socks faded into the night as he carefully carried the "shtump" home to his father.

As a correspondent attached to the U. S. Army, you call the Bavarian Press Club and they get you with a jeep. The boy who wanted the shtump had awakened me, and I saw a row of typical Munich redcaps, who were unchanged. They are old men, with homely, kind faces like those of very old, sad hounds. They wear long mustaches, and like taxi drivers, coachmen, and musicians are a race apart, and more stable in adversity than the citizen who has a business and ambition. One of these men gave me a moment of cheer. I smiled at him, he smiled back again—and looking into the city he shook his head and, with a gesture of disgust, swept his arm over the scene as if he were wiping it off——

"Yes, in the beginning you had to bite your teeth together hard so you didn't cry, when looking at it. But you'll get used to it. I got used to it. I don't see it any more now," he said.

The jeep then arrived and we drove through Munich. The sign DEATH IS SO PERMANENT hung over the main gate on the Stachus. There was also a passage, on the main artery past the Marienplatz, where traffic used to be particularly jammed, being funneled through an ancient tower, and while there is plenty of damage in other places the bombs had brought no relief here. The square is as jammed as before. Paradoxically, all that the Nazis built is undamaged. The immense Haus der Deutschen Kunst, which the Munich citizens call "The Athenian Railroad Station," is unchipped. The Towers of the Church of Our Lady, which are to Munich what the Eiffel Tower is to Paris, are also unharmed. The church itself is burned out.

If I ever build a hotel for difficult clients, I hope that the Major and his wife who were in charge of the Munich Press Camp will manage it. The two houses in which it is located were the property of the brother of Giesler, the Gauleiter of Bavaria, and of Amman, the former publisher of the *Völkische Beobachter*. They are comfortable, well laid out. There is no luxury, but comfort, a bar where you can get Martinis, and other drinks, at decent prices. The service is quiet and good, the kitchen plain, the house gives you the feeling of home, which makes it an island here, and while you are technically under the orders of the Major in command, his regime is so tactful that you find yourself his guest. I never saw any drunkenness there, and the only pandemonium I witnessed broke loose when a Scottish Major played badminton in his kilts.

In going about Munich on the second day, I found an epidemic of headless statues. In the railroad station every statue has lost its head, and before the Palace of Justice is another with its head gone. Also the statue of Liebig is decapitated. There was the beauty of ruins, in an arrangement of all the martial emblems of victory that had fallen off a triumphal arch and were carelessly put together at the left base of this monument. It achieved the heroic effect that the photographer Hoyningen-Huene gets with pieces of Greek statuary, fragments of helmets, broken lances, and pieces of shields.

With those you have known, old friends whom you visit, something like this happens. They are for a second so happy to see you that they don't know what to say—and then they look at you, at your fat, at your face, at your clothes. After this inspection they ask you to sit down. There is nothing they can offer you, they don't have anything they can afford to give you, they accept what you give them with a mixture of gratitude and ashamedness, and they look at the floor as they tell you, all of them, that

they feel guilty, that they should have done something, and all those I knew admitted that they lost the war and that Germany, or rather "the Nazis," had started it. This over with, they look at you again, and it is as if they were saying, "And what are you doing here—why did you come to look at us, now?"

Their eyes fill with tears because they think also of the past and bring out this or that happy memory —and then they sit still as you are about to go—a blank stare comes into their eyes, and it is as if you had visited a person once dear to you who is now in an asylum and no longer recognizes you and is no longer the person you knew.

I took a jeep on the third day and went driving out to Dachau. It is immense, and there are some ten thousand men of the S.S. behind the wire now, awaiting trial. While I was there the Flossenburg Gang was being tried. After a thorough check of identification papers at the entrance, we drove through the great stone portal on which sits the eagle that held the party's shield and emblem. Then we drove alongside a brook and came to the entrance proper, to the doors of the concentration camp, to a building that was called the Jourhouse. There, at a great iron door on which was written "Work shall free you," you are checked again. There are plots of grass and flowers everywhere, and neatly laid out walks. The driver parked the jeep in front of the Jour Building, and I went in to attend a session of the trial. The papers were checked again, and then an M.P. showed me to the press table in the courtroom. Outside the window was a bunker, and the accused, among whom was the doctor who had killed some ten thousand men with his experiments in Flossenburg, were called out, by their Polish guards. There were forty-two men, for all of whom the prosecution hoped to obtain death sentences. I had time to watch them, as they stood about, coming out of their cells. They looked no different from other people—that was the first shocking impression—not especially vicious or stupid— just like people that walk in the streets. They were told to get in line, and at the door of the courthouse the American M.P.'s took them over and lined the passage to the large box in which they sat. Every one of them climbed to his seat, and every one got a block of note paper and a pencil, and they talked to each other and relaxed until the Judge walked in.

The trial proceeds, with all the rules observed. Besides two German attorneys, there is a hard-trying defense battery of American officers assigned to the Flossenburgers, and opposite them the prosecutor has to fight point for point.

The prisoners themselves, after the court is seated, relax and watch flies or the M.P.'s, who remain stiffly where they stand. The accused shift in their position and doodle on their pads. They send messages to each other or to their German attorneys, and they have written messages or slogans on the backs of the cards that hang around their necks and bear their number until identified by a witness. The card is turned so that the number is not visible.

The witness of that morning, a little man, with the emaciated face of the concentration camp inmate, had been sworn in, and sat in a raised chair next to an American soldier who acted as interpreter.

Q. *"Wie lange waren Sie in Flossenburg?"*

A. "I was two years in Flossenburg."

Q. "As an inmate?"

A. "Yes, as an inmate."

Q. "Why were you there?"

The witness started to make a speech that he had not believed in the Führer, and always had been against the Nazis, that he had supported the Allied cause and therefore was in Flossenburg.

The examining officer cut him short and asked:

"Just tell us why you were in Flossenburg."

"Because I did not like the Army."

"You were a deserter?"

"Yes, I deserted."

There was a general look of disgust from the Flossenburg officials, in the direction of the witness.

Q. "You say in your deposition that while you were an inmate you never saw anyone beaten."

95

A. "That is right, I never saw anyone beaten."

Q. "Did you see anyone hurt by other means?"

A. "I never saw anyone hurt."

Q. "How was the food?"

A. "Good."

Q. "How did the prisoners look, after they were in Flossenburg a year or two?"

A. "They looked well."

Q. "I mean were they weak or strong?"

A. "Some were weak, by nature, and others were strong—just as on the outside."

Q. "Look at the defendants in the box, and point out the one who was the camp eldest."

The accused at whom the prisoner pointed stood up and turned his card, so that a large number showed. The identification was correct.

A. "That is the man who was my block eldest."

Q. "You say that he never beat any of the prisoners, or disciplined them in any way?"

A. "That's right—he was very kind."

On the paper before me, the opening statement of the trial, on which is listed what the prosecution tries to prove, there is the following under Number 21, which was that worn by the man being tried:

"Mathoi comes from Füssen, in Bavaria. He was convicted as a war criminal and served as a prisoner himself in Dachau, Auschwitz, and Flossenburg. He became a capo [a kind of noncommissioned officer within the camp] in Flossenburg. At Flossenburg he was camp eldest. His job was to maintain order, arrange for meals and baths. He has beaten many with his hand, fist, metal whip, and shovels. He was so feared that when he entered a room prisoners hid under a table or any other available shelter."

I asked a court reporter sitting next to me why they didn't keep that witness here too.

"Oh, that's nothing," he said. "You should hear the testimony on other days—this is very mild."

"Why does he give that kind of testimony?"

"Most probably that guy there has something on him. Or his family. Or else he does it for money. Also there's the possibility he's a fanatical Nazi now."

There was recess, then, and the prisoners were fed in the courtroom. I walked out, and along the corridor a door was open. I entered a room that was filled with green light. In large glass containers that were like those in which photographers hang plates to develop, and also like those used for electric bat-teries, were the various results of the researches and experiments of the doctors of Dachau floating in alcohol . . . frostbitten feet, kidneys, lungs, a head sliced in half with the lips sewn together and wearing the agonized expression of the Gestapo victim. There were various skulls showing, progressively, artificial atrophy of the brain; the most advanced was shrunken to the size of the tooting horn bulbs on children's bicycles. All were properly labeled and numbered. I was glad to get out in the air. The court reporter said, "Take your jeep and drive around to the right, where you see the long building with the tall chimney. That's interesting too."

When we got there I said to the driver, "Come along," but he shook his head and said, "Thank you. I've been here before."

The building, again on nicely landscaped grounds and among plots of grass, is neat. You might take it for the garage and laundry on a millionaire's estate. The chimney is a little high and wide, but cleanly designed. Its weight bears down on the rest of the building. It is as if Frank Lloyd Wright had experimented here. Outside is the pale blue Bavarian sky, and the line of the Alps drawn loosely as with chalk is visible over the roofs of the wall that surrounds the grounds. From here must have gone the last hopeless looks of people out to the sun and to the mountains up to the sky and the flight of birds. And then they were asked to undress. The pretext was that they would be resettled, and get new clothes and be put on a train.

There is the door through which they passed. It's a steel door, painted in a friendly color. And over it, in lettering such as you find spelling "Rathskeller" or "Restaurant" in that gay kind of sign painting, you see written here *Brausebad,* which means "Shower." This room forty by forty feet accommodated a good many people, and on its ceiling are the shower heads, and the small openings through which the gas poured in. And you now can stand there, and nothing happens except that your knees are weak. And you can also go out through a side door, backstage, and see how it was done—and peer through the little slit, heavily protected by two layers of glass, where the operator could see what he was doing. Like the basement of a large apartment house, overhead run heavily wrapped pipes, with wheels on them from which the gas and the warm

The old painter

water were sent into the room. And there are signs saying "*Vorsicht*"—"Be careful."

I went out of the door into another room, and there came upon a sight so awful that I needed all my discipline not to run away. Here former inmates of the camp had made life-sized puppets, and dressed them as prisoners. They hung and stood about in this room, showing the various punishments they suffered. I observed that crudely made figures like these, with staring eyes in badly cut and painted faces, are much more powerful than good art would be. The whole had the effect of a Chamber of Horrors at Coney Island, with dirty figures behind chicken wire.

I went next to the battery of ovens where the bodies were cremated. They are the least shocking thing here, because in them all terror came to an end. They are built of brick, with ashes and dust on them, and the long hooks and scrapers of iron next to each. Beyond the ovens there is a room where those less kindly treated than the customers of the *Brausebad* were prepared for the ovens. That room is solidly bloodstained up to the height of five feet, and beyond up to the ceiling are the marks of clawing and smears that have turned to a brown color.

By the grace of God you can walk out of this now. In the carefully planted plots of grass stands the hanging tree, a pine that has a heavy deviating branch, like an arm and an elbow, at the convenient height of seven feet. On this arm prisoners were exe-

cuted, but there is nothing awful about this tree. It is in the open, it has shed its old needles. Neither is there anything grim about a wall against which people were shot, because after you come from the crematory you come out of hell into light. There is one more detail of particular awfulness: a room in which small cans are stacked. In these the ashes of prisoners were dumped and sold. It was done with a small gardener's shovel out of a large garbage-type can in which the ashes of a group of anonymous dead were collected. The little cans were filled and sealed and those sentimental relatives of the deceased who sent the required sum to the camp received the ashes. The victim's name, typed on a label, was pasted on the can. Prisoners did this work.

"Have you had enough now?" said the driver. I said yes. We drove back to Munich, where we went to lunch at a place where they had calf's-head vinaigrette, but having seen the bottles with brains and kidneys and the half head, I just had some coffee.

"We're going to meet some good people tonight, who are celebrating a birthday. Intellectuals, who are all right," said a member of the Bavarian Press Club, a man who works on a publication issued by the occupation authorities.

The house in which this party took place was, like all other apartment houses in Germany, marked on the outside with a wide white line such as is painted on streets to keep traffic in its place. On houses it directs rescuers, in case of bombing or collapse, to the spot where the shelter is located, and an arrow at the end of the line points to where the digging is to be done for survivors.

The men at this party were like the furniture in their rooms. There wasn't a piece that was whole. A chair, the best one, offered to me, had one leg missing; also all the men were maimed or broken, pinched, pale, in need of clothes. They observed the rules of party-giving, as if everything were wonderful, and with gaiety greeted the arriving guests, smiling and showing them to the broken sofas and the wobbly chairs, hobbling along with the support of a cane, motioning with generous sweep of the one arm to a buffet on which a small bowl of potato salad and some plates and bread waited. There was music played on an old victrola, picked up by a worn needle and played with half the melody lost. With this accompaniment they danced, in curious fashion, holding each other apart, but rotating, and swaying back and forth, in wide, loose, waltz figures.

They were flushed from dancing and, after the excessive motions, had to rest when they talked. It was inevitably about the war, and one said that every German was guilty, and that they had known that something should have been done to stop it. I then asked that one whether the people knew what was going on in the concentration camps, and he said, "We would have been unable to do anything about it, but I swear to you that we didn't know until the last months. Nobody who came out ever talked, and few came out."

He told me a joke current toward the end. A man came out of Dachau, and he was asked how it was in there. "Ah," he said, "marvelous. Your breakfast is served to you in bed at nine, then a little tennis, after a walk in the park."

"But So-and-so," he was interrupted by his questioner, "told us it was terrible."

"Yes, and that's why he's back."

There was a little cheese, thin sausage, potato salad, and bad coffee at this party, and one bottle of liquor that we had brought along made them deliriously happy and was emptied with small drinks poured in cups and glasses.

I had a pack of American cigarettes and opened them and pulled out a few so that I could offer them. A young man next to me watched it, and as I handed the pack to him, he suddenly grabbed the three cigarettes that were pulled out and stuck them in his pocket, and then he turned red and got up and walked away. He wiped his face in a corner. He didn't smoke one of the cigarettes. Such tragedies in miniature are all around you, and people who formerly behaved with painful correctness now often forget themselves. After a while you get used to it and you know how to ignore it.

You drag yourself home to the rooms of the Press Club every night, and there you wash your face and your soul, and find yourself on an island. In the morning you have a good breakfast, with white bread and butter, eggs and bacon, and then you go out again into the ashes. I didn't suffer from the ruins, on the third day. I also had found that, miraculously, all the very good and beautiful places in Munich were saved or had suffered little damage.

On the third day I went looking for a man whom I remembered as an individual of indestructible humor, of courage, who had managed his life intelligently and gotten much out of it. I was told that he had never joined the Nazis, he was respected and lived in comfort.

This once happy man, whom I shall call Rupert von Hentzau, possessed all the attributes that went into the hero's character of Graustarkian novels. He was a horseman, he drank well, his hair was black and curly, he was always in love. He admired the Americans and did not suffer from the inferiority complex that Germans usually have toward the English but considered them as cousins, fortifying this with frequent references to the Almanach de Gotha and Burke's Peerage. He had invested in the United States and in South America, and traveled everywhere. He spoke his mind during the Nazi regime with reckless disregard for his safety, and he was somehow left alone. This immunity was due most probably to the fact that in the First World War he was an ace, and a member in Richthofen's squadron. He lives in one of the numerous villas built on the side of a mountain and in the style of a castle, overlooking a pale blue lake; he has four Irish tweed suits left, the jackets of which have the peculiar cut, with two slits at the sides instead of one at the back, which proclaims the wearer a horseman. Proudly he lets you smell the lapel to prove that the cloth is the genuine thing, vegetable-dyed. He has the horses that are indicated by his costume. There is a tackroom with a dozen saddles, but in the stable only two horses are left. He can't feed more, and he is reduced to one great Dane and her pups. He has helped people; he hid a Jewish banker and his family and protected them for months and finally got them out of Germany into Switzerland in their own Maybach-Zeppelin car with all their luggage and in broad daylight. Drawing his portrait as carefully as I can, I must stop here and say that I doubt very much whether Rupert von Hentzau would have done that much for a shaking, cold Jew, who had not previously entertained him royally, loaned him money, and from whom Rupert had not fished away his beautiful Aryan mistress.

I hoped that here might be some bright piece of color—even the false glow of an orange spot placed on the last act of a Shubert musical, with the chorus raising empty beer mugs and singing a Rathskeller

hymn to joy. It turned out sadly and otherwise. Rupert von Hentzau slapped me on the back as in other days, and gave me a choice of hare, which was already properly marinated, and of wild duck. The two animals were gifts of an American Colonel who also brought him, regularly, copies of English and American magazines. My host further offered a capon just right at the age of eight months and to be prepared in simple fashion, *aux fines herbes*; he also had veal, pork, Spam, and ham. We decided on the capon and then went into the cellar, which was for this time and place in remarkable condition. He brought forth a dusty bottle of the dry St. Catherine Hospice Steinwein of Würzburg, which is liquid gold and my favorite wine. He carried it carefully and, followed by the great Dane and her wobbly, continuously falling down brood, we walked down to a boathouse that is built out over the lake, whose upper deck is a shaded veranda on which we reclined. He tied a string to the bottle and sank it slowly down to the bottom of the lake, as he had no ice and the day was warm.

On the lake were boats with soldiers which he called "Tschi Eyes," and it took me a while to get the meaning of that. He wanted to say "G. I.'s." The soldiers came close and waved. "They like to hear my Benny Goodman records," he said. "I play them down here evenings."

Rupert von Hentzau has arthritis, but he will not give up drinking, and the bottle of brandy I brought along was emptied after dinner. He wiped his forehead continually. His doctor, having been a Nazi, is not allowed to practice, and the subject of arthritis opened up a long and astounding discussion of the Reich, Adolf Hitler, and the world.

"The only man with brains in uniform that I have met was Patton," said Rupert von Hentzau. "You can't be a soldier and a democrat; if you try, you mess up everything. It is the beauty of the military life that it is simple and realistic, and honest. It's a faith like the Catholic Church—I mean you know what you have to do. I mean, soldiers should run the world. The trouble begins when politicians step in. After soldiers have cleaned up their last mess . . .

"Why can't my good doctor practice?

"Because he was a Nazi," Rupert answers himself. "Therefore they punish innocent people by letting loose on them a quack.

"The military make sense. Patton ran a hospital hereabouts, and it functioned beautifully. He had Nazi doctors, because he couldn't get any others that were good. If anybody is to be locked up, lock up the bad doctors. Anyway, the well-being of the population always suffers from this false idealism of politicians. They should have dealt with the Nazis and locked them up at the beginning.

"Here is another chapter in incompetence. They're putting all the ex-inmates of concentration camps into leading positions; they are the new saints and pillars of the country. They are now put in charge of everything. They are virtually running the government. Please follow me closely now. Number one. Tell me why. What have they done to fit them for that? In the early days anybody could have fought Hitler; the Nazis were only a handful when they started out in Munich. Where were these heroes, and later, when anybody could still have taken a shot at him? He rode through the streets, unprotected, standing next to his chauffeur, straight up front in the car, the chest and head exposed. And there was no ban on weapons. People with a thousand cameras crowded up to him, you could have built a gun into a camera and taken careful aim. You could have taken a carbine with a telescope and shot him from a window. And the others were good targets too. You wouldn't want a better one than fat Göring, or Goebbels who limped. And all of them were fish in barrels and continually on view. Did any of these heroes then take a gun? No. Not one. The attempts at assassination came late. And from the rank of Colonel upwards. They had no courage, the concentration camps' inmates. I will prove to you that they were fools besides. Every child knows that the lion eats the zebra. Now when he was in power and almighty and properly protected, when they had let things go that far, instead of being against him, they should have been for him, because to fight him then was folly. Also, what did they do? They mumbled, they huddled in dark rooms to listen to forbidden broadcasts, they got excited, called the Führer names, all ridiculous and petty offenses for which they let themselves be beaten and broken. That proves that they were stupid.

"Now they are out, and in position to lead the Reich into its next catastrophe. Time spent in a concentration camp doesn't make a man fit for running the country. By all means, give him privileges and a decoration he can wear on his chest, and a pension for the rest of his and his wife's days, but by all means retire him, because he was a mess, and he is through. All you have to do, when you see one of them, and you can tell them a mile off, is shout at them and they start to shake, and that is not the kind of people we need in the tough time ahead of us.

"You may quote me," he said. "I will give you something to write about. I have not been a Nazi, I refused to join the party, but now I am, and I wish that others like me, who held out, had joined.

"If the inmates of the concentration camps had been for Hitler, instead of against him, and that amount of people, those it took to guard them, that might just have meant the difference, and we would have won. We would have won anyway, except for two major errors.

"Number one, we should have fought the Russians first. If Hitler had been smart enough to do that, he would have had American and British capital on his side.

"Error number two: We should have left the Jews alone. And then we would have had the services of Lise Meitner and Einstein, and that means that we would have had the atomic bomb long before the rest of the world and it would not have mattered had the Americans gone to war with us or not."

"Do many people like you feel as you do now?"

"But certainly. I'm not alone, and most of the Tschi Eyes I know, and their officers, tell me that they think Hitler was right. Ask any of them out there on the lake. They'll tell you."

"What makes you feel as you do?"

"The fact that there is no plan, that there is a worse mess than there was before. We had a plan, believe me, and England would have India today if we had won. Look at the map of the world. See how small England and America are, and mark my words, you'll read the history of the next epoch in Hindustani and the Kaffir dialect, published in Moscow. That is what we would have prevented; we would, for a thousand years at least, have staved off the decline of the West. We were for the white man, and that is why, now, I believe in National Socialism."

He wiped his head again. "Have you been in Nuremberg, have you seen Göring, I wonder when you go whether you could take him a bottle of this wine. You know, I have a feeling that he and I shall sit here one day, just as we are sitting now, and drinking. I always liked Hermann. The trial is a farce, and between you and me, the execution will not come off. It will be announced, perhaps, but they will all be kept for the day when it starts against Russia, by next spring, and you will see, old Göring, he'll straighten out in no time, and Keitel, and the others. Streicher they can hang, and von Papen too, and Ribbentrop, and Hjalmar Schacht."

He lit a cigarette, and then he helped a man who worked around the house to rig up a hunting wagon and drove me around the lake to the station.

In the train back to Munich was a G. I. of that unhappy type that has been written and complained about. He is fortunately not as generally evident as has been reported or he would not stand out as he does. This one was a rare specimen, a nose-picking, pimply recruit, drunk, with the same four-letter word in every one of his sentences. He found himself a German girl who went well with him, and he smeared kisses on her. He threw an empty beer can out of the window of the moving train, and later he dragged the girl into one of the two second-class compartments of the coach, which is upholstered, pulled the shades down, and slammed the doors. He came out of the compartment finally and sat down next to me. With difficulty and lolling, he asked me several preliminary questions and lit a cigarette, and finally, poking a finger into me, he said that he had something very important to ask me; he wanted to know, what he was doing in Germany? I used his pet, four-letter word to answer him. And it was satisfactory, for he gave me his dirty hand and thanked me, saying "You're all right, bud."

There was another soldier who got on the train later, a serious man, who talked of his own bewildering experiences with de-Nazification. He couldn't get over it that frequently German denounces German, for no apparent benefit to himself, out of revenge or envy. He also said, "It's bad enough that no German here realizes that his country lost the war; they blame the whole misery on the Americans. God, I long to find the person who blames it on the Germans, even among ourselves."

And so I returned again to the Press Club, grateful for the reality of the good-sized twenty-five-cent Martini and the faces around the bar. After supper I went up into my room. After I had turned out the light in my room and tried to go to sleep, the cracks on the ceiling over my bed multiplied. Rupert von Hentzau's monologue ran through my mind, in every detail, and the air was as it had been in the *Brausebad* in Dachau. I turned the light on again and picked out a book from the library that has been left there from the former owner of the place. I chose a book of poems. I will translate the most insane of them.

THE FUHRER'S EYES

As breath and heart stood still before the fire
In wild advance through the villainous vales,
As our bodies cried "Impossible"
We felt thine eyes upon us
And severely and kindly they gave us new strength
And everyone was silent.

As we were barely able to lift our helmets
Death reached for us in fire-belching horror
As our souls complained and almost whimpered
  "Senseless"

We felt thine eyes upon us
And severely and kindly they gave us the command
"Storm on ahead, Flag, fly—!"

As ever fresh graves flaunted our sorrow
And without tears the hard rough soldiers' hearts
  moaned "What for?"
We felt thine eyes upon us
And severely and kindly you gave us the explana-
  tion
And that was—"Victory."

On the next day I stayed home and wrote the notes from which this is taken, and the day after I took a train and had proof again how German treats German. My face is round, and by this time my one

suit was unpressed for a week. My shoes were dirty, and so I could pass as a middle-class German, traveling.

At the railroad station, alongside of a train which was reserved for the military, stood a conductor in a Bavarian blue uniform. I got into the train and sat down. He came in and looked at me for a while, and then he approached me. I asked him in German what time the train left.

"Ah, I thought so," he screamed. "*Schwein!* Out with you, what are you doing in here, how dare you get into this compartment? This is not for civilians —out before I kick you and have you arrested. This is reserved for American Army officers. *Rraus!*"

An officer who was traveling with me came along

and explained to the German official that I was entitled to ride on the train, whereupon the conductor collapsed. He said that his life depended on his job and to please not report him, that his wife and his little children would be breadless, and he whined and abominated himself until the train was past Nymphenburg. "Forgive me, I thought you were a German," he said.

Most disliked by the natives are Germans who have taken jobs with the occupation authorities, and especially those who act as receptionists. They are called "Vorzimmer-Deutsche," or "Foyer-Germans." Most of them are girls. In that unpleasant fashion in which a German higher placed has always dealt with the one a degree below him, they

now interview petitioners at their little desks out in the hall, look at them down their noses, and, when they so desire, take out a slip of paper and write thereon, with a flourish, their Bavarian O.K., which sends the petitioner in to another German, and eventually if he is lucky he finds himself opposite an American official who can do something for him, and usually tries to.

There was an export show, of various articles manufactured in this zone. The exhibition was well arranged and, except for a fashion show, whose collection was designed with the most unfortunate initiative and shown by heavy-footed models, there was proof of thorough workmanship and quickly regained skill in manufacture. In the room in which

toys for export were exhibited was a plain couple, and the woman said, "We should have brought little Sepperl, just for a look."

"*Ja*," said the husband, "I would have liked to, but I'm glad we didn't. It would break his heart to see all these things and not have any of them.

In the villa in which the painter Franz von Stuck formerly lived now resides an artist who, through all of last winter and spring, painted with gloves on his hands, and an embroidered, heavily lined woolen kind of cloche on his head, which Hausfrauen used to put over coffeepots to keep them warm. The windows of the studio, which was one of the finest in this city, were all boarded up, and the artist was so badly off that when finally an American got him the first food package, he forgot to say thank you but, turning from his easel, stared at it, as it was opened by his wife, and just said, "Oh God, it's high time!"

People of this kind, and like the ones at the birthday party, the decent Germans, are lost and in hiding. They're not able to adjust themselves to becoming Vorzimmer-Deutsche, they know no tricks, and they have nothing to sell. You do not find them before de-Nazification boards, because they were in hiding also while the Nazis were in power. Your only means of identification is the decency of their faces; you see them walking in the English Gardens or in Nymphenburg and along the River Isar. It's usually man and wife, and they walk arm in arm, and the motto of their lives is the words embroidered on the artist's coffeepot hat, "I'll remain faithful to you."

You think after a while that the hope is in the child. The child unfortunately still goes to a German school; the Nazi teacher is de-Nazified, but he is still a German. That means, he is wonderful at imparting to you some technical skill, and beating a language or a set of numbers into your head so that you will never forget them, but for the soul of the child someone else would be better.

To me the German tragedy has come from the schoolroom, from heartless corporal punishment, from a discipline tougher than that of a reform school in America. The school set the pattern for the treatment of the child at home. It instilled from earliest youth fear of parent, of teacher, fear of the policeman and of anyone who wears a cap with insignia or a coat with brass buttons. The Nazis could accomplish what they did only with an absolutely obedient population. The benefit of that training still is ours. They offer very few police problems. They are happy to receive commands, and commands that they can let someone else carry out are a delight to them.

In one high school a type of teacher rare in Germany, a true pedagogue, who earnestly tried to help his pupils over the tragedy they are going through, kept his teaching free of all political, patriotic, or religious mention.

After months of patient work he had their affection, and after assuring them that none of the faculty would see it—that the names of the writers would be kept secret—he asked that they compose an essay on the future of Germany. The following document, from the pen of a quiet boy, was typical.

ON THE FUTURE OF GERMANY

I was a member of the Hitler youth, and I am not sorry about it. I was a Nazi, and I was happy that I was one. I am a German, and I shall always be one. I can be forced to give the outward signs of another belief, but what I keep in my heart is mine forever. I can say what is desired of me, because only I will know that I lie. A lie that advances us is no sin. But truth that does damage to us is. Because we love our country we must, as in the hard days of the fighting, take our hearts into our hands again, and we must not mind the misfortunes that will befall us. We must be proud, and work freely. O my God, I love Germany, as she is now, a hopeless wasteland, and I will walk into this wasteland and, with only the power of my hands, create a paradise therein, more beautiful than that in the Bible. This shall be my future way!

"I think," said the teacher, "that the people of any country would be proud of such children."

There isn't much happiness traveling hereabouts. You can laugh for an hour in Munich, but it's in a theater, a show along the lines of a Cochran Revue, in which most of the jokes are on the occupation. The Americans there laugh louder at sketches about themselves than the Germans, and it is to the credit of the occupation authorities that the jokes are allowed on stage. There is a story which sums up the mood of Munich and of Germany at this time:

A German came to a psychoanalyst and said that he was deeply unhappy and depressed and wanted to die. The analyst tried to console him and told him that life was beautiful and that everywhere there was hope, but the patient argued with him with such conviction that the doctor could only wring his hands and nod his head and say, "You are right. Everything is black." There seemed to be no consolation. The doctor thought a while toward the end of the session, and he worried about how he could help his patient, and finally he said to him, "I know what is the matter with you. You have forgotten how to laugh."

"True," said the patient.

"Here," said the doctor, writing down a name. "This clown is the funniest man in the world. He will make you laugh again. He performs at the circus twice a day. Go and see him."

"I can't," said the patient.

"But why not?" asked the doctor.

"Because I am the clown," said the unhappy man.

Story of a Bavarian

AT THE BAVARIAN PRESS CLUB in Munich I took a jeep, which you can hire at the reasonable rate of $1.50 an hour, and drove to Regensburg. Along the route in this agricultural latitude I saw fine horses, and immense pigs, choice cows in the fields, and had continually to avoid hitting fat geese. These are again force-fed here as they were in olden times. The peasant women hold the geese between their knees, and—feeding good-sized dumplings, about thirty of them, into the birds, first forcing their beaks open—insert the food and then, by forming a ring with index finger and thumb, slide down the bird's long neck, forcing the meal clot down its throat. The children too, in the small villages along this route, seem well fed, and have fat rosy cheeks.

There is no evidence of destruction in the small towns and villages that you pass on the way. While the Autobahnen are bombed, the less important roads are undamaged. The tiny, hard apples that hang in the trees planted alongside them, and that would make a kind of crabapple jelly, were left on the branches, although they were ripe. There are a good deal of hops grown, also barley and potatoes. Regensburg itself suffered little damage, except on the outskirts. After I arrived I took a city directory and looked under *P*, for the name of my old friend

Pappelmeier, with whom I spent some unprofitable and dreary times on the hard benches and in the lockup of the local Lyceum. The professors of this institute tortured us in vain for three years. We repeated the same form, again and again, and were both held up as bad examples to the rest of three classes of pupils that passed us by.

My schoolmate Josef Pappelmeier, I found out on my arrival, had passed away during the first months of the war. The pieces of the story that follows were told me in a small garden along the Danube, by Pappelmeier's wife and daughter-in-law, and also later by his son Pepperl, who was in a camp.

My late friend had been of such extraordinary appearance that people who saw him for the first time turned their faces away, hid behind handkerchiefs or pocketbooks, or tried to turn into side streets. Caricature could only flatter him.

His face was like a Picasso drawing, where the model is seen from two sides at once. His crossed eyes sat so close together on the bridge of his nose that both could be seen when looking at his profile. It was like the arrangement of eyes on the face of a flounder. He had hair of the most improbable shades of red, and exposure to the summer sun and also to the cold

winters of Regensburg turned the skin on his face to flaming patches of orange, carrot, purple, and old rose, all of it illuminated with a coppery sheen of the peach fuzz that covered his features. As he grew to manhood the comfortable cooking at his home and an unquenchable thirst for the rich local brews fitted him into the oval outline of the funny-paper-type German of happier days. He completed the caricature with two Dachshunds and a green hat, to which was attached the usual bobbing chamois brush. The undertaker told me that, mercifully, he kept the lid on his coffin. He was mirth-provoking, even in death.

Because he found himself always surrounded by laughing people, Josef Pappelmeier was well adjusted and became a successful and happy man, learning his father's trade after he was, together with me, thrown out of the Lyceum. He was envied later for the courage with which he wooed one of the nicest girls in Regensburg, who to the great surprise of all straight-eyed people agreed to marry him, and everyone in the old town breathed easier when the child of that union looked like a normal citizen at birth.

His proud father named him "Pepperl," which is the Bavarian dimunitive of Josef. He grew up, a

healthy boy, impeded only by a slight speech defect, a liquid kind of stammering, which forced him to issue a few inarticulate, explosive sounds before he could express himself properly. He was, in school and on the street, called "Pappelmeier Pepperl," and, according to a teacher at a clinic for speech defects, this foolish appellation was responsible for his stammering. "You just try and say it," said Dr. Küssmaul. "Try and say 'Pappelmeier Pepperl.' How would you like to go through life with a name like that? Of course you'd stammer, and feel insecure, and fail in school, and want to run away."

Pappelmeier Pepperl's father was a Regensburg bon vivant, reveling in dishes cooked with red cabbage and sauerkraut, spotting his waistcoat with goose grease and the sauces that dripped off the various kinds of dumplings and *Spaetzles* that are the regional specialties.

When Pepperl was a baby my friend always took him along to restaurants and fed him on his knee. Pappelmeier was the only German I know who was unashamed to push a baby carriage through the streets of the old city, or carry his baby wrapped in flannels into the park—a job strictly assigned to women. He also refused to punish Pepperl in the good old-fashioned way, which recommends beating boys regularly like sacks of walnuts to make men of them, and that, many people said, and still say, was responsible for the tragedy of Pappelmeier Pepperl.

Old Pappelmeier had in years of hard work established himself as an independent manufacturer. He owned his own house, which stood on a square called "The Golden Opportunity." The façade of this building was so wide that on a black band, three feet high, between the windows of the second and the third floors there was room to spell out in letters that were broad and golden "Josef Pappelmeier—Atelier für Präzisions Mechanik." On the two ground floors were the drafting and work rooms and above them the living quarters of the family. Frau Pappelmeier led the detached life of the women of her kind. She

lived a silent, obedient existence in the back of the house, more wishless than that of the one girl they employed to help her. On Sundays she followed her husband, who wheeled Pepperl in his carriage along the Danube to a piece of property on which the precision mechanic eventually hoped to build a villa, such as all the better people of Regensburg owned. The practical family man hoped to construct its solid foundations with the heavy boulders that formed the remnants of a tower, once part of the defenses of Regensburg. He wanted to call the place, which was on a hill overlooking the valley of the Danube, "Belvedere." His wife now remembers with sadness and remorse, as if it had been a prophecy, that she had said to him, "Leave it, Josef, as it is—ruins are so beautiful [*Ruinen sind doch so schön*]. Now we have lots of them," she says.

He followed her advice, and in the romantic weeks of his life he erected an arbor on this property and planted a grape vine, the fruit of which never ripened in the raw climate of that latitude. The grapes stayed green and hard, like those made of glass and used for decoration. Asparagus grew, and some pears, hard and sour apples—there was no idle time in Pappelmeier's day. Pepperl as a baby showed promise of equal amounts of energy. His mother remembers how he perpetually headed on all fours toward the fence that enclosed the property. She did not suspect then that it was the first manifestation of his wanderlust, which was eventually to be his undoing.

In this garden, some years later, on one of my previous visits to Bavaria, Pepperl's father told me of his worries about the boy. He had said then:

"I don't know what's to become of Pepperl. He's not like my own flesh and blood at all. He's all thumbs, he has fingers like sausages—but that wouldn't matter if only he took an interest in the business—but he doesn't listen to a word I say—he leans on a drawing table with his chin in his hand, and when I'm through talking to him he looks like somebody that just wakes up out of a dream. 'What?' he says, or sometimes he doesn't answer me at all. I say to him, 'Look, Pepperl, it's all right with me if you don't want to be a precision mechanic, if you think it's beneath you. I understand. If you want to go into something else, and become a doctor, or into another trade, and be an aviator, or a brewer, or something else, I understand—I'll look around and see what I can do. Look at me,' I say—then he looks at me like a dead calf, and then he stutters, 'N-no, Papa,' and then I say, 'All right, you tell me what you want to do, Pepperl.' Then he leans over the table again and looks out through the window and he says he doesn't know what he wants and his mother talks to him. She says, 'Pepperl, look at this beautiful business, your papa worked so hard to build it up for you—look at this golden opportunity. Why don't you learn to be a good precision mechanic like Papa? We can leave you money, but money gets lost, or there is an inflation, but here you've got something that nobody can take from you, no matter what happens.' But that's all for nothing—he stands there and looks and I don't know what to do. They say beat him until he is soft as a wet diaper and break him—and make him do it—but I can't see that it would do any good, and anyway, I can't do it. The worst thing is, I need somebody next to me, in my business.

I've got a few things on the board, a new injection pump for Diesel motors, and some clasps and mountings that I have designed, and I don't want an outsider to have to hand it to, but I need somebody, and why should I have to take in a stranger when I've got my boy?"

The period of indecision lasted several years. Josef Pappelmeier wrote me that he finally had to take in somebody, a poor relative, a young man by the name of Franz Hinterwimmer, who had served his apprenticeship under a respected and well-known master mechanic in Nuremberg. I saw this young man the next time I came to Regensburg. He had the ideal elongated fingers for his delicate work, a face as sharp as if it were laid out with a triangle, and eyes deep in their sockets, just right for gripping the black, tubular magnifying glasses with which precision mechanics and jewelers do their work.

"I thought," said Pappelmeier to me at that time, "that perhaps this boy, this relative, Franz, who is ambitious and quick as lightning, would shame Pepperl into going to work, or make him jealous, but the boy has no pride at all. He stood there and watched the other, the one who worked at the bench that was rightfully Pepperl's, and he looked at him as if the other one were an idiot, and after a while he just turned his back on him and walked away. I said to Pepperl, 'Hinterwimmer will be at the head of this business one day,' but Pepperl just pulled up his shoulders and walked out, and promenaded along the Danube—and I say, how much longer can this go on? And his mother talks to him every day—'Look at this beautiful business lying here, waiting for you,' she says. 'Why don't you become sensible, Pepperl, why don't you go and learn the business just to make Papa happy?' But he doesn't seem to hear anything you say to him."

The poor relative, Franz Hinterwimmer, advanced from the workbench to the drafting table and the inner office. The uncertain dreamer Pepperl eventually changed. He came out of his shell and revealed himself at first in the halting words of the inhibited and oppressed and later in fluent speech. One day he said to his parents that he wanted just one thing and that was to travel, mainly to get away from Regensburg, from the house in The Golden Opportunity, and from the ambitious relative Franz Hinterwimmer.

His father took a long walk with Pepperl, and they came out to the ruin in the garden along the Danube and sat down on the weathered bench and table in the arbor. Pappelmeier Pepperl became articulate again while his father was speechless at the son's queer logic and un-German outlook. The boy had thought a long while, he said, and taken everything into account. He said, "Look, Papa, if you make any more money than you are making now, we only have to hand it to the government in taxes. Now you had a hard life building up this business and I am properly grateful, but you never had any fun, never any real fun, because you had to worry all the time and think about your work—and what have you now—still worry. Now why don't you give me the kind of youth that you would like to have had. I don't ask for much—I just want to live my own life and get a little happiness out of it."

Papa was surprised. He had a funeral oration all ready for his son's plan, but when he looked at Pepperl's face he buried it, for he truly loved his son. He sat back and watched a paddle steamer splash in the Danube, and then he got up and led the way back home. He went to his favorite brewery and sat down in the restaurant thereof, at his usual table. He was so upset that he did not discuss the problem with either the jaundiced municipal councilor or with the canon who came there to meet him and play cards nightly.

The next day he went to his house and he said to Pepperl, "How much do you think you'll need?" And Pepperl had his calculations made to the penny and ready for him. The father then arranged for the necessary funds and reached into the till to supplement the sum with some petty cash. Several days later, after the mother had counted his linen over and over again and added to his purse from her own household savings, the traveler bid good-by to the old house, and with the curious eyes of the poor relative on him he walked out with his parents to the railroad station. After a bitter time during the buying of the ticket, and a last meal in the restaurant of the terminal during which his mother stared at her plate and the old man was unable to swallow his beer with any degree of pleasure, at last the train was announced, the signal bell rang, and seated in a compartment third class (he wanted to travel in plainest fashion and cost his parents as little as possible) Pappelmeier Pepperl left aboard the local train for Munich on his first journey.

In the Bavarian capital he was like Goethe in Italy. His first journey was reported in four letters that found space in Regensburg's newspaper. They reflect the mood that once was in that romantic old town whose token signs are the twin towers of the Church of Our Lady—steeples that do not stab at the sky, but rather look like two old, green umbrellas held up into the sky by pilgrims in russet-colored cloaks.

Free of all worry, young and in a new suit, Pappelmeier Pepperl roamed happily through beer halls, museums, royal palaces, and the English Gardens, drank tea at the Chinese Tower, and watched flowers being painted on royal Nymphenburg porcelain. He made excursions to the castles of the Bavarian Kings, listened from the medium-priced seats to Wagner and Mozart, read the story of Lola Montez, watched the peasants in the fields, and observed the customs of people who lived in small villages in the mountains. If Pappelmeier hoped that

his son would return to him saying that he had found the world dull and had enough of wandering and wanted to settle down and learn to be a precision mechanic, he was sadly disappointed. Pepperl returned only to entertain the silent dinner table with anecdote and travelogue. He supplemented his meager wardrobe with a gray suit, arranged his finances, and he was off again, this fateful day in the other direction, towards Nuremberg.

The traveler of today may tear out the pages of his guidebook that concern themselves with the treasures of this city, but at the time Pappelmeier Pepperl came there, it was rich. He was privileged still to promenade along the mysterious, slow waters of the two rivers that join there, see the city's gilded fountains, and stand in the churches, whose ancient stones had the texture of Roquefort. In these hushed retreats stood wondrous carved wood altars, in gilt and faded colors, dusty and worm-eaten, cut by Riemenschneider, whose every angel's face, saint, bird, leaf on small tree, dog and drapery was executed with religious devotion, high artistry, and patience. In the footsteps of the many English and the Americans, who loved this comfortable patrician town, Pappelmeier Pepperl tramped past all these wonders.

One day, crammed with much emotion, he started to visit the famous Albrecht Dürer House, feeling pride.

From there he went to the old fortress, and with awful thrills stood fascinated as a guide demonstrated the workings of the Iron Maiden which stood inside the tower, and cried out with her rusty hinges, as the heavy figure was opened, disclosing her spike-studded interior and the sieve through which the victims' blood was drained off. Pale as the other tourists, Pappelmeier Pepperl came out of the tower and wanted to get to his hotel, where he lived under an arrangement that included his meals, at five marks a day. He never got inside of it that day. He found himself in a thickening mass of people, which enfolded him, so that he gradually lost the freedom of his arms, and did not have to walk, being

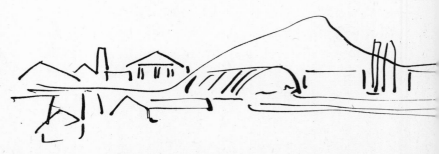

pushed along through flag-draped streets. Stuck in a vast sea of faces, he was washed along and came to rest after having been carried past his own hotel, to the front of another, which was called "Deutscher Hof," and there the crowd shouted and cried and sang, until Adolf Hitler appeared on the balcony. The hysteria of the mass transferred itself to him, on that first of the *Parteitage*. He shouted himself hoarse and was pushed out to the stadium, and he came home to the hotel walking over the dead and trampled flowers with which children had covered those streets of Nuremberg through which the Führer had passed.

Pappelmeier Pepperl, who usually was of good appetite, had missed his midday meal and he now let his evening soup get cold. The patriotic exercises to which he had been exposed continued within him, there was shouting and marching in his head as he lay back on his pillow. He heard the Führer's words over and over again: "Germany shall live in all eternity." He felt hot tears flowing down his cheeks and saw himself, with the talent for melancholy that is in the make-up of most Germans, in a faraway soldier's grave, but covered by a wreath that would never wither.

Early the next morning Pappelmeier Pepperl, presented himself at the headquarters of the party; he was referred to the proper authorities; his answers to a questionnaire that had been handed him were satisfactory and his spirit admirable. He was told, however, after a physical examination that he would be a soldier of the head rather than of the heart, and he was told to wait, pending the investigation of his person and record.

In the meantime, he was to return to Regensburg and wait. At his father's house, the returning Pepperl found the poor relative seated at the family table. There had always been an undeclared war between them, but this suddenly ended as Pepperl spoke of his last journey, of the Führer and the *Parteitag*, of Göring's address and of the jubilation and the crowds. During this exciting recital the poor relative Franz Hinterwimmer sat stiffly in his chair, his deep eyes steadily on the speaker's face. At the end Pepperl turned to his father and announced that he had applied for membership in the party.

At this the father left his mouth open, but the usually silent Hinterwimmer turned over the lapel of his gray jacket, showing a button with the emblem of the S.S. Jumping up and coming to stiff attention, he greeted Pepperl as a blood brother, gave him the party salute, and became agitated. He appeared to be an altogether new person. He repeatedly jumped to his feet and often hit the table as he engaged in a loud political confession of faith and drank the health of the new-found Nazi.

Old Pappelmeier shook his head when they told him that he too should join the party. "I'm already a member of all the things I want to belong to," he said mildly. His wife now remembers and admits, sadly, that she advised him to join. "Everybody is doing it," she said. "Just wear the uniform occasionally, Papa, to show where you stand, and all you have to do is attend a meeting now and then, and once a month collect on street corners for the party."

He shook his head and said no, but Pepperl's party membership, and the ability and energy of Franz Hinterwimmer, brought untold benefits to the firm. As time passed a large building was put up outside Regensburg, which manufactured the products of the firm of Josef Pappelmeier, and it was proper and beneficial that preliminary talks concerning the contracts for this undertaking took place in Munich and Nuremberg with the S.S. Lieutenant of the Reserve Franz Hinterwimmer, now no longer the poor relative but a member of the firm, who appeared in a long dark cloak at S.S. Headquarters. The final papers were signed by Parteigenosse Pappelmeier Pepperl, who for these purposes slipped into the gray greatcoat of a lesser branch of the service, that of an ordinary party member, but one with a relatively low number, entitled to special privileges, because he had joined early.

His mother again says with self-accusation that she was proud when she saw him walking through Regensburg in his uniform coat. "He was so elegant," she says, "with gloves always, just like an aristocrat. And everybody in Regensburg who looked at Pappelmeier's new factory and its big smokestack and its wire-enclosed entrance for its

two hundred employees now envied him his smart son.

"*Ja, ja,*" says Frau Pappelmeier, "it was all too wonderful and all on account of Pepperl's journey to Nuremberg."

Pepperl, himself, became tired of praise and success, and he also found the uniform too stiff. He left the glory to Hinterwimmer, and everything might have been all right if he had not gone traveling again. He went to Munich and went to one of the best tailors there, the firm of Kielleuthner and Cie, and ordered himself an extensive civilian wardrobe. He also went to Budapest, and he changed to first-class compartments and sleepers, and returning to Regensburg he astounded the city with his elegance. He became engaged to the only daughter of the richest brewer there, not because of her riches, but because she had the allure of the women he had admired on his recent first-class travels, whose slim calves he had watched as they hopped the steep steps of the fast trains he rode. She was the only one that was as languid as the beauties he had seen at the Walterspiel Restaurant in Munich and at the Bristol in Vienna. Sylvia had style.

She had been christened Liesel, but she changed it almost as soon as she could speak. She pouted into all the shop windows of the Regensburg couturières and, protesting their offerings, she walked about covered by a white, severe, tailored raincoat and a small sport hat. Her heavy ginger-colored hair was not braided but rolled down over her shoulders, and in spite of the Führer's dictum, she painted her lips and rouged her cheeks. Sylvia and Pepperl had recognized each other immediately; she pleased him, although she was disapproved of by his parents and even her own father, who told her that she looked like a streetwalker. After a hasty marriage which everyone in Regensburg prophesied would end in disaster the happy and elegant couple provided again a bitter farewell for their parents, for after the wedding breakfast at the Hotel Maximilian they drove away in a new, pale gray Mercedes Benz cabriolet; the honeymoon was to be spent in Berlin.

At this part of the story, Frau Pappelmeier, who told it, sitting in the arbor along the Danube, patted the hand of the beautiful woman who sat next to her, and who was Sylvia, her daughter-in-law. Pepperl's wife then walked away to the fence, where her own little girl stood, rooted with fascination, watching two colored soldiers of the American occupation forces swimming in the Danube.

Frau Pappelmeier continued then, "I was wrong—we all were, I must admit. I didn't have any hope for the marriage, but it turned out good. I don't know what I would do without her now. She has eyes for no one but for Pepperl."

As I said, they went to Berlin, and in a cabaret they were seated next to a man who was also with a young woman who was smartly dressed, and this man also wore the party emblem in the lapel of his coat, and he had the manners of a man of the world. He smiled across to Pepperl and his wife and he started to talk—first about Berlin, and life, and his travels. He seemed to have been everywhere, and Pepperl became very interested. The stranger then asked him about this and that, and Pepperl told him about his own travels, and about how they were just married and how he had joined the party after seeing the Führer in Nuremberg and how beneficial it had been to his father's business. Pepperl did not put his light under the table, but spoke about his philosophy of life, and the man admired his spirit, and told him how lucky he was, and how rarely one found anyone so young, and from a provincial town like Regensburg, with so wide a horizon, so sure a grasp of the meaning of things. He also said that he had great connections and that he might be of help to Pepperl in advancing him further into a position where his talents could find their proper sphere, and he suggested another meeting. The two men had found themselves in complete harmony on every question, and they left the restaurant together as friends.

The stranger and his companion then called on Pepperl and his wife at their hotel and took them on a tour of the city's most elegant places, and over wine and liqueurs the men discussed the Fatherland's needs. It was in the week of the crucial decision over Poland. The stranger came to the point quickly and said it meant war, and he asked about the capacity of the Pappelmeier factory in Regensburg.

Pepperl set his forehead in wrinkles and in strictest confidence gave his new-found friend the latest statistics on production in the Pappelmeier factory for precision instruments. He told him about the number of gauges that were manufactured for the Messerschmitt factory, whose huge new plant had been built right next to the Pappelmeier works, as well as the number of precision instruments for submarines. He gave his estimate of the number of planes that were flown away from Regensburg, and offered to find out the latest figures as soon as he got back. The man said that he would come to Regensburg and visit Pepperl and have a look at things himself. As they got up he gave a proper and stiff party salute and a "Heil Hitler." As they stood in the lobby of the Femina night club, while the girls were getting their cloaks, he quickly checked the information once more. After a second martial good-by, he left with his companion.

There were elaborate presents of flowers and perfume for Sylvia the next day, and then the stranger vanished. Pepperl saw him again several months later, when he appeared in Regensburg. Soon after that he saw him for the last time in a Nuremberg courtroom, after the friend from Berlin had been arrested as a spy. Under order from a Nazi judge the man identified Pepperl, and somebody read the information Pappelmeier had given to the debonair man in Berlin, and which that one had put down in a small book, in a code that the efficient Gestapo broke as quickly as they had the accused. The accused pleaded for Pepperl; he remarked, without being asked, that Pepperl had been his victim, that he was a good follower of the party, and that at any rate he was too stupid to have had evil intent.

Pepperl's mother told me that part of the story with a trace of annoyance. "He's not stupid," she said.

After the trial Pepperl was allowed to go home and told to wait. The poor relative came into the room which the son of the house never left and without a word placed his service gun on the table, indicating thereby that Pepperl should shoot himself. What followed then we hear from Pappelmeier Pepperl's own lips:

I was lying with my wife on the sofa in my old room, and I spoke to her. I knew that something was in the air, because one day before, I had a kind of warning. I spoke to her, about what we should do with the child that she expected, if I were to be sent away and if all our property were to be taken from us, and she cried quietly. Then the bell rang and there were two men in civilan clothes outside and one of them said, "Good afternoon, Herr Pappelmeier. We are here to check papers and passports. You travel a good deal; give us your pass if you please, and may I have a look at your papers." I had all my papers in the best possible order. "Good," said the one who spoke while the other one looked around the room. "Have you any books or papers here that concern the activities of the party?"

"Yes," I said, "I have various books. It is among my duties to read them."

"Yes," said the one.

The other went to a bookshelf and looked at the books I had indicated. "Have you weapons of any kind?"

"No weapons," I said.

"Good," he said, while the other replaced the books.

"We regret very much," said the spokesman, "but we have to search the apartment."

"That is perfectly all right," I said, "go ahead, allow me to show you the rooms."

I must say that they were very polite and correct. When they were finished looking around they said, "We have one more request to make of you, Herr Pappelmeier. Your superior at headquarters would like to have a word with you this afternoon."

"Certainly," I said. "I shall take a streetcar and hurry to see him right away."

"*Ja*, Herr Pappelmeier, there is no need of that, because we have a car downstairs, we shall drive you there," said the man, and at that moment my knees were weak. The men suddenly stood at my sides.

"Come, Herr Pappelmeier," they said.

"I would like to say good-by to my wife, if I may."

They were again polite, I must say, and let us say good-by. I had a ray of hope. One always hopes that there is a mistake, and I went down to the car. There was a chauffeur in uniform. It was a closed car with-

PAPPELMEIER PEPPERL IN BERLIN

They stood in the lobby of the Femina Night Club

out insignia, and again I had hope. One of the men got in, and the next one motioned to me to follow, and then the other got in, so that I sat between them, and the car started off. And I said, "We are going in the wrong direction, the headquarters building is that way."

The car drove awhile. Then the one who had been silent said to the other, "Have you told Herr Pappelmeier already?"

"No, I haven't told him yet," said the other.

"I regret," said the second one, "to inform you, Herr Pappelmeier, that you are under arrest."

"I thought you said that my superior wanted to speak to me," I said.

"*Ja*," said the one. "I said that, but now we're going to the depot to take a train."

Then I said to myself, "Oh, God. Now things are suddenly different."

At the railroad station the car stopped not at the regular entrance where I had always bought my ticket but at the end where it's deserted toward evening and where freight is loaded. It was getting dark and there was an enclosure. The two men walked me to the gate.

"Oh, one more of those swine," said the guard at the door and let me in, and with a group of others I found myself waiting in a shed. After an hour we were marching out on the platform and then assigned to a car. In every one of its small compartments were about ten men and one guard. There were two benches facing each other on which we sat down, and the guard sat on a chair at the end almost in the corridor. Five and five of us sat facing each other in front of him. None of us knew how to behave ourselves, but we gradually learned that. He was an expert at striking anything with the butt of

114

Story of a Bavarian

his gun. He balanced it precisely and used it like a javelin. We sat for a while, and we heard some crying and whimpering in adjoining compartments. The journey started. The man next to me had a cold and reached into his pocket for a handkerchief, to blow his nose. That is where the butt of the guard's gun came flying the first time and stunned him; it smacked him square on the side of his face. He bled, and the prisoner who sat opposite him said to the guard, "Excuse me, but he only wanted to blow his nose." The gun butt sailed in again, this time to the head of the one who had made the excuse, and he cried out in pain.

"You are much too friendly toward each other," said the guard. "We don't encourage friendship. You on the left there," he said to the prisoner who had spoken, "smack that man, opposite you, the one you worry so much about. Hard. Harder. Go on." The man had hit his opposite twice, halfheartedly. He hesitated and the guard lifted his gun again. Then the prisoner did as he was told. "Now you there on the right, smack him back, the one that hit you." The other man obeyed. "Don't be afraid, don't protect one another [schont euch nicht] or I'll teach you how to smack," said the guard. "I want to hear it, keep it up until I say stop," and so the two with the blood streaming from them smacked each other until the guard said, "Halt."

"We're not traveling for pleasure," he announced. "They won't like it if I turn you in without a little

Nuremberg

damage showing. But I am not like other guards. You may not think so, but for a Dachauer I have a heart. You're supposed to stay awake until we get to Dachau. I would let you sleep except that I think you are stupid. You don't know how to sleep yet. And I'll have to teach you, and I'll teach you, also, how to wake up; that's because if the controlling officer comes in here and sees that my prisoners sleep, I'm in trouble."

Now he said, "Listen carefully. You sit at attention, absolutely still, you have your hands on your knees, and keep your head up. You look straight ahead."

He watched us, and then he said, "Now let me see how quickly you can go to sleep. Upon the command 'Schlafen' I want you to close your eyes, and get down with your heads, because that's how you sleep the very best way, and when I say 'Wake up' then you wake up, but immediately, because the one who wakes up last gets a reward from me." He balanced his gun again and held it ready.

He must have played this game often, because after he gave the command "Sleep" he quickly banged his gun on the heads of all those who did not bend quickly enough. At the command "Wake up" he hit two. At the next command of "Go to sleep" everyone ducked his head so quickly that he bumped it against that of the man sitting opposite him. It was of no consequence whether a man went to sleep fast or slowly; if he did not crack his skull against a fellow prisoner he was hit with the gun butt of the guard.

The guard amused himself with issuing commands until he finally was satisfied and tired of playing with us. "Sleep," he commanded once more and made himself comfortable. "Now that I have taught you how to sleep, God help those of you that don't wake up properly," he said and closed his eyes.

We left Regensburg about eight in the evening and we arrived in Dachau at ten o'clock the next day.

We marched in through the gate of the camp and came to the place where you give your name and profession, and there was one who asked me my trade. I hesitated for a moment because I was confused about what I should say, what was best—precision mechanic, party member, traveler, or what. At any rate, while I was thinking what to say a guard hit me in the stomach and then swung his fist into my face so that I spit out teeth and blood, and I had to write down the answer. I wrote "precision mechanic."

"Get out!" he screamed then, and before I could turn I was hit again, by somebody I did not see, and then I fell and I heard a humming sound like that of bumblebees in the summer and it felt like a very hot summer day and I landed on the floor, softly and with unimportance, as if I had decided to lie down under a shady tree. It was quiet and I was comfortable. They must have dragged me out. I was wet and there was a voice that woke me up and it came near. A man took shape. He stood in front of me. I was one of a row of men. I was standing up and I felt blood running from my mouth and nose, but I had already learned how to behave and did not lift my hand to wipe it away.

"I want to be able to hear a needle fall," said the man in charge of us who talked. He was our superior. I learned later that he was an habitual criminal, as were all the block eldest who were responsible for the bunkers in which we lived. They had been transferred from regular prisons to concentration camps and been given charge of the barracks in the capacity of noncommissioned officers. They were to be addressed as "Herr Unterscharführer." *Unter* means under, *schar* is a small group, and an *Unterscharführer* is the leader of a small group.

These civilian criminals were feared and called "capos."

"I am going to tell you now in few words," he said, "how you are to behave yourselves. In the morning, first thing, the cells are cleaned. Then we stand at attention and each man reports. First he says his name and number, then his cell number, and then he says why he is here.

"You understand, we stand against the wall, hands down, at attention. We sing out the information, loud and precisely, the head up, or else there's unpleasantness, you understand."

"Yes," said the men. "Yes."

"Yes what?"

"Yes, Herr Unterscharführer."

"Yes, Herr Unterscharführer," said the group.

"Next we take the night bucket. And with that we advance, in double time, to the latrine. We do everything here in double time, you understand, or else there is again unpleasantness, you understand?"

"Yes, Herr Unterscharführer."

"In the latrine we empty the bucket, and then we let water into it and then we rinse it out, and then we run back and we put the bucket on the floor in the corner of the cell and go to the washbasins, and there we wash ourselves, but all that is done like lightning because if any of that takes as long as it takes me to tell it, then there is unpleasantness.

"There isn't any talking at all here, ever.

"Have you heard of me, any of you? Have any of you ever heard of Gneissl?" He looked up and down the line, and there was one face he didn't like, that of a fat priest. He went to the man and put his fingers around his throat. "I want to know whether you have heard of me," he screamed. The man opened his mouth, and the capo used his fist on him. I looked away. There was a moan, and then a series of slaps and punches, and a sucking sound as if the last of the water were running out of a bathtub. We all stood and looked straight ahead.

When the capo was through he said, "We'll leave him here. He needs fresh air." And then he wanted to see how quickly we could run, and then he told us that he was famous for his discipline, and then we were put into our solitary cells.

I remained there in the same shirt and trousers in which I had arrived, and only once did anyone talk to me. The capo, Gneissl, came in, and he had a piece of paper in his hand, a small, brown piece of paper, with something written on it with a pencil.

I stood at attention as commanded, flat against the wall of the cell, the hands at the sides, and the head up, and announced the number of the cell, my name, and that I was here on account of being a traitor.

"How long are you here now?" said the capo.

"Four months, Herr Unterscharführer."

"Look at this carefully," he said, and held up the little piece of brown paper. "I found this in the cell next to yours. Now if you were me, what would you do about that?"

"I would punish the prisoner, Herr Unterscharführer."

"Good, and what kind of punishment would you give him?"

I thought for a while. We were fed every sixth day, so I could not say, cut his rations. We had only one blanket, so I could not say, take that from him. And we slept on a wooden bunk, so there was no mattress to withhold.

The capo came near me. "Well, how would you punish him?" he yelled and reached for my throat, just as he had done it the first day with the priest.

My knees were weak. "I would," I said, "take his exercise away from him, Herr Unterscharführer."

"You are crazy," said the capo. "You seem to think that this is a sanatorium. First I'm going to give him a thrashing, and then he will stand, he will stand day and night with the window open. He will not sit down or lie down. He is going to stand twelve days."

He took his fingers off my throat and left the cell, and I held my ears then, because it started again, next door, just as before, the punching bag and the sucking sound. He had left me alone to save his strength for the man in the next cell.

I came out of solitary confinement one day and was given the striped uniform of the regular prisoners, who are called "Ka-Zettlers," a term that is derived from *Konzentrazionslager*, meaning concentration camp.

I was assigned to a barracks with several other men, and it seemed unreal that when the new capo had left the room for a moment we all bowed and introduced ourselves to each other. There was a traveling salesman for the Eberhard Faber Pencil Company, an administrator of a charitable institution, a manufacturer of woolen goods and a man who had been active in the repertory theater, a Catholic chaplain and an architect for tunnel construction.

We all had said "formerly" when speaking of our professions, but there was somebody here who, even at this low tide, tried to impress and used the present tense. He bowed stiffly and said, "Von Domhoff— I'm the chairman of South German Electric." He continued as far as saying, "I'm the director of thirty-six—" when the theater man shut him up, saying, "O.K., my lord." The term "O.K." had then already been taken over into the German language. The old von Domhoff disappeared soon after, and most probably went to the crematorium; he was no good at digging in the peat bogs, and he had a lot of gold in his teeth.

There is much that I can't remember any more, because it was so terrible. The barracks were immaculate, and around them were plots of grass, and

Here my paints gave out. I tried to sketch the crematorium and the tree on which they hanged people and also the inside of several of the buildings here, and the room with green bottles; but it didn't lend itself to my hand.

I picked up a photograph in Dachau, taken by a photographer of the Signal Corps. It would make a nice Christmas card for Hitler. It shows one of the many prisoners on the high-tension wire, the way the Seventh Army found them.

It is a good thing for the Germans to remember forever that no Russian, Frenchman, Englishman, or American, and no Jew entitled to revenge, has done to the Germans what other Germans have done to them.

this grass was not allowed to be shorter or longer than ten centimeters. It was carefully watched. There were the most exquisite flower beds everywhere; there was the strictest order. The various prisoners were marked with different identification tags; political prisoners had red triangles, pederasts rose-colored disks. I must stop here, also, to say that those, the homosexuals, were the only ones to retain some humor. They were courageous, kind and often heroic. They set an example in how to bear injustice. There was dignity about them. The Jews had yellow marks; incurable loafers (*Arbeitsscheue*) were designated with blue tags, and habitual criminals, who were in supervisory positions and the most favored of the concentration camp inmates, wore green. There was the most marvelous order. When I say that, I can't remember something because it was so terrible. I mean, for example, I can't remember how we managed to keep the floor in the entrance hall of the barracks, where we had to take our shoes off, as clean as it was. The floor was of a bright red, battleship linoleum composition. We came home from the moor pits and on rainy days our shoes were covered with mud, and the shoes had always to stand out in that entrance hall, orderly in line and always shined; even the strip of leather at the bottom of the

shoe between the heel and the sole had to be shined, and somehow that was always done, they were always clean and in a row, and the floor was shining. There was also a dental laboratory that cost one million marks to install and was the most modern in the whole world—but that was to show to people who came visiting, and to inspect the concentration camp, and when they saw how everywhere there were plots of grass, and flowers, and they saw how neat the barracks were, and often they were shown through the dental laboratory, and saw painted on a wall WORK SHALL FREE YOU they took pictures of it, and they said to themselves and to the people back home, "It is impossible to treat prisoners better than in Dachau. They have everything."

There were several forms of punishment, and the first time I ran into trouble was with the supervisor of the first barracks I was in. I was very well behaved and did everything exactly right and he watched me carefully.

One day as we lined up for mess this man took my mess kit out of my hand and said, "This mess kit is filthy." I had been extremely careful not to get in his way. I had been warned by the others, and I had painstakingly cleaned my mess kit. I said nothing.

"Don't you see how dirty that mess kit is?" said the capo, turning the metal dish this way and that in the sun.

The kit sparkled in the light and was spotless, and I said, "I beg your pardon Herr Unterscharführer, but I don't think that it is dirty."

He swung the mess kit by the handle. He hit hard and struck me across the face. "You see now, don't you, that this mess kit is awfully dirty?" he said mildly, like a father.

"*Ja*, Herr Unterscharführer," I said, "I see that this mess kit is awfully dirty."

He hit me with the edge of the mess kit across the mouth then and said, "You learn quickly. There's hope for you."

He reported me the next day for infraction of the rules and for lying, and my punishment was hard labor. That means that for three months I had to work every day until nightfall, and Saturday afternoons and Sundays I had to go out to the peat bogs as well. There were people among us who would have had the courage to jump at one of the S.S. men, or the capos, and bite them in the throat and kill them that way, and it was sometimes discussed, but it was impossible, because the consequences would have befallen the entire group. In that connection there was a man who was confined because he was a homosexual. He was in our group, and he had no time to finish his food, and so had put aside a small piece of bread at messtime. And because it was strictly forbidden to put any food into the pockets of the prison garb, he squeezed this piece of bread over his ear inside the rim of his cap. As we marched out to the peat bogs, we met an S.S. man, and whenever that happened all the caps had to be pulled off quickly, and as this prisoner did this he lost his bread. It fell to the ground. The S.S. man saw it, and the entire company was sentenced to work for the next three months without caps. Our hair was cut short and the sun burned down on us, and it was a great punishment for us. Sentences of three months were a favorite stretch of time with them.

I also remember a scene that occasionally was enacted when a man who had succeeded in escaping was brought back. They were almost always caught soon after they left, and then at the end of the working day there was a parade. The band marched ahead through the camp, and in back of it the con-

vict who had been returned. He was in his prison suit again, and around his neck was a string from which hung a sign. On this was written, "*Ich bin wieder da.*" Normally that would be a nice warm sentence — "I am back again." With this he marched, and then he disappeared to the place where the screams came from and where they killed them slowly.

It was the devil himself who invented these things —or perhaps not even the devil: human bestiality only could think them up. There was also another disgraceful punishment. You had to report to the house where the administration offices were, and around this house, perpetually at attention, stood those who were ordered there, and any S.S. man who went in and out there and was in the mood came up to you and hit you in the face or on the body with just his flat hand, his fist, or anything he had in his hand. That was for a day, and if you fainted you were taken away, but you had to come back for another day until you served out the whole day.

When my sentence to hard labor was over I had another trouble. I had great pain in a tooth, in one of the molars on the right side of my jaw. The man who lay in the bunk beneath me whispered, "Why don't you go to the dentist?"

I said to him, "I would rather die," but he couldn't sleep below. He could feel how I twisted with pain in my bunk and how I turned from one position to the other all night.

"Go," he said, "go to the dentist."

The third day I reported on sick call. I was taken to the wonderful dental office, and the doctor stood there, an officer in a white dentist's coat, with a gun strapped around him outside his coat. I assumed the proper position and said, "Prisoner 783365 reports for treatment."

He put me into the chair and looked into my mouth. I only had the back teeth left, the others had been knocked out.

"How do you stand it?" he said, examining my jaw. He started to work on me, very carefully. After a while he drilled, and I twitched just once as he came on the nerve.

"Does it hurt?" he asked and stopped.

"*Nein*, Herr Doctor," I said.

"But you twitched," said the dentist.

"*Ja*, Herr Doctor," I said.

"But then it must have hurt," he said.

"No, Herr Doctor," I said, remembering the lesson with the mess kit. "It did not hurt at all."

"It isn't supposed to hurt," said the dentist. He continued to drill. A second later I twitched again. "But," he said, "you're not telling the truth. It does hurt, because you twitched again."

Oh, what new devil's invention is this, I thought, and I looked at him and said, "Yes, it hurts a little."

He said, "Why didn't you say so right away?" He stopped and got the needle to deaden the nerve, and I had to wipe my eyes because I cried. I thought I was dreaming, such a thing could not happen in Dachau. I sat up and looked at him carefully once more—at the white coat and the revolver strapped around him—and he stood there and he did nothing to me. He made me a very good inlay, which I still have today.

I would not give you a true picture if I did not tell you that some people were kind even in Dachau. I will never forget that dentist. Dentists until then were people to whom I did not pay particular attention. That happened in the fine dental hospital I told you about, with the most magnificent X-ray machinery and all the latest equipment.

"This isn't possible," I said one day later when I found myself in a room and there was a sign on the wall that said, "Work shall free you," and a picture of Adolf Hitler and some chairs on which twenty of us sat down. We never sat down, so it was an extraordinary occasion.

We jumped to attention as an S.S. man came in, and he sat down at a table, and looked at us, and then he folded his arms.

"You're going to be discharged by special kindness of the Führer—why, I can't understand. Before you leave, however, I want to brief you. We don't expect you to go back and tell them on the outside what a good time you had here. We don't want that at all because then they'll break the doors down trying to get into Dachau. Neither do we desire that you go back and tell them that you were mistreated, you understand."

"*Jawohl*, Herr Lieutenant," said the chorus with enthusiasm.

"We don't want you to say anything at all about Dachau, because if you do when we come for you you'll be able to say that you were really mistreated —you'll get twenty-five across the bare backside every day. And speaking of that, if it were up to me, before you got out of here, just before you left, as a reminder, I'd give you the twenty-five, but frontside, because the temptation to whine and talk will come when you're back with your women, in the night. Remember my words, and also remember that we have a long arm—it reaches all the way around the world. You can't run from us. There is no place on earth you can hide and no disguise that we won't tear from you. That's all I have to tell you. They'll give you a suit and a ticket home and some pocket money. Heil Hitler!"

I think one must be born German. Otherwise how is it possible that one can feel so thankful? I have never felt so grateful to anyone as to the capo who handed me a suit and money. There was a railroad station there, close to the crematorium, and it had also its ten-centimeter grass and its flowers, and we were separated from it by a fence. At this station was a fruit stand, and I said to the Gruppenführer, who was in charge of us, in the fashion in which permission for everything had to be asked: "I beg most obediently [*Ich bitte gehorsamst*], Herr Gruppenführer, may I buy myself an orange?"

And he said, "*Ja*, as soon as you have changed your clothes you may buy yourself anything you wish."

That is how close I was to freedom. In the room in which we were turning our clothes in, suddenly and terribly, my name was called, and somebody said, "Doesn't he go?"

"Yes, he goes," they said, "but not with this group."

I was then again hoping for the impossible error, saying to myself that a mistake had been made that I had been called for the wrong train, but they opened another door and I found myself with a contingent that went to another camp, and that was because I had stated, when I came to Dachau, that I was a precision mechanic, and there was a camp where such skills were needed.

I traveled with a group of people to Flossenburg and was assigned to a special unit.

I was put on a work table, and a tray of various delicate wheels was put before me, and I was to assemble them. It was perhaps something very simple, but I sat there and tried my best to put the puzzle together and couldn't. A prisoner came after a while and took away my tray—the one on which should have been the assembled mechanism—and brought me a new one, with new wheels and springs, and I sat again and stared at it, and then the Gruppenführer came, and stood by my side for a while and watched me. My face was hot. The water was running off my back, but with my untaught hands I was unable to assemble the mechanical puzzle. I was also forbidden to speak.

The Gruppenführer's face brightened as he watched me. He smiled and then he called an S.S. man who also stood awhile and watched me. Then they both left, and an hour later, after I had stared my eyes to a kind of blindness, looking at the tray, I was taken outside.

There stood a wooden horse, and in a triangle all the men of my barracks assembled about it. Next to the wooden horse was a big man who had a whip in his hand. My feet were tied to the wooden horse, and then I was told to remove my trousers. I was then strapped down over the horse and my coat pulled up, and I had to count loud, and if I had missed the count, then it would have started all over again. At the side of the horse stood a doctor with a white coat and a gun strapped around his waist, like the dentist. If a man fainted he listened to the heart, and he gave the signal when the punishment could be resumed. I received twenty-five lashes that day; the last was always a double smack, so one could really say that it was twenty-six lashes.

They left me alone for two days, and then I had light work for three more. There was a group that trimmed the lawn, which was to be kept as exemplarily as it was at Dachau, and there was another detail that kept the paths in order, but these paths were already so in order that nothing could be done to them, and the camp commander therefore had ordered that one of the prisoners was to fill his apron with little stones and rubbish and go ahead of the group, sowing the stones and the trash onto the path, and the others with small baskets followed and cleaned up again. We had to sing, and we had to walk in a bent position that was the invention of the particular commander of that camp. For a while my back burned, and when I lay still I thought of poor Papa and Mamma, and how they had begged me to learn to be a precision mechanic, and how all this would not have happened to me if I had listened to my parents. After my back had healed I was sent back to the workrooms, and they must have known that I wasn't a good mechanic, because I still couldn't assemble the pieces, and they assigned me to some simpler work.

There is a kind of collar button that is worn by officers of the German Navy, which is worn in back of the neck and has a double loop, one inside the other; the larger folds down over the cravat, once the collar is attached to the shirt, and the smaller folds upward. In the room in which I worked now, these collar buttons were assembled, and I was given a tray again on which were the parts of which the collar buttons are made. It's simple to put them together if you know how. But as I have said, my fingers are clumsy and I had no mechanical skill whatever, and while the others worked fast, the pieces on my tray turned very slowly into completed buttons. Although I missed my meals and thought of nothing but making these buttons quickly, I did not turn out the required number.

"I've watched him long enough," said the Gruppenführer to the S.S. man again as he stood in back of me. "He's obstinate, he hasn't learned his lesson."

And that afternoon there was again the triangle of comrades, and a small wooden footstool, and they wound a stocking around my wrists and then folded them in back of me, and tied them with a chain, and pulled my arms up—and then they kicked the stool from under my feet, and my arms were almost torn out of their sockets. They marched away and I was left hanging there. I hung thus for a long, long time, and my arms went to sleep.

"Ah, look who's here," said a voice I knew. I twisted my head in agony, because I had been given a shove, so that I swung back and forth like the pendulum on a clock. Franz Hinterwimmer was in the uniform of an S.S. Captain now.

"Congratulations, you've done a good job," he said. "The factory is gone, they came and bombed Regensburg, the Messerschmitt works too are gone." He looked at me for a while, then he said, "I'd like to stay longer, but I came here on business—I must leave you now," he said. "I have to pull out—I have to get back to work and repair the damage—we're back in the old house now at The Golden Opportunity, thanks to you."

As if he were my friend and shared his troubles with me, he added, "I had a terrible time getting on the four-o'clock plane to Regensburg. I thought of driving here but then I figured it would take me away from home too long. I must tell you about your wife. She's gotten off her high horse. She doesn't make up any more. She's learned to conform —she's a clever girl and she understands the times. I think you should also know about your father— he died.

"I'm leaving now," he said, and gave me another shove. The pain in my shoulders was so great that I fainted. I don't remember when they took me down.

After, I was with the gang singing again and clearing the paths. We followed the man who threw the small stones from his apron and my arms ached as I picked them up. We were all bent, and once we came close to the fence that enclosed the camp. The Gruppenführer who supervised us told us to stop singing. He turned to me. "You're obstinate," he said, "and useless. You're no good to us here, but I'll make it easy for you." He tore the cap from my head and threw it into the wire enclosure. "Run, fetch it," he said, as one says to a dog. But I knew that the moment I would run and come near the fence, I would be electrocuted by the wire or shot by the guard in the tower. So I refused. "Oh," he said, "you want to live—you refuse to obey orders." And so I was punished, and that night I forgot where God lives.

They came for me, and put me in a small dark room. It was filled with water to a height of two feet, and in the center of it was a stool. I sat down on this and because they had taken my shoes away I pulled up my wet feet. They were cold, and I sat down on them, and then they became numb. I slept and prayed, and begged my parents' pardon, and I cried, and I forgot to think for long spaces of time, and I forgot time. I was sorry then I had not followed the Gruppenführer's order and made a run for the cap, and I remember that I thought of the agony of Christ, and I said, O God—after all, what was that compared to what happens here—Christ's suffering lasted only four hours. I thought of my wife and my child, and I cried for hours, and when they came and let me out, I collapsed from the light. And the comrades in my barracks told me that I had been away for six days. From then on I led a life so care-

ful, so quiet, so without any sign of revolt, or even the smallest violation. I did not even dare to show discontent on my face. I was left alone, and in steady, quiet fashion I became nimble, and actually learned to be an expert mechanic. I thought only of my work and of Sylvia. I had her engraved on my mind, on that dense screen of blackness that is before you when you close your eyes, and in the one thousand six hundred and eight nights that I was there she was always before me. No one knows love like a prisoner.

The war was going badly for us, then. There were many rumors—that the concentration camp would be evacuated, and that those who could make the journey would be marched to Dachau, and the others shot.

The Captain in charge of our unit, who was a friend of Hinterwimmer's, had me brought before him. He had arranged something very carefully. He had me brought to his office, and he spoke in almost conversational manner with me and did the unheard-of thing of asking me to sit down. And he asked if there was anything I wanted him to tell my wife. He looked at the door several times, and it opened, and a man brought in a package, and on it I could see my mother's writing, and a letter from my wife. He said to the soldier, "That one doesn't need anything any more—put it on my desk here." He took me by the arm and lifted me, and said, "Stand over there. You can think about the message you want to give me while you wait, while we get a few more together." I said nothing. I floated in the air, as if I didn't care. I didn't feel any more. "Don't you have anything you want to say?" he said. I didn't answer him. I wanted to cry, but I kept my face dry. Not even my lips trembled, I wept inside. I think I cried with my stomach. They brought two others, and there was a guard for each, and so we marched out, along the barracks and plots of the nicely cut grass, and the clear path, and a man opened a gate and let us through, and there was a wall, and everybody had known all along by the sound of firing that regularly came from there what it was for. At that wall we halted. Hinterwimmer suddenly was there, and his friend said:

"Now I'll give you some good advice—lean forward, with your head touching the wall, then you'll fall right, and close your eyes. I promise you, you won't even hear anything. I'll do you a further favor, Herr Pappelmeier. I'll let you be the first."

I did as he said. I was without will. I waited, then I heard two shots that made me deaf and I felt the blast and fell and there was a great pause and then I heard him laugh. I was confused, not knowing whether I was dead or alive.

"He's still afraid to die," said Hinterwimmer, and then the guard yelled, "Get up, march, march, back to the barracks. We'll keep you for later." It was all a joke.

Two days after that, the Americans came. Of that I remember only that one gave me an orange, and that I went to a hospital.

"He weighed seventy-six pounds when he got home," said Pappelmeier Pepperl's mother. "But then everything was all right—all the people who came out of concentration camps were given a special identification mark, a crown of thorns, to wear, and they were immediately allowed to operate their business, and they received special food packages, and Pepperl was honored and the Americans gave him their wrist watches to fix, and everything was fine.

"It would have been all right, but then Franz Hinterwimmer is behind the wire now, in the S.S. compound at Dachau waiting to be tried as a war criminal, and he needed some witnesses to say that he had never mistreated anybody and that he was there only for a short time and because he was ordered to be there and had to carry out orders. So his sister came, and cried, and said what a disgrace it would be if Hinterwimmer were to be hanged, and that if Pepperl would go to Dachau and testify before the Americans, as an ex-Ka-Zettler, then everything would be all right.

"But Pepperl refused, and so the Hinterwimmers got together and dug up the old story of Pepperl's having once belonged to the Nazi party, and denounced him to the authorities, and they proved that he was one of the first to have joined, and it was true. So his crown of thorns was taken away from him, and his privileges, and the food packages, and the time he had spent in Dachau was all for nothing. And he is behind the wire now. He will go on trial, and get maybe a year or two in prison—but he can go to church, and he isn't beaten any more, and he gets enough to eat and has two blankets on his bed, and we can bring him a little something now and then. And this too will pass, and maybe the judges will take into account what he has suffered already. Oh, he is cured, and you know when he comes out, he will get all of Papa's old customers—because now Pepperl is a wonderful precision mechanic. He can fix anything and put together the most complicated instruments—and also, he says, he doesn't want to travel any more, he just wants to stay in Regensburg, at the 'Golden Opportunity'."

Gypsy Music

Gypsy music

They sat in groups
    around one of their tribe
        who strummed a guitar

Among my friends who are photographers one stands out for resourcefulness as well as high enthusiasm. He is Raymund Marivilya. He traces his ancestry back to Cervantes, and often, after he has said something imaginative, I remind him that he should write. He always answers with a shrug and the words, "Perhaps one day I shall." He looks sadly out into space for a while, then he disappears under the black cloth that hangs over his old-fashioned portrait camera, looking through the ground-glass viewer at whatever he is going to photograph, and humming intricate passages of classical music. His talents are many.

As are most of his colleagues, Raymund Marivilya is what is called a frustrated artist. He has, however, a brain that provides him with perpetual invention, and for a decade editors of fashion magazines, advertising art directors, and hard-bitten manufacturers of the products he photographs have failed to pick it dry. Now fifty, and after having changed, in the difficult past, his technique as often as his domicile, and in the process rescuing his files and equipment from Budapest by way of Vienna and Paris, he finds the unending tournament with the fierce women of the editorial chair and the salons of high fashion merely pleasant diversions. In a constant war of prices, ideas, and uncertainties, while the shapes of perfume bottles, handbags, and hats forever change about him, while the colors of lipstick and powder are altered and renamed and editors and entire staffs of magazines disappear, while lesser photographers wilt, the five-foot four inches of Raymund Marivilya remain statue-strong.

His hair is still carbon black and a slab of it, shaped like the fin of a shark, hangs over his forehead. His face is pock-marked and dark as a gypsy's. He climbs ladders all day to look down at the complicated or naïve arrangements of objects he is about to film. With fingers whose nails are stained by acids, he adjusts the dresses on elegant women and with the aid of his camera continues to seduce the more important ladies of the trade. Year in, year out, he matches the monotony of their ecstasies. He calls them, with a mixture of affection and contempt, "my old beauty queens."

The ear of Marivilya is less acute than his eye. He has never learned to pronounce the *th*, and says it as a sharp, hissing *z*. Yet he is a polyglot in his con- versation and uses the words of three languages. His speech, while rapid, is further complicated by colloquial phrases and expressions he has picked up from his delivery boy and darkroom assistant, and flavored with the italics of the *chic* patter of his old beauty queens and their assistants.

When Marivilya makes photographs or becomes excited over an idea he closes one eye and the other comes almost out of its socket and is then like the costly lens of his large camera. With this orb he seems to focus and calculate the light, and while describing anything he envisions he retains this same glassy stare. As is proper for a photographer, gadgets, shapes, imagery, and color have his foremost attention.

I met him one day on Park Avenue, while it was softly raining. "It is nice zat you go wiz a cane when it rains," he said, pointing at my walking stick. "Everybody else would walk wiz an umbrella." He took my arm. "I appreciate zat, because I hate umbrellas. I hate zem because my fazzer was a manufacturer of umbrellas, and in ze rain or in ze snow, in Berlin, he made halt before every umbrella shop. While I stood at his side, jumping from one foot to ze ozer in ze bitter cold, he carefully considered ze construction, shape, and infinite detail of every damn umbrella in ze window."

As we walked together down the avenue, I told him that soon I was going to Europe. "Boy, you're lucky," he said. "I'd give anything if I could go with you, but I have to stay here with that big fat balloon bitch who is running the advertising over there now." He motioned toward Fifth Avenue, where stood an imposing store which was one of his clients. "Come to my studio—this morning we are photographing overcoats worn by famous dogs. I wish I had the patience to write something about that."

At the studio one of his assistants was putting small dishes of water before various agitated dogs.

"Let's go in the other studio," said Marivilya. "You can't hear yourself talk in here with those mutts. Where are you going this time? To the South of France? Oh, then—then I will give you something"—his eye assumed the lenslike look—"God, I'd give anything if I could pack up and go with you. I have discovered something in the South of France that nobody knows about, and I will give it to you—listen!"

One eye closed and the other protruded from its socket. He delivered himself of an essay that went something like this:

"From Marseille you go to the country of Daudet and you come to a place that is called Les Aigues-mortes, which means the 'Dead Waters.' Here a warm wind that is named after the poet Mistral blows over the lands of the Camargue. You drive through a stretch of land emerald green, relieved by patches of water in which porcelain blue sky reflects itself. In these paddies rice is grown. This arrangement of nature changes soon to scenery like that of the prairies of the American West, but here the sandy earth is used for the raising of superb asparagus and marvelous strawberries. You come eventually to dunes and salt grass, and in this part of the Camargue cowboys on white horses herd the wild, fiery-eyed black bulls that are used in the *Corridas à la Provençale*—the exciting and, for the

bull, humane, bullfights, in which no killing is allowed and not even blood flows—only the man gets hurt. In this direction on the shore of the Mediterranean lies a forgotten fishing village of a few houses whose name—mark it well, for you will find it on few maps—whose name is Les Saintes Maries de la Mer.

"Once a year to this lost place come the gypsies of France. They travel on the one road that leads to the island in violently colored wagons, predominantly green, pulled by pathetic horses. Alongside each wagon walks the man, the wife, the children, and a monkey or a donkey. The reins are in the hands of the grandmother, who is in the driver's seat. She smokes a pipe which has a piece of cloth wound around the stem so that she can hold it between her gums. In spite of that she is magnificent and you will want to photograph her. The gypsies congregate at the village of Les Saintes Maries de le Mer, before the fortresslike church of *Notre Dame de la Barque*. The barque is a miraculous relic in which stand the two Saintes Maries after whom the village is named and who, according to the Greek religion, were the sisters of Christ and fled from Palestine together with their faithful servant, the colored Sainte Sara, after whom the Saracens are named. In the middle of the night, by the light of thousands of candles, from the ceiling of the church a jeweled casket is lowered. In this are the bones of Sainte Sara, the patron saint of the gypsies. Then starts a tumult that transforms the ceremony into a pagan ritual, and at the end of this the new King of the Gypsies is elected. Naturally, everyone present is a musician, and the church organ is drowned out by unwritten melodies played on ancient instruments, wild music that comes from their blood and excitement. Ecstasy mounts like a river in flood-time. The scene becomes more like a Harlem ballroom than a church. Even the priests take part in this *auto-da-fé*. It is exactly as it was six hundred years ago—or a thousand—and it is the one thing in this world, besides the Taj Mahal, which, when you actually come upon it, does not disappoint you. It keeps its promise. I give it to you. And what I have told you is only the first scene of the first act of this opera. During the night, while the church is filled with singing and dancing, the cowboys, who are called *gardiens,* ride out to sea. The Mediterranean is in-

129

Les Saintes Maries de la Mer.

The barque is a miraculous relic

credibly shallow at this point and the cowboys can ride their horses beyond the horizon without losing ground. They take with them the barque on which the two Saintes Maries originally landed here with their maid, the dark Saint Sara, and a trunk that contained their clothing. As the sun rises the gypsies, led by a bearded Patriarch of the Greek Church in magnificent robes, walk down to the sea—the women in their most colorful costumes, with spit curls and holding in their arms the young that were born during the last year, and all look out to sea, waiting to behold the barque.

"As the barque is sighted there is a fanfare of trumpets, and the Patriarch, followed by his acolytes, wades into the sea until his beard touches the water, and there he awaits the barque. After welcoming the Saintes Maries and Sainte Sara, he turns around and leads the procession out of the lukewarm waters back to land. The wet jewels on his robes now sparkle in the sun. The children born during the year are baptized in the water that drips from his

sleeves. They are allowed to touch the robe of Sainte Sara, and are thereby given the promise of health and happiness for their lives, and their parents know that they will never belie their faith. Since it is against the tradition of the gypsies there to stay in one place longer than three days, the village of Les Saintes Maries de la Mer is deserted on the third day and goes back to sleep as it awoke. If you crave the absolute in solitude, there you can have it."

As Marivilya stopped speaking, the door was opened by an assistant bringing a tray on which was a pitcher of milk, some graham crackers, and a dish containing small red radishes. Marivilya rearranged the objects on the tray as if he were going to photograph them, then he poured some salt on the tray and, holding a radish with three fingers, he said:

"This is how the gypsies cross themselves in Greek Orthodox fashion, with three fingers pressed together, and that is why they are called 'salt pinchers.'

Gypsy music

"I give all this to you—and here, take this with you." He took a camera from a shelf and handed it to me. "For God's sake don't lose it. Take some pictures of the gypsies and other things. If my old beauty queens should hear this story they would go crazy over it," he continued, his lenslike eye shining, "and immediately steal the idea. They always get excited about travel subjects, and they are beside themselves when it is elegant travel, like these Saintes Maries taking along a maid and a trunk full of clothes. They call that a 'tie-up.' It's good for at least six pages in color."

The assistant came into the room and announced that all the dogs, except a Yorkshire terrier named Kitty de Belvedere, had arrived, and that the camera was set up. Marivilya rose.

"*Alors,*" he said, "good-by." In the door, with his hand on my shoulder, he added, "You and I, we are people of the better class. There are people to whom nothing ever happens, and then there are people who never have anything to tell, and then there are the others like you and me, and to us an adventure comes every day of the year." He limped away. "*Auf Wiedersehen,*" he said, and went to photograph the aristocratic dogs.

A month later I was on my way to the shrine of the gypsies. The road led through prairies of the Camargue alongside the delta of the Rhone, past

As the sun rises, the gypsies walk down to the sea

vineyards that produce the *petit vin du pays*. There were green fields shaded by umbrella-shaped pines, and rice paddies that reflected startingly blue sky. The desertlike stretches, however, produced neither the asparagus nor the strawberries Marivilya had promised, but innumerable stones of astonishingly equal size, larger than pebbles—a little too large for throwing and not big enough for building. Apparently they were good for nothing. The road to Les Saintes Maries de la Mer was devoid of romantic gypsy wagons, pipe-smoking grandmothers, and decrepit horses. Instead, motorcars and modern trailers bore the gypsies in great numbers to the fiesta, and they rushed past the taxi which carried me at twenty-seven francs a kilometer. Further, my taxi was frequently forced to the side of the road by huge busses which took thousands of tourists to the rendezvous of the "Bohemians," as the gypsies are called in this part of France. In addition, to the left of the road were tracks bearing special excursion trains which were crowded to the steps.

Officers in charge of traffic at the entrance to the village of Les Saintes Maries de la Mer dispatched the streams of vehicles to various parking places, and the confusion and noise were equal to that which confronts you in Paris at the dangerous spot where the traffic of the Rue Royale pours into the Place de la Concorde.

In the center of the village and near the sea were the encampments of the gypsies. Pictorially, these were exactly what the word "gypsy" implies. The women had shiny dark faces, matted hair, and wore many dirty skirts of somber hue. They tormented the tourists with menacing insistence, offering junky trinkets and pictures of Sainte Sara. Others were attempting to quiet their half-naked children along the sidewalks, and some were busy cooking inside their trailers.

The men, who I learned were generally menders of broken casseroles and umbrellas and shearers of dogs and sheep, stood about mostly idle. Some industrious ones, who owned tents in which their women consulted the stars and read palms for small fees,

were busy patching canvas or hammering stakes into the ground. Others, near the bastionlike church, were unloading small, battered, and once white wooden horses and suspending these on rusty chains from the canopy of a shaky, blue-and-gold merry-go-round. Here and there walked one in an ill-fitting but sober business suit and cap.

Later they sat down on the running boards of their cars, on tables under lampposts and trees, and ate, sometimes with knife and fork. The oncoming darkness came to their aid. The appearance of the flea-bitten wanderers was improved in the deep shadows around the church and along the sea. Presently the street lamps and the moon edged their silhouettes with golden light as they stood and sat in groups around one of their tribe who strummed a guitar. I thought they all looked depressed.

The church was crowded to the point of danger; the smells of unwashed clothes and bodies were intensified by the warmth of candles on many altars and were mingled with the sweet odor of incense. On a side altar was the barque of the two Saintes Maries. The saints were rendered with touching simplicity and painted in bright colors, but neither the trunk nor the servant Sara was in the small ship with them.

It developed that the gypsies were not salt pinchers, and that there was no Patriarch of the Greek Church to bless them. Besides, the Saintes Maries are not sisters of Christ, and the Saracens are not named after Sainte Sara. The devotion of the gypsies, however, was deep and real. Next day the ceremonial of the pilgrimage was presided over by a Vicar General of the Catholic Church, who did not walk into the water. Therewith the second act of Marivilya's opera collapsed.

Not at dawn but at the comfortable hour of eleven, the morning of a lovely day, the procession headed for the shore with the barque of the two Saintes Maries. With a greater amount of enthusiasm and louder singing from the gypsies, the statue of Sainte Sara followed them.

Of the Saintes Maries and Sainte Sara, the official *Manuel des Pèlerinages aux Saintes Maries* says:

"Sainte Marie Jacobé and Sainte Marie Salomé were the close relatives of the Holy Virgin. Some say that they were cousins. According to respectable opinions found in several ancient writings at Arles,

Lyons, and Rheims, they were her sisters. In all we know for certain by the Evangelium that they were the mothers of four apostles: of the two Saints Jacques and besides of Saint Jude and Saint Jean. We find them at the foot of the cross, at the side of the Virgin, and at the tomb of Christ at Easter. They were present also as he arose and, as did the apostles, so did they receive the Holy Ghost. For twelve years they stayed in Palestine near their children and witnessed the rise of Christianity, and after as the apostles were forced to flee, the saints were set adrift in a small barque without oars or tiller and abandoned to the winds and the sea, but the angels themselves conducted the barque safely across the sea and deposited the saints in Camargue."

Besides the religious tradition, there is the pagan legend which has been preserved by Jean Aicard in *The King of Camargue,* and told in verse by the poet Pierre Gauthier: When the saints had landed on the coast, accompanied by Sara the Egyptienne ("gypsy" comes from "Egyptian"), a payment was

demanded of them by a boatman who had helped them disembark. These saints were in a state of extreme poverty, so one gave a sprig of rosemary which had touched the lips of Christ; the other, one of Christ's blond curls. As for the poorest of them, Sara, she had nothing to offer but the garments she wore. These she took off, but God, says the legend, covered her nudity with a nimbus of light, and the boatman, thus dazzled, prostrated himself before the holy women. This is probably a confusion of two legends, one concerning Sainte Sara, the contemporary of Christ, the other concerning Sara the Egyptian, the converted courtesan who lived much later, in the fifth century.

The Catholic Church is vague about Sainte Sara. Therefore the official shop, which is located in the rectory, offers souvenirs to match individual beliefs. One may select postal cards depicting a barque containing only the two Saintes Maries, or one may choose other cards which include Sainte Sara and the trunk, too. In the crypt of the church one sees a statue of Sainte Sara, her altar, and her relics. The Bohemians honor her as their patron, especially on May 24. According to them, she was one of them, a native of the region, the first one to be converted by the saints and their servants.

As far as Bohemians are concerned, the dark Sara was not a servant. She was one of their own. She was, they believe, a young and ravishingly beautiful gypsy princess, the daughter of the King of Anatilia, a place that has sunken away into the sands of the Camargue. Walking on the beach, Sainte Sara was the first to perceive in the dawn the barque in which the Saintes Maries tried to land. Immediately struck by faith, Sainte Sara swam out to them and, making a sail of her dress, brought the little vessel ashore.

Thus, according to the gypsies' legend, Christianity was introduced into Gaul by a gypsy, and one

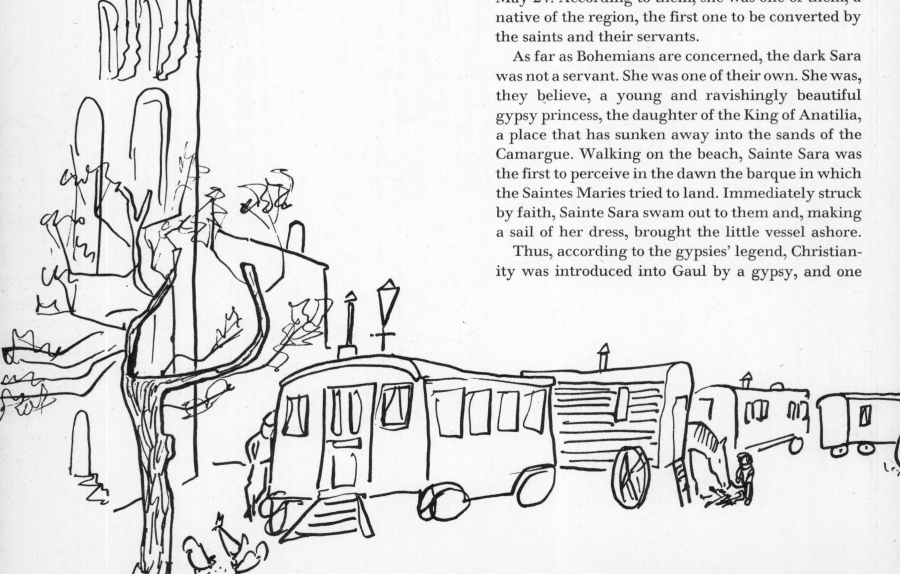

can imagine the impatience of the people of her race in seeing her relegated to second place in the ceremonies of the pilgrimage, and furthermore neglected as the one of the three in the boat not properly canonized, having to stand beside the altar and not upon it, in her shrine in the crypt of the church at Les Saintes Maries de la Mer.

On the third day of the festivities, tired from the glare of sun and sea, and hungry, I entered a crowded restaurant whose one harassed waiter looked near collapse. I sat at the one free table in the corner, loosened my collar, and had pulled the camera strap over my head when I was yanked to attention by an unmistakably American voice.

"My God, there is the man from the airliner," said one of two motherly-looking women who, I later learned, were sisters. Both seemed ruffled by travel and the heat. Having been an air passenger to Europe, I looked around, but they pointed to a man in the corner opposite mine.

"Oh! The time we've had to find anybody that speaks English!" shouted one of them over the tables. She then turned to a gypsy who stood beside their table. He weighed over two hundred pounds, but his flesh was hard, and he had the head of a Roman Senator. It was covered with shining, tight black spirals. He stood out from the rest in a pair of fawn-colored corduroy pants and a clean, brick-colored shirt.

"Here—*signaiz ça*," said one of the ladies as she pushed an illustrated program of the pilgrimage toward him and, making the motions of writing herself, indicated to him that she wanted his autograph.

The gypsy took the pen offered him and studied the paper.

"We're a couple of good-will ambassadors from Missouri," said one of the ladies loud enough for everyone to hear, and, smiling in the direction of the man from the airliner, her sister said to the gypsy, "We're going to show this to President Truman when we get back. President Truman—you *comprenay?*"

"*Ah, oui,*" said the gypsy, "*le bon Président des Etats-Unis.*"

"*Signaiz ça,*" repeated the first.

"We're from Independence, too," said the other woman.

"*Pardon?*" said the gypsy.

"Independence," said both of them, and one said, "You know—*Fraternitay, Egalitay,* Independence—"

"*Liberté,*" said the gypsy, and nodded with vehemence.

"It's the same thing," said the more articulate of the sisters. The whole restaurant was listening and nodding approval.

"He's the King of the Gypsies," shouted one of the women to the friend from the airliner, and the latter got up and made his way through the crowd to their table.

"You here alone?" one of the ladies asked him.

"No, I have a friend," the man answered. He seemed to be a French businessman, yet he spoke American English with only a slight accent.

"Well, bring your friend," said one of the ladies from Independence. "Hey, waiter, *psst—garçon—* get a chair for our friend."

"Ask the King to sit down, too," said her sister.

She went on, "My God, just think of it, a week ago this time we were in Washington—and now where are we?"

"Well," said her sister, "the world is just getting to be a shriveled-up little old place." She looked around for the waiter. "*Du* water," she said.

"*Evian, Vichy, Perrier,* madame?" said the waiter.

"Oh no—just water, you know, from the faucet." It was the sister who had handed the gypsy her pen. Now she illustrated turning a tap with her hand.

"*Ah, de l'eau nature,*" said the waiter.

"And bring us four champagne cocktails, no, make it five, one for the King."

"My friend does not touch anything," said the French businessman, pointing to a young man who had sat attentively, making amiable faces, but until that moment had been ignored.

"That's all right," said the lady seated next to him.

"Give it to the King," said the other sister.

"He was in the underground the entire war," said the man from the airliner, pointing at his compatriot.

"Oh, he was," said one of the two kind ladies with slow and important words and large eyes. "My, that's interesting, I bet he's got some stories to tell."

"Unfortunately, he does not speak English," said the Frenchman, while the underground member looked at the table, ashamed.

"Well, tell him he's going to have a good time from now on," said one of the good-will ambassadors. After the message was translated to him the resistance fighter nodded and said, "Zank you."

"They don't have any champagne cocktails here," said the Frenchman, "but the wine of the region is very good."

The ladies then said loudly how much they had enjoyed their visit to the Saintes Maries. The resistance fighter began to tell a story to the man from the airliner, who translated it for the sisters from Independence. The gypsy left after he had joined in a toast to President Truman. The place was enhanced by the presence of the ladies, and they were the best kind of ambassadors of good will. Like all things that are good and true, they shone and gave out happiness, and it would have been a completely successful and happy excursion for them if at the end one of them had not suddenly screamed, "My pen!"

The French businessman got up and with determination walked to the door of the restaurant, and then ran out on the sidewalk. But it was the third day of the feast, and the trailers of the gypsies were rolling past the restaurant and out of the village.

As if he were reciting the end of a travelogue, the Frenchman said: "Well, and now you may say *adieu* to your beautiful ball-point pen—"

"And I just got it new the day we left Washington and it was fourteen-karat gold," said the good-will ambassador from Missouri, miserably.

After several of the wagons had passed, the village square became visible, and in its center still stood the largest and most shiny of the trailers. Close to it a gendarme sat astride his bicycle with folded arms, putteed legs firmly set on the ground. He was watching several gypsies loading on a truck the last of the merry-go-round horses.

"Let's go and see," said one of the ladies. "Maybe that's the King's trailer."

The Frenchman asked the gendarme, who nodded and pointed toward the comfortable home on wheels. "It is his, all right," said the French businessman. From inside the trailer came a complaining woman's voice and the crying of a child. On the trailer steps stood two pairs of baby shoes covered with fresh whiting. A door slammed, muting the voices, but for a while there were sounds of objects being knocked about in the room apparently closed by the door that slammed. There, probably, the Queen had retired, for one could hear the rumbling basso of the King, also complaining. Then there was quiet. The Frenchman looked up from the baby shoes and knocked at the door.

Gypsy music

The gypsy King opened it and, standing there with pen in hand, said something unpleasant. Then he recognized his visitors and his face cleared. Pushing his glasses to his forehead, he invited them in. "I am glad to shake you by the hand," he said to the Frenchman. He picked up a paper from the table. "I don't know about America," he grumbled, "but the French government knows how to be malicious. One can say that with candor after looking at the forms they hand you to fill out." He let the long printed form go; it sailed back and forth and then settled on the table. He raised his voice again and turned his face in the direction of the closed door to the next compartment: "Life in France is a scandalous affair today," he cried. "First of all you try to liberate yourself of the debts imposed by your installations, then you try and prepare a little capital for your family. After that you begin to think of old age and do your best to amass enough so that you will be exempt from material needs. *Non*, they won't let you. They harass you with undecipherable forms and send gendarmes to see that you fill them out. But it is most bitter when those to whom you should be able to turn for succor and understanding, and of whom you must ask co-operation, fail you, and also turn against you. That is all I have to say."

A provocative "Ha" was heard in the other room, and another door was slammed so hard it would have rocked an earthbound house. Here only the gladiolas in a vase on the dining table were disturbed.

The King put the ball-point pen into his shirt pocket and smiled. He rubbed his hands and smiled again, took a key from his pocket and, stepping to a built-in desk, opened one of two small leaded doors that were decorated with stained-glass lilies.

"A little Mirabelle," he said, taking a bottle from the closet. He stuck the fingers of his other hand into five thick liqueur glasses as if they were thimbles and thus transported them to the table.

"What do you call a ball-point pen here?" asked one of the good-will ambassadors of the Frenchman.

"Oh, simply a *stilo*."

"Tell him we have a *stilo* just like his," said the other sister as she pointed at the gypsy King's shirt pocket.

The Frenchman translated.

"*Ah, non!*" said the King. "You cannot possibly

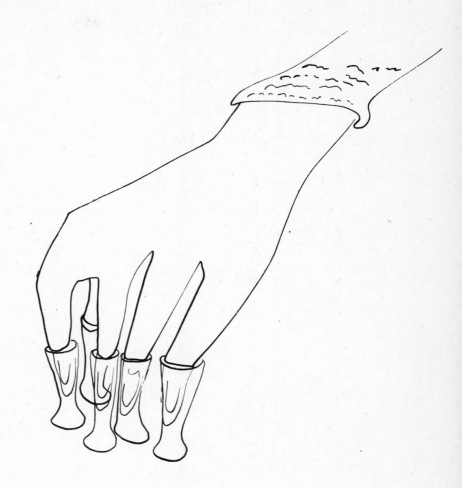

have one like this! I have tried them all, whatever name they come by—Le Montblanc, Le Triomphe, Intermonde, Mon Ami, Succès, and Météore, but this, mesdames, messieurs, is the best of them all. I will show you why." He took the pen out of his pocket held it up. "This is the regular end." He removed the cap, exposing the ball-point. "Now let us assume that we have a breakdown at this end. Your inspiration, *alors*, is not wasted, you continue to write! You simply turn the pen around and—watch"—he removed the cap from the other end of the pen—"*voilà!* you have a fountain pen of convention which actually writes. You finish your poem, your testament, your letter; your government will not be disappointed, for you will not stop filling out the forms. Always you are at ease and in accord with the world!"

I was afraid that the gypsy would turn out to be the sole local agent for the marvelous double-ended pen.

"May we have a look at it?" said one of the ladies.

"But certainly," said the King. "Please try it out.

Here is some paper." The pen wrote beautifully with either end.

"No, that's not our pen," said the good-will ambassadors to the Frenchmen.

The gypsy King showed the visitors his combination radio and phonograph, and four small fans attached to the ceiling in the corners of the living room. He demonstrated an intercommunication system between car and trailer, and with special pride he opened the doors of his icebox. Outside, he displayed eight laying hens in a traveling coop that was slung beneath the trailer, where also hung a charcoal-burning stove of his own invention. Running the length of the car was a locker that contained his fishing tackle.

The gendarme, in his original pose astride his bicycle, was still waiting for the form to be filled out. The wooden horses and other parts of the merry-go-round had been stowed on the truck, and at last all of the King's possessions had been admired by the good-will ambassadors. The French businessman, who had looked with reserve, finally asked coldly if, *par hazard*, the King had put the ladies' ball-point pen into his pocket at the time he had given them his autograph.

The King looked a little hurt. "*Alors, non,*" he said. "I don't do things by hazard." He remembered clearly that he had given the pen back. He took his cap off and said he was sorry, but the annual rendezvous of the Bohemians had come to its end. Bending over, he picked up the two pairs of baby shoes as he had grasped the liqueur glasses and announced that he had to leave.

Later, at the restaurant, the underground leader, who wanted to write down the address of the good-will ambassadors, reached into his pocket and there found two pens, his own and that of the ladies, which he had put there by mistake. But it was too late to apologize to the industrious Bohemian, for beyond the limits of the small village of Les Saintes Maries de la Mer out of the indigo night shone two bright red lights, the tail-lights of the gypsy King's trailer. Or, perhaps, they were "ze eyes of ze wild black bulls" which my friend the photographer Raymund Marivilya had told me "graze in ze endless salt marshes of ze Camargue."

Les Saucissons d'Arles

Les saucissons d'Arles

"ONE REGRETS," said the waitress of the Restaurant Au bon Coin in Arles, "but one has no Saucisson d'Arles. There is a kind of Saucisson d'Arles that I can offer Monsieur, but it is not the *vrai* Saucisson d'Arles, which, as Monsieur undoubtedly knows, is made from the meat of Donkeys."

The waitress, who had the face of the true Arlésienne, a narrow oval commanded by an aquiline nose that has a smaller upper and a longer lower concave edge, looked at me with the brown eyes that go with this type of face and waited for my answer. Since few things in this world are *vrai* any more and made of the stuff they once were, I ordered the imitation Saucisson d'Arles.

"After the Saucisson may I suggest Monsieur la Truite au Bleu," continued the waitress, handing me a soiled piece of cardboard with a Kindergarten kind of writing on it. Then, pointing with her pencil stub, she said, "After the Truite, perhaps the Côtelette de Veau Provençale with a small salad. As to the order for the dessert, I will come back for it. To drink I can recommend to Monsieur *le petit vin du pays*. It has no name, but it is a good, light wine."

She wrote out the order in the same hand in which the menu was written, on a block of cheap paper. I kept nodding and she turned after every dish and sang out its name in the direction of the kitchen. The cook was listening through a window-like opening through which he had stuck his head, nodding acknowledgment of the orders from the other end.

Halfway between the table and the kitchen, behind a bar, sat a woman with the calm face of the Mona Lisa, who listened, smiling with approval, and after the wine was ordered she turned majestically to take a small carafe from a zinc-covered bar and filled this with the *petit vin du pays*.

The Guide Michelin lists no famous restaurants in this region, and I had come to the Restaurant Au bon Coin upon the recommendation of a taxi driver I found standing in front of the Hôtel Jules César, which is the best in Arles, comfortable, but not of the luxury class. The Restaurant Au bon Coin is located in an old building, to which a cement box has been added by way of a terrace. The terrace has four windows at each side and a set of French doors that run the width of the structure. There are no fly

screens, and, as in all such establishments, the selection of the color or material of curtains has not troubled anyone much. The tables in such places are sometimes alike, but the chairs certainly vary in design, or else the chairs are the same and then the tables belong to several styles.

Here there were four small tables seating two people each, two tables for four, and one large enough to seat ten to twelve people. The parquet hardwood floor ended where the French doors folded back, and at that part it was much scraped and cut from the gravel which extended from the doors to the sidewalk. On the day of my visit two of the small tables were outside on the gravel, and the one at which I sat down was shaded by a near-by tree.

The chef, who looked like a young mechanic rather than a cook, accompanied the waitress, who carried the Saucisson d'Arles, and he excused himself for allowing it to come out of his kitchen. "It is regrettable," he said, "that people who have come from such faraway places as America to eat the real Saucisson d'Arles in its place of origin have to content themselves with an imitation," which, he ex-

plained, was made of pork. The waitress staggered back through the gravel, then walked on the hard floor and took a tray from a stack; the woman at the bar handed her the small carafe of wine, which was placed on the tray—together with a glass—and brought to the table.

Into one corner of the terrace leaned a man dressed like a groom; he wore a tattered sporting jacket several sizes too big and an old cap. He came to life as another man, dressed in the same fashion but in clothes that fitted, came running through the restaurant. The well-dressed one was busy pulling on gloves, and as he came out on the gravel he was met by a third man who handed him a whip and led him to a waiting horse and cart. After a clicking sound and cracking his whip smartly, the man with the gloves sailed down the street behind his trotter. His jacket was visible long after the shape and the color of horse and wagon had become uncertain.

The sound of the hoofbeats fell away and the crunching of feet in the sands, to which I turned, announced the waitress, who poured the wine and asked for the bread ticket. I had just carefully detached the badly perforated token when the clop clop clop of the trotter was heard again, and as the horse came back up the boulevard, the entire staff of the restaurant ran to the door, the guests arose from their tables, and everybody shouted encouragement and praise. The cart went past, the driver lowered his whip in salute and smiled with ownership's pride. A puddle of water near the curb briefly mirrored his jacket.

"Monsieur is not eating his Saucisson d'Arles?" said the waitress with concern as she turned to the table, after having waved at the horseman. She snapped her napkin at several dogs and eyed my table. "Go away, Diane. Give me peace, Azore," she shouted. As the dogs moved under the other tables and inside the restaurant the solicitous waitress said: "But they are not as bad as all that, the Saucissons, Monsieur." She pushed the plate toward me, put my fork on the plate atop the six thin slices of Saucisson d'Arles, which resembled disks of greasy red marble, and then she went to another table, where she busied herself ladling Potage Santé into the plate of a man who had the unmistakable symp-

toms of a regular and satisfied patron of the establishment.

I poured myself another glass of wine from the cloudy glass jug, whose neck was full of fingerprints, and ate the sausages, which were good enough. Again the hoofbeats became audible, the staff once more rushed to the door, and this time the cart halted in front of the restaurant.

The magenta-colored nostrils of the horse distended and contracted; it was unhitched and taken to one of the trees, to which it was tied facing away from me, in a position that allowed it to swish the flies from its haunches as well as from my table.

The waitress came and wiped her face with the napkin and then threw it under her arm as she took away the plate on which the Saucisson d'Arles had been. She said, "Don't derange yourself," forgetting the third person address, "I shall be with you in a second and then I will not budge from this table again—the trout is on its way."

From then on, until the salad was cleared away, there was a crowd in front of and around my table, feeling the horse's legs and patting its rump. The

The house where Van Gogh lived in Arles

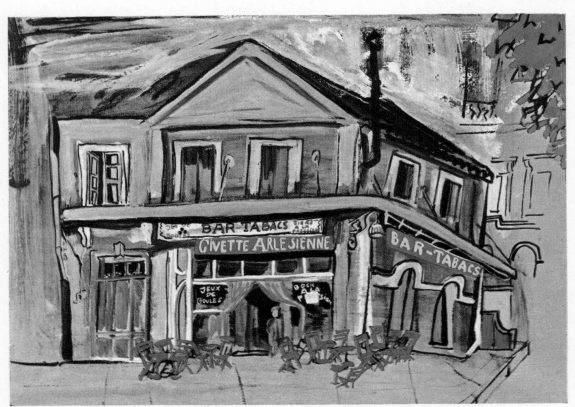

chef found time to bring out carrot greens and feed them to the horse, and the owner stood with folded arms looking out into the street. Now and then he was almost pushed off the curb by the animal, which rubbed its head against the back of his multicolored tweed jacket.

He turned suddenly and put an end to the adoration of his horse by screaming for the waitress, whom he ordered to serve champagne to everyone. He took off the jacket and hung it over the vacant chair at my table and explained to me that he had acquired the horse that morning.

The Arlésienne let everything lie where it was and occupied herself with the order of the sportsman. She came back with champagne of an unknown brand, but, in the way of wine in France, nothing that comes out of a bottle is altogether bad, and this champagne, which had the color of thin light beer and its fragile white foam, was drinkable, and with the loud textiles it aided in establishing the free air of risk and reward that properly belongs around horses.

There was some singing later, and then after his coffee, whose piece of gray sugar he took from the saucer and sacrificed to his horse, the owner picked up his coat and, after brushing it with his hand,

hung it over one shoulder. He untied the animal, looked at it once more, and led it away.

The waitress leaned against the tree and examined a bite on her arm inflicted by a horsefly.

"Who was that man?" I asked. She looked after him. He and the horse were stiffly walking down the exact center of the Boulevard des Lices.

"Oh, he," she said. "That is monsieur the proprietor of this restaurant." She sucked the bite on her arm.

"And madame," I asked, "is she the lady at the buffet?"

"*Non*," answered the Arlésienne, "Madame and Monsieur have been divorced a long time. Madame lives in Paris."

I offer this overdetailed report on the character and personnel of this restaurant partly as a description of an average place in which I had a fair and reasonable meal, but chiefly to undo a cast-iron set of characters that live in the literature of travel. They are the half-witted, jovial owners of small restaurants and regional eating places who are usually called Papa or Mama, or *le bon Père So-and-so* or *la bonne Mère Catharine* or just *Monsieur le propriétaire* or *Madame la patronne*. They all suffer from the saccharine idiocy that infests Walt Disney's bunnies. Whether in Normandy, the Midi, or Provence, the cute innkeeper of these reports always comes out of his kitchen rubbing his hands to explain the *specialités de la maison*, and madame then comes trotting from behind her buffet, from her arrangements of homemade, delicious pâtés, her special Céleri Ravigotte, from the secrets of her small andouilles, her priceless tartelettes and macédoines. She joins *le bon père* at the table of the tourist, and with many sad "Oh's" and shakings of the head they both bleat about the bad times one lives in, and add to this a recital of their occupational ills. Later they speak of the past, nodding now with nostalgia but saying "Ah" instead of "Oh." The conversation of these figures is as static as their design, and you will hear them speak as they do now in articles written in 1898. Now as then in these stories they agree with every opinion, religious, political, economic, scientific, or gastronomic, which the guest puts forward, and as that one tears himself away to say adieu—always after the most memorable meal of his life—they both come to the tavern gate and wave after

Whether in Normandy, le Midi or Provence

him. I have met all kinds of *hôteliers*. In my travels I have looked in vain for monsieur and madame.

Before I left the Restaurant Au Bon Coin in Arles I asked the waitress to tell me where the house that van Gogh lived in stands. She looked at me without understanding. I then pronounced the name in every way possible—van Goff, van Goch, van Hoch, van Choch. The painter, I said. She shook her head and then asked the lady at the buffet and the remaining guests, but nobody else in the restaurant had ever heard about him. I walked to the Hôtel Jules César and asked the chauffeur who had recommended the restaurant to me to take me to van Gogh's house and to one of the bridges he had painted. He said he was sorry, but he didn't know of whom I spoke. I walked to the Hôtel Dieu, the hospital where the painter had been treated after he had severed his ear and the painting of whose garden is one of his best known works. It was there also that he had done the self-portrait with the white bandages wound around his head. The garden is there exactly as he painted it, but the doorkeeper said he did not know anyone by that name, and asked whether he had been a patient there recently. No—

long ago, I said. The rule of the prophet being least remembered in his home town holds true of the painter as well. While Arles was not his home, here van Gogh painted himself into recognition.

I came to the Musée Arlaten, its vast rooms filled with local antiques and objects of nature. Rows from the typical life of the Arlatens. On the third and last floor of this museum at last I found paintings. The largest room, well lit, was hung with the original oil and water colors of local artists, all of them burdened with sentimentality. In many of them, and in the largest, appears the poet Mistral in cape, flowing hair, and with ecstatic lifted face and pose. There were several sketches and water colors, all of them painted and drawn with the determination to make nature more beautiful and interesting than it is. Past this exhibit, in a small side room which I carefully measured and which is exactly twelve by sixteen feet, I found van Gogh's work at last. In this room hang reproductions of several of his best known canvases and one that I had never seen before, called "The Sand Barge."

I went to the museum several times and once took my camera along to photograph a large and interesting statue of St. Christopher which stands in the courtyard. I was up in the van Gogh room again when a man who could have posed for one of his pictures, an old bent creature in a plum-colored almoner's suit, came wandering into the room, followed by a woman. He looked at the prints with weariness. He was about to go but stopped and, pointing after a while at the wall where most of the pictures hung, he moved his dry lips and, with the heavy peasant finger waving at the exhibition as if he were admonishing the painter, he spoke to his companion with much effort and barely audibly: "They say that he was a great painter. I knew him well, madame, and I tell you that he was a madman." He left the room in haste. I walked after him and asked him whether he knew where the house stood in which van Gogh lived. He told me that it stood no longer, it had been blasted in a bombing raid. "Nothing of it remains," he said.

Later at the hotel at dinner I talked about van Gogh to a Frenchman. I told him of my difficulty in finding anyone who knew him or his house, and I quoted the old man at the museum. I also told him about how esteemed and well known van Gogh was in the United States and how many originals by the great painter hung in American museums and collections. The Frenchman looked coldly across the table and said, "Ah yes, I believe you. You buy ev-erything, and you have the paintings, but don't ever forget it is we who have the painters."

Leaving the Musée Arlaten, one takes with one the impact of van Gogh's design and color, for the reproductions of his painting that hang there are good—much better than most of the mass-produced color-poor copies that have been thrown on the market in America. On walking through town and field, and along the canal to the bridges he painted, one can see his color everywhere. The brightness of the large sun over Arles explains his brilliant palette —the tortured trees that appear in his painting still stand there, the water is his blue, and his yellow is smeared on fields as if it were pressed out of a tube. Of the famous bridges, however, only the foundations remain.

In Arles there is also an amphitheater made of rows of stone blocks in an oval arrangement around the oval arena in the center.

The bloodless bullfights that take place here and have been much publicized are only occasionally bloodless. In between them the real corrida takes place, with the bull put to death in Spanish style. The humanity of the bloodless bullfight is also questionable, for while it is true that the animal is not killed in the ring, the bull, even if he wins, is not turned loose but is led around the corner to the butcher, where he dies without glory.

In the center of Arles is the Place du Forum. After the fury of van Gogh's design and color, the visitor comes here upon a new mood, a small-town idyl, a poetic backyard that is best looked at from the sidewalk tables of a café called "L'Union des Corses."

The awning of this café is like a sultan's tent. In front of it, around three in the afternoon, a Moor in a long blue robe and with a red fez on his head appears. He pulls a cart and props it up in front of the sidewalk tables. He orders an apéritif and, after slowly sipping it, lies down in the cart. Folding his hands under his head, he looks up, losing himself in the greenery of the plane trees, of which four shade the square. Children play on the pedestal of the statue of Mistral; the statue itself was melted down by the Germans, as were all others in France whose metal was of use. There also comes a man with a little girl, and he sits down on a bench. He has lost one leg, and after he has made himself comfortable the child, using it as a toy, takes one of his crutches and, placing her cheap doll on the handle in the center of the crutch, drags it around.

To the north the square is dominated by the Hôtel du Nord Pinus, into which, like jewels into gold, are set the remains of a Roman arch. On the balcony of the hotel a chambermaid who was beating carpets sang to the music of a violinist who stood in front of the competing establishment, the Hôtel du Forum. After a while the violinist turned and shouted up to the maid, "Mademoiselle, please sing a little less strongly if you please." The violinist, who, besides popular airs, played songs by Reinaldo Hahn, distinguished himself further by squeezing his umbrella to his side while playing.

Into this square came also three German prisoners of war, who signed contracts as voluntary workers. They were still in their old field uniforms and walked about unmolested. One, leaning on a broom, listened to the Frenchman with the crutches, who had lost his leg in the war in which the Germans fought—yet he nodded and said to the prisoner, "Until tomorrow," as he left. Another one of the Germans read the menus on the outside of the various restaurants with great interest. After a while the prisoners all started to sweep the square, and then watered it down, under the direction of a Frenchman who worked alongside of them. At the end they shouldered the brooms and with free hands in pockets they walked slowly back to their barracks.

The leniency extended to them backfires occasionally, and they don't always walk back to their barracks. I translate in this connection a story which appeared in *France Soir* in the issue of June 10, 1947:

In conducting to the police station his German rival

A DECEIVED HUSBAND WINS AN AWARD

When Maurice Tireau, last evening, brought to the police station the German prisoner of war Walter Dietrich, whom he had found at his domicile at number thirty Rue Piat, he learned to his surprise that he was entitled to an award.

He would have welcomed with joy this good news, if behind his feat there had not been hidden the saddest conjugal misadventure possible. M. Tireau, by profession a traveling salesman and committed to long absences from home, had in effect found the fugitive at the side of his wife.

The German came from the camp of Blonville-sur-Mer, in the Calvados district. In this region, where the prisoners enjoy a certain liberty, he had made the acquaintance of Madame Tireau, who was then visiting there, and after this meeting and the return of Madame Tireau to Paris, the prisoner thought of nothing but of how to reach the capital, *where eventually the young wife was to offer him the most tender refuge. Walter Dietrich arrived in Paris on April 21, 1947, and immediately went to the address in the Rue Piat, taking there the place which the traveling salesman left, alas, too often vacant.*

The presence of the five-year-old daughter of the Tireaus contributed to the almost perfect domestic idyl that began to develop in the small apartment. The German never left and walked about clad in the salesman's comfortable red, petit point slippers embroidered by the hands of Madame Tireau.

It was only upon M. Tireau's return last evening that an angry encounter took place. The German tried in an approximate French to furnish explanations and stated that he had signed a contract of voluntary worker and thereby attested to his sincere love for our country. The deceived husband put an end to these protestations by a punch, and led the prisoner away to the commissariat, where a soldier was called to take the Don Juan, who was still wearing M. Tireau's slippers, into custody. Monsieur Tireau said he was sorry about the whole affair. He reluctantly accepted the reward and in parting promised the commissaire that he would forgive his wife.

An old street in Arles

Venice

Upon beholding Venice for the first time, and also on repeated visits, there is no solution for the newly arrived or the much traveled person but to say with Dante that "she strikes us dumb with amazement" (Dante's words are: *Di stupor compiuto*).

Before one gets on the train it might be a good thing to look briefly into a Baedeker, the *Intimate Guide to Venice* by Valeri, or Professor Daru's foreword to *The Doges of Venice*.

It is not a rare thing to see great emigrations of peoples occupy a country, and change the face of it, opening up to history a new epoch. But that a handful of fugitives, cast upon a sandbank some hundreds of yards wide, should there found a state and conquer a territory; that a numerous population should come and cover those moving sands which offered neither vegetation nor drinking water nor materials of any kind, not even the space to build upon; that from the industries necessary for subsistence, and to consolidate the ground under their feet, they should reach the point of presenting to the modern nations the first example of a regular government;

that from out of that marsh should come ever-renewed fleets of ships to go and overturn a great empire and gather to themselves the wealth of the East; that one should see these fugitives hold the political balance of Italy, dominate the seas, reduce all the other peoples to the condition of vassals—in fine, render impotent all the efforts of Europe leagued against them—here surely is a development of the human intelligence worthy of study. And if the interest it inspires should awaken a desire to know what was the part of glory, of liberty, and of happiness which befell this nation, all we have to do is to glance at the history of its progress and its misfortunes.

The best train from Milan gets you to Venice at night. You arrive in a modern, relatively undamaged railroad station of cement platforms, gates, lighted clocks, signal lamps, and baggage trucks, walk past the usual arrangement of customs offices, waiting room, and ticket windows, to a door beyond which there is a stone quay, and here the magic starts. A porter, as casually as if he were getting you a taxi, calls a gondola.

Your baggage arrives, he waves his arm, and one of the romantic vehicles that seem to be constructed as are violins detaches itself from darkness and rides with perfect balance to the quay. Your bags and even a trunk go aboard.

On such a night the Grand Canal is properly gilded by the moon. The moon belongs to Venice as the sun does to the Sahara. Its reflection places a wide golden band in the center of the canal. This waterway is busy all night long. *Vaporetti*, the streetcars of Venice, small tough little steamboats, toot and maneuver to the docks; the smaller motorboats overtake them. Launches with Allied soldiers float by, and occasionally a spick-and-span speedboat with a solitary English officer races by. The gondola is surprisingly steady in the disturbed water, its gold-and-silver trim shimmers, it carries you out into the canal, and on the way to your hotel it swings into the dark narrow canals, where the gondoliers shout, warning each other of their approach at intersections. Again you encounter the band of moonlight. It is twice reflected with dazzling effect—on the water, and from there upward onto

care, receives you. Inside is a regulation hotel lobby with soft music, intimate bar, and two American air-force officers with their wives, four dry Martinis, and a bowl of pretzels and potato chips.

You must reserve a room in advance. The key to it is attached to a wooden egg so large that you can't possibly put it into your pocket.

Later, on walking out of the hotel, there are six people who offer you various rates for the dollar. The paper money here is stout. Thousand-lire notes are handed you in packets; they are sepia-colored, stiff as playing cards, and uncomfortable to the hand and pocket, especially if you are used to the beautiful blue air-mail tissue on which French currency is printed. It buys a little more, but it is as easily spent, because the shops are full.

On the short walk you notice for the first time that the children of Italy don't seem ever to get to bed—not only the juveniles who stand in doorways and on bridges with their cigarette trays, openly selling black-market tobacco, but also very little ones who play bundled up on the streets, listen to music in front of sidewalk cafés, or amuse themselves by climbing on and off the bronze lions and other ornamental animals at the bases of monuments.

You find yourself sitting in one of the thousand uncomfortable metal-and-canvas chairs that are in front of various restaurants on St. Mark's Square, and at last you are part of the scene which you have seen so often in picture post cards, prints, and photographs. Now it is alive with the sound of people's conversations at the tables close to you and the music of several orchestras playing an assortment of tunes that overlap each other like the waves in the wake of passing gondolas in the canals.

It isn't necessary here to reach for a simile. It isn't "like" anything else. Once you have looked at the Square of San Marco, it will remain in your memory and come forward whenever you seek the picture of glory in architecture. If it must be given a little more bell-ringing, then one can say that especially at night it appears an indoor, rather than an open-air, place—it is a grandiose ballroom, with the open sky for a ceiling. It is easy also to imagine that the devout, when they awaken in their heaven, may find themselves sitting in a place like this, in the antechamber to the throne room of the Lord, and that, as here, silver horses, bronze lions with

the arches of the bridges through which you pass. The buildings float by in every tint and dye of the night. There are alleys black as pitch and soot and walls washed with indigo and a fine golden dust sprinkled on them. Here and there you see people looking from windows and bridges, their faces like alabaster. You can fall overboard with enthusiasm. All the promises of travel literature fall flat before reality. The beauty of Venice is true. You can only regret that even at the snail's tempo of the gondola, the cut-glass and marble scenery passes too fast, and you suffer from a visual kind of indigestion as ever new beauty comes at you.

It is doubly enchanting, as everything seen standing up repeats itself in mysterious pattern below the level of your eyes in the water of the canals. This circumstance is most probably responsible for the fact that the artisans of Venice have turned to mirrors and glass to express themselves.

Nowhere is the mood jolted—everywhere is history and melody and the setting for Renaissance painting. The magic ends and you awaken when, after being borne through this magnificently mildewed storehouse of grand opera scenery, your gondola is punted up to the steps at the door of your hotel. A working boat, filled with crates of syphons, and the launch of a British officer are tied up there, and the night porter of the Albergo Luna, tailored with

Venice

wings, and golden-fleeced sheep pasture beyond on the shores of the emerald lagoons. If I were to do a motion picture with a scene of the beyond then instead of the low-lying studio fog that always rolls over unlimited spaces and blankets the feet of Claude Rains, who as a heavenly dispatcher is busy checking off passengers on a departing or arriving plane, I would borrow from the enchantment of St. Mark's Square, which entertains your eye, compels you to devotion, and gives work to artisans.

Seated in your chair, you turn most often toward the Cathedral of St. Mark. It shares its majesty with humor; it is rather like a theater than a church, a capricious edifice that seems now made of ice, now of gold, depending on the light that plays upon it. It is mostly so diaphanous that you doubt whether it actually exists and will still be there when you look again. You turn your face from it, and listen to people talk, and watch the life on the square, and then look again—it still stands there. It floats, as all stone does in Venice, and it retains its peculiar fluvial quality the next day and as long as you are there. As the Cathedral has its very own character in Venice, different from anything anywhere else, so you feel the water through your shoes, but without dampness—it is a matter of weight—it lightens you.

If this water in the canals the next day is foul and sickening when you look at it closely, it still serves as the mirror for the exquisite façades. Written in chalk on a stone wall close to the hotel, I read: "Venice is a gondola that dances and swings, it is made of stone, sun, gold, and love."
(*Venezia xe na gondola, che balda, che se dondola La xe fata de piera, de sol, de oro e d'amor.*)

Venice is also made of wood. The buildings are constructed almost like those of the early lake dwellers, but in magnificent style. Whole forests were brought by main force from the valleys of Cadore, and used for the foundations. The wood was generally oak, but there was elm, larch, and poplar. The

building stone was shipped across the Adriatic from Istria.

The piling was driven into the soil beneath the lagoon in an upright position, closely packed, and one pile against the other. It became blacker and harder with time, and in consequence, the old palaces and churches stand now on a base as hard as iron. The subsoil of Venice is formed of a stratum of compact clay seven or eight meters deep, with beds of peat here and there. To drive the piles the Venetians still use a simple rammer, and it is surprising with what slowness the piles sink into the earth. On the side of the canals, the masonry is always encrusted with stone, mostly marble over which the tidal waters flow without causing disintegration. As you pass through the city on the waterways, you are astounded at its smallness. If, for example, you were to put all the little islands in New York Harbor together—I mean that on which the Statue of Liberty stands, and Governor's and Ellis Islands—you would have the territory of Venice.

Over some five hundred bridges you can walk as well as float from one end of it to the other.

On both ends of the Rialto Bridge you are reminded of New York again. In these two streets are the life, the noises, the smells, and the colors of the pushcart neighborhood around our own Canal Street, in New York.

Close by is the fish market, and not far from it a gambling palace, more elegant than Monte Carlo's Casino. The milk route is seagoing, the iceman cometh in a barge, coal, wood, and building materials are transported in long narrow boats, and the legend that the Italians are a lazy people is dispelled here as it is all over the country. The young as well as the old work with the same intensity with which they gesticulate as they talk. There are traffic arguments here exactly as there are on land, and the screaming of "Head of veal!" and "Sunday chauffeur" that one hears in narrow Paris streets is here translated into *"Va remengho!"* and other ready insult, which ex-

tends also to ancestors. Important arguments when ended are followed by elaborate making up. To restore friendship the combatants go and have what they call an *"ombra,"* which translated is "a shadow" and means a glass of wine.

The gondolier who rowed me around was sixty-five years old and wore a sailor suit with a straw hat that had two long, black ribbons hanging down the back. He had been a gondolier since his thirteenth year, his father before him was a gondolier, and his son will be one if he ever passes the difficult examination. He lives, so to say, in the suburbs, on the Isle of Giudecca, which cannot be reached except by boat. His greatest professional worries are the weather and the government, in the order named. He cares only for a government interested in tourism.

The older gondoliers want to know nothing of communism. In spite of this, I saw all over the city, along the waterways, stenciled on houses in red paint, the prow of a gondola and the hammer and sickle. Under fascism they did well, but then as now their diet consisted of polenta, a bean soup, fish, and a glass of cheap wine. Meat they could not afford, except on holidays. There are 450 gondolas of the kind that take tourists about. Of these, only half are in service at a time—that is, they work in two shifts. Of the 225 that are rowed at a time, about a hundred are busy working at the *traghetto,* which is the ferry service on thirteen points along the Grand Canal. Since only three bridges span this artery, the *traghetti* are very much in demand. They have no season, work in any weather, and charge double at night. In consequence, the ferrymen are envied by the others, who gondel around with tourists. The next best off are the gondolieri stationed at the railway terminal and at San Marco. At present the best customers are the Swiss. In previous years it was the Americans and the Germans, the English and the French, in that order, according to the size of their tips. With care a gondola lasts twenty-five to thirty years. The old man said that the gondolieri regretted the fact that the aristocrats no longer can afford to keep private gondolas, or to replace them, as they sold them previously at reasonable rates and in good condition after but a few years of use.

The gondolieri keep aloof from the boatmen who handle freight, and they get older than the average

Venetian on account of the light exercise and the outdoor life. The gondolier said that his son, an apprentice gondolier, was a student at the Berlitz School of Languages studying English in preparation for the expected masses of tourists. He also recommended to me a paper that had been written on the gondola recently by the head of the Society of the Gondolieri.

With the aid of a professor of the local Berlitz School, this essay was translated from the original in Italian. The text as handed to me is as follows:

IN ORDER THAT THE GONDOLA SHALL LIVE

The gondola—this typical means of conveyance, unique in the world, which besides being an instrument of work and life to a great deal of workmen, represents in all its characteristics a symbol of genuine Venetianity. The gondoliers live by honest work in the most spontaneous and free discipline, observing the tariffs and also their own dress and with their gondolas in the best order, are besides respectful to the citizens, Italian as well as foreigner. The gondolieri are proud of their brotherhood that offers them gratuitous medical help, their own physician with ambulatory service and black gondola destined for the transport of their corpses. . . .

During both wars, when steam ferries and motor launches disappeared, the gondola suffered enormously through rough wear and tear in accomplishing alone the task of keeping up communications in the labyrinth of our streams and canals as well as between Venice and the Islands.

The gondola, a craft unique in its kind, executed in the purest lines of the most difficult shipbuilding technique, has risen in price from a pre-war sum of 3,000 lire to the present-day cost of 300,000 lire. Besides, there is difficulty of finding the materials for the gondola itself. It is almost impossible today to obtain the accessories, furnishings, such as carpets, curtains, lamps, etc., and decorative materials. . . .

"THE FATHER OF THE GONDOLA"

To save Venice and for the preservation of the gondola and for the assistance to the gondolieri a benefactor had to appear and he did with humble and flowery actions. Owing to his refined Venetian taste and to his courage the repairs which had meanwhile and still are becoming more and more urgent have been started. Achille Gaggia is this benefactor who is shunning all this publicity. . . .

Beyond this, there appeared in December 1944 the following notice in the papers—:

Five thousand seven hundred and eighty-seven pawn tickets are at the pawn brokers' offices of Venice and these pawns can now be redeemed gratuitously by order of an unknown benefactor to give the most humble homes a token of comfort at Christmas. And so a spirit of goodness punched holes

in the old pawn tickets, underwear as well as watches and loved keepsakes as well as blankets, mattresses and tools returned to happy homes, and many a piece of furnishing for the gondola also, such as headlamps, pads and carpets, and of course everybody knew that the unknown benefactor was none other than Achille Gaggia—so much for the darkest hours.

THE ANXIETY OF THE GONDOLIERI

After so many sufferings which had an end in the joy of all the people and also of the gondolieri who were the first to sympathize with the allied troops, there came again a cloud for the gondolieri, but it passed, without shedding any rain, due to the solidarity with which the gondolieri went on the first strike of gondolieri ever recorded in Venice. It was against an order of the Allied command who wanted a reduction of fifty percent in fares for the Allied soldiers. Soon after, however, there was a feast not to be forgotten in which a superb train of gondolas filed off in the Grand Canal and drove together with the people and the authorities to the Altar of the Nicopaia Virgin of San Marco, in order to thank

God for having saved our city from the destruction of war and having preserved intact all its invaluable artistic and historical patrimony.

The gondola as we have seen, has been divinely kept above the waves of bad will as an eternal part of the city. We must safeguard it with a careful discipline and put an end to the turbulent running of motorboats which provoke waves dangerous for the buildings and the palazzos of the canals, at the same time bringing the gondolas to their ruin. The motor tends to dominate all of life with its mechanical insistence, rendering it the slave of a sterile mechanism. Let us preserve at least here in Venice the possibility of enjoying happily and slowly the marvels of Art and Nature, and for this it is necessary that the gondola shall live!

Some of the citizens of Venice seem intensely patriotic in an extremely local fashion. "You know why the gondolas are black?" asked my gondolier. He answered: "They are in mourning for the end of the Venetian Republic. We're not Italians, and we don't want to have anything to do with them. I worked in New York once—wops, you call them, and Dagos. That's right. We're not part of them—

read our history and you'll see. We don't want them here." In support of this opinion, which I came across in several instances, you see lettered on buildings: DOWN WITH THE NEAPOLITANS! and a crude skull and bones painted under that. It is frequently said that Venice is a sad city. Thomas Mann wrote a book entitled *Death in Venice*, and Maurice Barrès called it "a great tomb suspended above the waters." Wagner wrote *Tristan und Isolde* here, and himself died at the palazzo that is now the Casino. It is a scene of tragedy in Shakespeare's plays. Yet, unless you bring that mood with you and, as Wagner did, come here to die, the macabre is totally absent. It is in fact more like the Japanese island on which no one was allowed to die. In Venice the tombs are on another island, one called Murano, to which the funereal gondolas take the departed. The contagiously ill are on their own island, as are the insane.

If anything, Venice has too much life.

My room at the Albergo Luna was on the third floor and faced out on a narrow alley in back of the hotel. On this, as on every street in Venice, were several restaurants, the celebrants from which walked home arm in arm, singing Italian songs and in the richest trebles they were capable of. At three in the morning I gave up the idea of sleeping, but filled the ample basin of a portable *bidet* with water and poured it down on the next group of singers that came along. They stopped and, dripping, looked up and shook their fists, and I again had proof that Venetians are not fond of other Italians because, among angry insults such as *"bastardo"* and *"va a remengho,"* the ones they screamed most often were *"Napolitano!"* and *"Siciliano!"* For a while they kicked with their feet against the iron shutters of shops, thereby waking up the whole street. Eventually, hooking their arms together, they went up the alley singing louder than before.

A friend in America had given me a letter to an Italian official who is the equivalent of a police captain in America. He is a heavy man, who could play a Roman emperor or the chief of a band of pirates as well as the Chief of Police. He has some trouble breathing; I suspect a sinus condition. His handkerchief is in his hand most of the time and his eyes are puffed and watery. The Italian mind as I found it here lacks the lively choreography of the French; it is sadder, as flamboyant but not as elegant in its

elation or complaint. There also was in this official and in others more of a shoulder-shrugging attitude than you would find in a Gallic one. The Chief frequently said, while holding a large handkerchief to his large, sad, and watery eyes: "Anything is *possibile* in Venice"; he placed the accent on the second *i* in *possibile*, and with that he shrugged his shoulders. Before we had come to a table at the Café Florian in St. Mark's, he had looked in on his one prisoner, who sat on the wooden platform which was his bed in a roomy cell. The Chief asked him how he was. What the prisoner answered would have got him a bust in the jaw from an American, but there too the Chief had shrugged his shoulders and made a face that said, What can you do? He had given a coin to a beggar woman who sat on one of the bridges and then headed for the table.

Before I met the Chief, I had found an Utrillo in an art gallery and priced it. The man who showed the painting asked a million and a half lire. Now he came across the plaza, called the Chief by his first name, and asked to sit down at our table. He pulled out a pack of Camels and offered the cigarettes to us. The Chief said, "Thank you, no" and, pulling out a pack of Camels of his own, said to me, "Don't take his, take mine, they are real—those he has are made in Rome especially for the black

The children of Italy don't seem ever to go to bed

market." The art dealer pulled a magazine from the pocket of his coat and said, "Perhaps you have a doubt about the genuineness of the Utrillo you looked at. Well, here"—he opened the magazine—"is a reproduction of that picture." It was in black and white, and with it an article. "This magazine," said the man, "is published here, and in this—here, you can read it—Utrillo says that it was himself who painted this picture." "Who wrote the article?" said the Chief dryly with his sad eyes looking at the art dealer. "Oh, a professor," said the art dealer. "How much will you really take?" said the Chief. "Oh, make me an offer," said the other—"but a good one. You know, this street in Montmartre which is the subject of this picture, Utrillo painted that with his old palette—before he started to do postal cards en masse." He waited awhile and added: "How much do you offer? It is worth two million lire, at the present rate of exchange. We are asking one and a half million lire, but if you offer one million, that will be enough." I thanked him. "Come and look at it once more—tomorrow," he said and left.

"That man there," said the Chief, "in that corner, is a rich man, a Senator from Milan, the old-fashioned type of Italian, still rich, and with him is a woman. That is his wife. She is German, and she is Jewish—came from Hamburg—lost her parents, both gassed—and has no reason to do good to a German. They were rich people in Germany before the war. The Senator rescued her by marrying her and bringing her to Italy. She now rescues German prisoners from the Russians. These prisoners are in camps around here, which are being broken up, and they are sent back to where they came from. This kind lady, when she hears of one who is to go back into the Russian zone, writes to some people in other zones that offer to employ these boys—most of them are now only twenty—and then after she fixes things they can go to the American, French, or British zone. For others she obtains permits to stay in Italy—illegal papers—everything is *possibile* in Italy— and the Senator gets mad, because sometimes they stay at his house while they wait, and sometimes a prisoner of the right size even wears his suits."

"Senator" usually means a person of weight and stature, in Italy as anywhere else, but this Senator weighed only about a hundred and thirty pounds and looked like a small St. Francis.

"Now look at that beautiful girl coming down the arcade," said the Chief. "Her father was the owner of one of the biggest corporations in Italy, and the fascists threw him out, but they hired him again because nobody else knew how to run the complicated works. Eventually he was shot, and in a bombardment of Milan she lost her right arm. The hand with the black glove is artificial, but that British sailor who is following her—he does not know that yet, and by the time he finds out he will not mind. She is a lovely girl, and has great success. Perhaps he will not find out at all, because he may not take his eyes off her face. There is another one like her. She picks up customers sitting at a table in a little restaurant near the statue of Goldoni, and she has to do that because she has a club foot, but she also is very beautiful—and she works hard making men fall in love with her face so much that they go with her anyway. Look at the table of the Senator now. One of the German prisoners has arrived—I'll ask him to come over." The Chief—who, like most Italians, found it difficult to pronounce the *H* in Herr—called 'err Krause and motioned to a chair.

Herr Krause came and bowed and then sat down. He was young, with hair the color of light beer, an open shirt collar, and also the most open expression in his blue eyes. "*Ach, Sie sprechen Deutsch,*" he said to me smiling with even, white teeth. "*Ja,* then I have a lot to tell you." The Chief said he understood German.

"Tell him about the camp," said the Chief.

And as if there were no Italian within earshot, Herr Krause said loudly: "*Oh, die Italiener!* What a people! They steal everything. I will explain to you. You know they wait outside of the barbed wire of the camp. All we have to do is throw things over the barbed wire, and an L.K.W. is awaiting outside. What is an L.K.W.? Oh, *ein Lastkraftwagen*—a heavy truck. Of German make? No, no—no, Amerikanisch—everything is Amerikanisch. All right, so let me tell you. I was on guard there—you know we prisoners guard ourselves inside the enclosure. The English guard us on the outside, but they also steal—everybody steals, not only the Italians." At this the Chief of Police nodded gratefully and offered the prisoner a genuine Camel. "All right, I will tell you how it goes. So one night we were on guard there, and forty of those small tents had to go over the wire—hoppla—one after the other. The L.K.W. was waiting outside, and I was checking them off. And then blankets, and then tires—the Italians wanted tires most of all—and there was one, he wanted a special size. We found that size, but it was on the wheels of a gun, and that Italian who wanted those special tires said, 'What will I do with the cannon?' It was a Bofors antiaircraft gun. 'I only want the tires.' But then the English Sergeant who was selling that lot and who gave us a commission was called and he said to the Italian, 'Do you want the tires or don't you?' so the man said: 'Yes, I want them very much.' 'Good, then you buy them with the gun, or not at all.' So the Italian bought the gun also for the value of the metal, and we took down the barbed wire and got together and moved it out. The Italian took the cannon with him and paid for it.

"I have a fine machine gun for sale—Amerikanisch," said Herr Krause to the Chief. "Do you know anyone who wants to buy it?" The Chief shook his head. "Cheap," said Herr Krause, and added, "It's a hard thing to sell. I must find somebody, maybe somebody who has property to defend and needs to defend himself, because if I don't sell it to someone like that, a communist is likely to buy it. I also can get the ammunition for it, any amount."

"Go on with the camp," said the Chief—"tell him how you steal and how the English also steal."

"Well, it's the German drivers that are the richest men in camp," said Herr Krause—"everybody knows it. It's because they can drive out of the camp any time they want to, and into town. They always take spare parts, tools and tires along, and sell them. We all wear two uniforms, one over the other, and when we get a pass the one we wear over the other we sell."

The Chief interrupted Herr Krause. "I must explain about the uniforms," he said. "They are British, and the prisoners wear them. The only difference is that the prisoners, instead of an insignia, have a round patch on the arm. Tell him about the patch."

"*Ja*," said Herr Krause, "that is so—we stretch that patch over a cardboard disk, like so—and then we stick a safety pin inside the sleeve through the patch, on the outside, and we look like prisoners. When we are past the gate we just take off the safety pin, and the patch comes off. We put it in the pocket and we look like anybody wearing a uniform. Anyway, everybody wears parts of some uniform these days. When we go back to camp we take the patch out of the pocket and put it back again, simply with the safety pin."

The Chief of Police dabbed at his eyes.

"Go on," he said, "now tell him how the English steal."

"How do you get the uniforms?" I asked.

"Oh," said Herr Krause, "that is all arranged—that is very easy, from the Supply Depot—as you buy them in a shop, only we don't pay. We give a percentage later to the Quartermaster in charge. Everybody is in business, everything is for sale. For example, even the barbed wire. The camp was ringed with barbed wire, and the wire was held up with iron posts. These posts have three loops, through which the wire is threaded, and these posts also are disappearing along with the wire. Each of these stakes brings a thousand lire—but that's for the stupid ones. It's hard work to dig these stakes up and carry them around until you find an Italian who will take them off your hands."

"Tell him about the English officer," said the Chief.

"Oh yes, last week it was my turn to work in the mess hall, and I was afraid I'd be scolded, because the officer in charge there was lifting the chairs on the tables and looking under them and I thought it was because I had not cleaned them properly. But he did it only to take the numbers that are under the seat of the chairs. He was selling them.

"He sold six jeeps last week, before I left the camp," said Herr Krause. "In a way I am sorry it's over. You know, if you're really smart you do like the rich German drivers of our L.K.W.'s. They get themselves an Italian straw man, and through him they own villas and farms."

"He's speaking the truth," said the Chief.

"Everybody knows it," said Herr Krause.

"Everything is *possibile* here," said the Chief.

Herr Krause clicked his heels and walked back to the Senator's table. A waiter came. The Chief insisted that I be his guest, and he paid with two of the large brown thousand-lire bills. But although he was a police official, the waiter held the bills up against the light and looked to see if they were real. At the end of the square, again in moonlight, and looking exactly as it does in the romantic souvenir paintings that are sold to tourists, stood the gay Cathedral of St. Mark.

The Chief dabbed again at his eyes. "Well, you heard about the English stealing too—it makes me feel a little better. Everybody says only the Italians are thieves.

"You know," said the Chief, "once I took a vacation in Switzerland. I stayed at a good hotel, and I had my raincoat stolen. I was happy. I thought to myself, Well, good, here in this nice clean Switzerland—so real—so honest—so properly run and orderly—they have thieves too, thank God. That did me good—but only until the next day. Then the manager came and brought back my raincoat from the police. He excused himself and said that it would never happen again, and it had only happened, he added in a whisper, because a few days ago he had hired an Italian."

The sad official dabbed at his eyes again, and we walked along the plaza to the wing which Napoleon built, and through this, along the canals, and into the dark streets.

"Here you must be careful if you walk alone," said the Chief. "Before, we had wooden gates at the ends of some of these streets. They kept people from walking into the canals, but during the war people took those gates and chopped them up for firewood, and now it's dangerous." We passed several small and cheap restaurants, all of them clean. Here, as in France, the proprietor of even the humblest place is a patron of the arts, and everywhere there are paintings in frames, or done directly on the wall, with which hungry artists had paid for food and drink.

The large restaurants and the best in Venice don't compare with the French. The menu lists a starchy diet. The wines are so-so. In none of the restaurants do you find comfortable chairs. They are all for

In front of various restaurants on St. Mark's Square

small-bottom people, with cane seats and without arm rests, standing on mosaic or hardwood floors, or outside on the sidewalk, street, and various piazzas. There are several beggars that take up regular positions at mealtimes and look over the hedges and through the trellises of the various restaurants at the customers. One in particular, an appealing woman with a small child in her arms, is always outside the Trattoria al Colombo, but her performance is as languid and professional as that of several beggar women who drape themselves on the stairs of the bridges. Picturesque and part of the décor, they take their alms with graceful movement of hands, and slowly nod their thanks. In front of the Taverna la Venice sat a man with a small dog that wore a muzzle and was leashed.

"Venezia is a miserable place for dogs," said the Chief. "There are few lampposts. Most of them are so ornamental that photographers pose people against them all day long, and others have steps at their bases on which mothers and children sit."

There is no place to dig, as all the streets and squares are solidly paved. The one who loves his dog and wants to give him a run must buy a ticket and go to the trouble of taking the steamer over to the Lido.

The Lido, once the favorite spa of the international café set, and also of Herr Goebbels, is deserted, the hotels are closed, and along the roads is a lot of barbed wire that so far no one has taken the trouble to steal or remove. The little bathing houses are open and very comfortable. The water is lukewarm and without much motion, and if it interests you, you can sit there and watch young Italians make love most intimately and until closing time.

162

Promenade sur mer

THE TRAIN leaves the Gare Montparnasse at eight-twenty, and at one-thirty you change at Nantes and again at two-fifteen at La Roche-sur-Yon, where you take a Micheline, a rail bus which is propelled by a Diesel motor painted gray and strangely modern in all the ancient, rusted stable of the French transportation system.

The people try to get into the Micheline with such haste that it is remarkable that they pass the door, where they jam themselves into an arguing mass from which one after the other tears himself loose and runs for a seat. In this conveyance, in sticky midday heat, are the five girls of one family, the oldest twelve, all of them in large garden hats, and three carrying butterfly nets and garden tools, as well as their papa's fishing tackle. Each one also has a bag to carry. Anyone who is polite, and who wishes to get up to give the children or their mother his seat, can't because he is wedged in between three other people who together with himself sit on space designed for two. Opposite you is a sad-eyed ten-year-old boy, to whom his mother, who is also the mother of the five girls, says frequently:

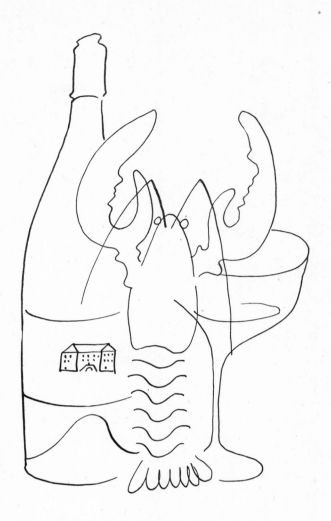

"*Philippe!* Stop swinging your legs." Philippe's legs are so thin that with all the crowding he has room enough to move them and knock with his heel against a box that is under his seat.

This activity slows down when Philippe sees something that interests him. Then he opens his mouth for the while that he looks at it, and if she catches him in such a stare his mother says: "*Philippe, mon chéri, ferme la bouche!*" He has a package on his lap. Other valises, handbags, fiber and reed containers, nets and bundles are in the people's arms, and all around them as if they had been thrown in, together with the passengers. Luggage also forms a wall in the small compartment that holds the toilet facilities, and this, during the entire trip, is occupied by six people who stand in it crowded together. The trip is short, but each of the little girls and Philippe are given some small repast. The word "Mamma" has big meaning here.

The women loosen their hair, start to fan themselves, and set aright whatever jabots and trimming on their dresses the air that comes through the small windows has deranged. In half an hour the smell of the sea, of tar and fish, pervades; all the people lean forward and then are jolted back as the Micheline comes to a stop. The door is opened and the outgoing jam starts. You are in the bourgeois seaside place which is called Les Sables-d'Olonne. The sands of Olonne are famous for their smoothness. The women of the region are called "Les Sablaises," which is not altogether fortunate, meaning "The sandy ones." Tourists come here, lured by the propaganda of the local Syndicat d'Initiative and the French Tourist Office, which allows no poster of Les Sables-d'Olonne to go out without showing at least two Sablaises dressed in the native costume. This is gay enough when black and more so in colors, and consists mainly of a skirt that comes down to a line midway between knee and hip. The legs are made the most of and are in sheer black stockings: the allure is completed by black hair, long lashes half down over dark eyes, and a snow-white, lacy headdress.

One of the Sablaises in the posters usually leans over, her chin cupped in one hand, the elbow of which rests on one of numberless posts that are part

of a cast-iron system of railings along the promenade. She gazes out to sea, which is beyond a wide beach.

It is a fortunate strip of land, where everything is as it was before the war.

The best, the Grand Hôtel and the Hôtel Splendide, offer good second-class accommodations, there is any number of reasonable rooms and small apartments in pensions, the houses are newly painted, and the prices about half of what they are in Paris. The water in the compact harbor is churned white all day by the propellers of fishing craft. The sailors in rubber boots and blue denim hand up tuna that are fat as pigs and as valuable. From other boats comes, on trays, the small change of the ocean, the sardine. Here it is has stripes like a tiger, alternately silver and the blue of polished steel. As it is carried close to the dark stones of the quay, it showers glitter on the mossy walls, it reflects light like the crystal balls that hang from the ceilings of cheap cabarets. The children play and run and the older people seem of the same weight and shape as before.

The short skirts are not on the young girls, who go to the pictures and dress in the fashion of their favorite actresses. The old fisherwives wear the short skirts, together with wooden shoes raised on elegantly cut heels. These formidable ladies, who shove wheelbarrows ahead of themselves and hang the gill nets on the cast-iron banisters to dry, give the impression of a brigade of veteran bobby-soxers.

All the marine charm of this region is packed into the old port. There is a really good restaurant of no pretension called Chez Georges. Fish just pulled from the ocean can't be spoilt by the worst cook, but here is one who is worth shaking hands with. The chef's name is Courvoisier, and on his letterhead is written, "Only a hundred meters from the beach. Moderate prices. Kitchen entirely *au buerre!*"

He has a sensible dish called Palourdes Farcies (the *palourde* comes close to being a clam, and you can try this with a cherrystone-size clam as well as with a little-neck):

RECIPE FOR BAKED CLAMS

First: *Wash the clams in a little white wine; remove one shell.*

Second: *Make the dressing. Mix the ingredients according to your taste: parsley, shallot and garlic, finely chopped, lemon juice, salt and pepper, all mixed with butter.*

Third: *Put the above dressing over the clams and bake in a hot oven from seven to eight minutes. This dish of some twelve clams is a kind of maritime* Escargot. *It is served with a very light wine called Muscadet from grapes that grow in the valley of the Loire.*

You eat here under a faded awning, and the wine costs fifty cents a full quart. Before you the masts of ships move slowly in and out of the harbor. Occasionally a small jovial man, with a belt let out to the last notch and with a face highly colored by both the weather and the bottle, will pass and look with sharp blue eyes into the restaurant and point to his ship, called *Monique*, and to a sign that advertises PROMENADE SUR MER. Then, nursing a Pernod and eating *moules* or the above-described Palourdes Farcies, he will wait for an offer. I went to look at his ship. It is twenty-one feet long, the deck is a mosaic of fish scales that are stuck all over it, and it stinks, but it is—like all the *sardiniers*—a tough little boat. The one life preserver that hangs on the wires that hold up the mast is thin, as half the ground cork has run out of it. But whether you like it or not, the *Monique* is the only boat here that occasionally lets the others go out after the lobster and sardines and makes the *promenade*—the captain is an individual and a gregarious man. Off the coast of this part of France is a little island, which you will find on some of the larger maps, called l'Isle d'Yeu. I had been to this island before the war, and I wanted to visit it again, so one day I spoke to the captain and, after the inevitable half hour of arriving at a price, I chartered the *Monique*.

We decided to start the following morning at five. There was an able seaman aboard, a Goya type— lean, maroon-colored, with blue-black hair and a complete upper set of gold teeth. After we got out of the harbor we went along the coast for a while, then the captain stopped, and after putting on large canvas aprons, we all pulled on wet rope, lifting lobster baskets from the water. The lobsters in them were, like the sardines, of metallic colors. In this case they were sky blue, with dark patches, and emerald green on the sides, turning to a porcelain white on the underside. After this, the sailor busied himself with a ship's stove to boil three of the lobsters, a bottle of the Muscadet was put on ice, and the captain went down into the low cabin of the ship. He brought up a square, battered box, with a few patches of varnish left on the cover, which contained the compass. This he placed between his bare feet and headed the ship toward the Ile d'Yeu. The sun rose, and soon the sea was green, the sky was

blue, and a little warmth came with the breeze that pushed the *sardinier* and cleared the stench from its decks. It was all as good and full of promise as it had ever been.

THE ISLAND THEN

On my first visit to the Ile d'Yeu I started out from a place called Fromentine—it was a year before the beginning of the war.

At that time there were three hotels in Fromentine, one as good as the other. All three smelled of wet sand and bathing suits. The one I stayed at had the best view, a glass-enclosed dining room, and a *piccolo*, which is French for a busboy. The piccolo was twelve years old and Spanish.

The dining room was decorated with aquamarine nets, dried starfish, pink streamers, and bouquets of mimosa standing on the table. Out of this room one looked at a beach, chewing-gum gray and halved by the scaffolding of a pier. Under this pier the sea rose and sank. It dragged garlands of seaweed up and hung them on splinters and on the rusty bolts and then took them away again.

Partly on the pier and partly on the beach was a Chinese pavilion dedicated to the sale of sand pails, shovels, and souvenir lighthouses and Eiffel Towers that were made of sea shells. As in all Brittany resorts, there was also a postal card which showed a bearded fisherman in oilskins leaning against a boat and holding a ten-foot oar. The card was always entitled "Un vieux loup de mer."

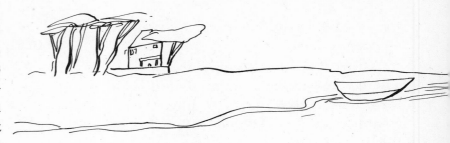

Back in the dining room of the small hotel a half-grown-up girl and the Spanish boy piccolo, who had been adopted by the proprietor, served the guests. About fifty people sat down to meals which were announced by a big brass bell at the end of a black handle. The bell almost swung the piccolo off his feet as he worked it outside on the terrace. The seaside patronage slowly crept up through the sand from the beach and arrived with vacation faces—burned purple—with crying children, matted hair, and ravenous appetites. The people who came and come here for two weeks of determined happiness are mostly from Nantes.

It was always a holiday in shirt sleeves, of loud singing and thumbs under suspender buckles. One shows here that one knows how to enjoy life. Toasts are drunk in *vin ordinaire*. Everyone bows and smiles to the right or left; there are no strangers. Coquettish young girls squeeze between chairs to their tables with an extra wiggle of the hips and shoulders; conversation drowns out the sea, the phonograph, the clatter of dishes; only the screams of children, and the service directions which the proprietor yells to the piccolo, rise above it.

In this dining room, then, there sat with me, to the right and left of a shivering, mouse-faced fox

terrier, a Madame and Monsieur le Baron. Monsieur le Baron (*"Tout est bon chez le Baron"*) was the owner of a pork store, a *charcutier* from Saint-Nazaire. He had the torso of a lion tamer. His mustache seemed made of cast iron and painted black; it was hard, heavy, and new. He had a habit of crossing his arms so that he could scratch both his formidable shoulders at the same time. The shoulders came out of a striped, sleeveless garment which madame explained to me was "American," bought at the Bon Marché in Paris, and she called it a "sweet shirt" instead of a sweat shirt.

The ample menu began with *"Les fruits de mer,"* which were usually mussels in a green cold sauce, followed by a kind of fish goulash highly seasoned and appetite-making. The soup plates in which it was served were cleared, and Monsieur le Baron wiped his mustache with a piece of bread, ate it, and turned toward the kitchen door. About then a murmur went through the crowd, there was a pause of expectation, and everybody looked at the door of the kitchen as it opened and the fifty pensionnaires of the Hôtel de Paris cried: *"Ah, les crabes!"*

The Spanish boy staggered into the room carrying a copper casserole of boiled crabs. He wore an apron that reached from his neck to his shoes, and sometimes under them. He brought six crabs on each trip from the kitchen. They were immense, the color and texture of imitation-leather bags; each one had six legs, and each leg was two feet long. The young girls arched their backs as he approached, and the legs of the crabs reached out for their shoulder straps, for the piccolo's black hair, and for the mimosa on the tables, once he put them down. He managed to serve them without anyone's coming to harm; he had a great deal of practice.

At that time one stayed overnight at Fromentine to take a ferry to the Ile d'Yeu the next day. Three ice-cream-colored villas and a few children warmed

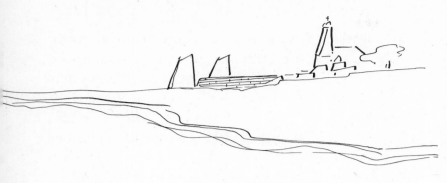

themselves in the next morning's sun. The seagoing motorship *Insula Oya*, brightly painted and newly commissioned, tooted. The Spanish piccolo of the Hôtel de Paris, wearing a green apron, came running with a small wagon, the proprietor pushed on one side, they brought the bags, bowed, and the ship left.

After an hour of calm, green ocean on that first voyage, there appeared first a lighthouse, then a church steeple, then—seven kilometers wide and nine long—the island itself. Another half hour, and the colors of the houses separated, windows and doors went into place, lettering was readable, and it spelled out Hôtel des Voyageurs, Café de la Marine, and Buvette du Port. The entrance to the harbor was like a bent sleeve, and where the elbow is, stood a lighthouse. The entrance was so narrow that a chain was thrown from the lighthouse and fastened to the bow of the *Insula Oya*, the captain spun the wheel, and she turned in her own length and entered the harbor.

The Ile d'Yeu was immediately beautiful, and at once familiar. Its round, small harbor was stuffed with boats—the big tuna schooners in the middle, in relatively deep water, and in a semicircle around them the *sardiniers* and lobster boats—the opaque green water shone up between the sterns and bows of boats, and one could walk across the harbor from deck to deck. Twice a day there was the creaking of hulls and tilting of masts as all the boats began to settle and lean to their neighbors, and only a Spanish ship, which had fled into the harbor in a storm and was beached, stood upright as all the water ran out of the harbor. Aboard this craft, which burned with rust, the orphan who worked as a piccolo had come to France. The *hôtelier* from Fromentine had come across to the salvage auction, bought the kitchen equipment and the crockery of the ship, and taken the boy back with him to Fromentine.

In front of the derelict ship was the Hôtel des Voyageurs, and not far from it the Street of the Sardine. This street, beautifully named, with houses on both sides that touch your shoulders, is comfortable only for a man with one short leg to walk in, as half of it is taken up by a one-foot sidewalk. There seemed to be only three kinds of people on the Ile d'Yeu: sailors in their hundred times patched, sensible, wide pants and blouses that came in every shade of red and blue, few children, but everywhere sets of two little bent old women, dressed in black, their sharp profiles hooked together in the island's gossip. Like crows they were, and rightly called "*les vieux corbeaux*."

Posing everywhere were fish and the things related to them and to their capture. The sardine was the banana of the Ile d'Yeu; you slipped and fell on it, it looked out of the small market baskets the *vieux corbeaux* carried home, its tails stuck out of fishermen's pockets, and it was dragged by in boxes and barrels. The other fish, the tuna, passed on the shoulders of sailors and was tied to bicycles and pushed by pairs of boys in wooden carts.

Stuffed and mounted fish hung in the Buvette du Port and the Café de la Marine. In addition to decorating rooms, they were carved in wood, brightly painted and sailed as weathervanes over houses and atop the masts of ships. Even in the kitchen the fish motive, together with the shapes of lobsters and crabs, was hammered into brass molds and served for the baking of soufflés and cakes.

Across the island is a small harbor called Port de la Meule, where the French novelist Georges Reyer lived in a shack with a donkey and a dog. He had a

small dory and a half dozen lobster pots. The dog ate only fish, and when he held a crab shell or a lobster claw between his paws he growled as angrily as another dog with a bone if anyone came near him.

The donkey, named "Tintin," stood near the water in patches of salt grass and sometimes lifted his head and answered to his name. He was driven to town for bread and cheese and a lot of wine in the rare moments when Reyer, who on account of his kindness was known as "Bon Georges," was in a hurry. He leaned forward from the driver's seat of the two-wheeled cart, and the donkey laid his ears back to meet the words of his master, and he heard him say: "Tintin, how beautiful you are—come now, and make like a little horse!" This flattery got five meters of trotting out of him.

The inside of the shack in which Bon Georges lived was underwater green. The light came through cracks in the wall, filtered through a mountain of empty wine bottles which were stacked against the weather side of the shack. An old sail served as an awning and was held up by two oars. We used to sit under that awning and eat the lobsters which we caught. Bon Georges called these meals "*une noce d'homard*"; after these fiestas we rested inside the shack on two bunks. Over one of them hung a picture of Léon Blum. Georges wore a pair of blue linen trousers turned up to the knees, an open shirt whose sleeves were torn off at the elbows, a pair of sandals, and a big straw hat. We often said that if the whole world should explode, here you would never hear about it.

I know all the roads here. One runs over rocky fields and past a pine forest, whose fallen needles, warmed by the sun, fill the air with their fragrance. On this road one comes to a blind curve at the right of which are some bramble bushes. Along here I bicycled home one day, carrying a sack of provisions which I had slung over my shoulder. I pedaled with one hand in my trouser pocket and the other holding the end of the sack, and I was on the wrong side of the road. Around the curve raced the island's only automobile, a four-horsepower Super Rosengart, belonging to the baker of Saint-Sauveur, another of the Ile d'Yeu's villages. This car was sympathetic to me until then. But that morning it threw me in a wide curve into the bramble bushes, and became a flour-covered, fragrant breadbasket on wheels. I took the car's doorhandle off with my elbow. I asked the baker to take me to the hospital in Joinville, but he said he was sorry that, according to French law, a car had to remain exactly where it was when the accident occurred, so that the gendarmes could make their proper deductions and see who was responsible for the accident. I tried to change his mind, and got mad at him when he repeated his statement, but he said: "Permit me, *alors*, monsieur, if you use words like that, then it is of no use at all to go on with this conversation." He spread aside the thicket and looked for his doorhandle. I went to Joinville on foot, and eventually a doctor came with a cigarette stub hanging from his lower lip, and as he wobbled a blunt needle into my arm he said: "Excuse me, sir, but your skin is very tough" (*Mais votre peau est extrêmement dure*).

And the doctor's needle wasn't too clean. Soon after, I left in a hurry to get to another doctor in Paris.

THE ISLAND NOW

As we approached the Ile d'Yeu aboard the *Monique*, the captain as well as his sailor was surprised when I offered to pilot the ship into the narrow and rocky harbor of Port de la Meule for them. I know the currents and the tide there well. We tied up the boat and I walked up to the hill where George's shack was. It is still there, but the light inside has changed—bottles have become valuable now, and the whole wall of them is gone. Now I stood again on this same spot and suffered the sorrowful emo-

guarded, patrols are in those pines, and they carry arms and are ordered to make use of them if anyone approaches. You say, monsieur, that you come from America. Then why in the name of God don't you send us bread?" She abruptly turned and walked away.

There is nothing new one can report about the Marshal. It is known that he is ninety-two years old, in excellent health, and gives the impression of a man of sixty. He walks straight, carrying his cane in back of him rather than using it for support, He is, however, allowed to walk only in the innermost, low courtyard of the Citadelle and not on the ramparts surrounding it, from which he would have a view of the sea which he craves. Madame la Maréchale, who has lived on the Ile d'Yeu for two years now, visits him every afternoon, walking from Port Joinville to the Citadelle and back. She has never been alone with him; there are always two soldiers present. He is alone with the curé, who hears his confession and reads mass there once a week. He is grateful for the devotion of a cat which has recently attached herself to him and keeps the mice from running over his chest at night. He makes his bed himself every morning, "*un petit lit de soldat.*" He gets the food which the soldiers eat, and eats it with good appetite. Madame la Maréchale receives many packages from all over the world, some from faraway and unlikely places, and the greatest amounts from the United States and the Argentine—mostly coffee, cocoa, and cigarettes. She gives all that away. The Commandant of the Citadelle allows her to bring Ovaltine, of which the Marshal is very fond, into the prison. Flowers—even a small tree for Christmas, or any kind of gift—are forbidden him.

As you walk toward Joinville from the Citadelle, there is toward evening, before the light breaks, the shimmering stippled effect of a Seurat painting. The sky is butter-colored; the foliage and the flaming berries on bushes, the pebbles and the roofs of houses, even the water, are as if done with little dabs of color, as acutely chromatic as the scales of fish. After a while there is a change to pure color. You approach the village, and on its outskirts are many white houses, all of them the same. They are called "*kers,*" and fit well into the scenery. As the sun sets, the shadows that one house lays on the other make it seem that everywhere structural

tions that run through one that are the funeral for a piece of time out of one's life. The finely traced lines of the shore lost themselves in vapors, below the small *sardinier* shimmered in sunlight, and the captain swayed up the path and said that he wouldn't mind if I paid him now and that if I wanted to walk across the island he would sail and meet me in Port Joinville.

The island has now become the prison of Pétain. It takes an hour to walk to the Citadelle, where Pétain is incarcerated. On the road where I had been knocked off my bicycle I met one of the Ile d'Yeu's *vieux corbeaux.*

"The Marshal," she said in answer to my question, "certainly he is in there, but we have never seen him, no one has seen him, no one is allowed to go in there, and I advise you to continue on your way to Joinville without trying to. He is well

The Dining Room
of the Hotel
des Voyageurs
Isle d'Yeu.

changes are taking place. The houses at this hour stop blinding you with their whiteness. They are now the white of paper inside a room, and their sides the color of lead. You look into their interiors through large open windows, and in each of these houses sits one of the old women, with arms folded and dressed in black, looking with steady dullness out into the street. It is quiet, and then with a yammering wail the bell in the tower of a church, which is built in the shape of a lighthouse, begins to set the scene to its proper music. You hear footsteps and turn, on the road from the Citadelle appears a French officer who looks like Leo Durocher, and then in a while he is gone. The small and incredibly lonesome figure of the Marshal's wife passes the same way. And you know that there are sentences worse than death.

"For heaven's sake, monsieur, don't ruin me! Don't waste my water!" screamed the proprietor of the Hôtel des Voyageurs in Port Joinville as I held my hands under the cold-water faucet, because the

warm one did not answer. He put a plug into the basin, let the water run in, about a teacupful, then he closed the faucet with a tight turn.

"Excuse me," he continued, "but that is all I can let you have because the problem of water is one of life and death here on the island. There is never enough, and now all my reservoirs have dried up and I have to buy it. It is bad enough if you have a little house and your own well—there is always some water—but here in this hotel of thirty rooms with everyone washing himself whenever they feel like it, it is catastrophic. We have to use water for cooking, for washing dishes and linen, for the flowers in the window box. We used it also to make ice, but that we have stopped altogether. And ice, monsieur, is also a problem of our existence. Look out the window and see how empty the harbor is; the reason for it is the scarcity of sweet water and of ice. Each of the large tuna schooners needs a minimum of six tons of ice before it puts to sea, to refrigerate the catch. Since we have no water and no ice,

172

most of the boats have left the island and are fishing out of harbors on the mainland. There is hope someday of making ice from sea water, but that, alas, is still in the domain of the laboratory. I would have further grave observations to make on how all that affects the economy of the island, but I must leave you now to see Madame la Maréchale, who eats early. A room I have for you, but no bath, of course."

I remembered then that in the house I had rented when I was in the Ile d'Yeu before there was a well and it was always adequate, because we drank a lot of cheap wine; now there is no cheap wine and no cheap water here.

The portions of food and the bread ration were smaller than in Sables-d'Olonne; there was no rice, and the dessert was a blob of brown stuff. Thanks to Madame la Maréchale's packages, the coffee at least was good.

I walked out in front of the hotel after dinner and counted the ships in the harbor. A fisherman walked by, holding a few sardines in his cupped hands, and one of the old *corbeaux* looked at them and admired the child who stood beside the man. "Just enough to fill her stomach," said the fisherman, "but it's better for her than the bread we get these days." The sardine, alas, is no longer the banana of the Ile d'Yeu, and you don't slip and fall on it any more. One finds great differences in the way people live, drink, and eat, in the distance of a few miles.

I went back and sat down at the table which Madame Pétain had vacated, to sketch the room, as it is the typical dining room of the hotels of this region. A buffet with bottles stands in the center. Most of them are for decoration, and many are empty and used for display. Through them the light is filtered as it once was filtered through Bon Georges's bottle wall into his shack. On one side of the buffet is the desk, and the icebox that doesn't make ice any more. There is a coatrack and a holder for post cards—the post card with the "Vieux loup de mer" is still there—also the board on which room keys are hung.

The restaurant of the Hôtel des Voyageurs is distinguished from all other marine eating places by a pair of stag antlers that hang near the entrance.

The proprietor sat down with me after I had finished my dinner and excused himself again about the water. He said that he was worried because his hotel and all available rooms were solidly booked for the season and nobody would be able to take a bath. He also said that if there were plans to let the Marshal go home, as had once been rumored, no one on the island, including madame, knew about it. She lived in one room on the first floor, and a month back a man had suddenly opened the door and photographed her. The photographer slammed the door shut after saying hastily: "Oh, pardon, I have made a mistake," and that was the only time when the Marshal's wife lost her composure. The picture appeared in a magazine and in the text it was stated that madame had posed for it. "That is not true," she said, "but otherwise the press has been extremely considerate of both of us."

I looked for the captain and the sailor with the golden teeth, and found them in the Café de la Marine, where they sat among local fishermen, on benches which are no wider than a hand, and much polished from sitting. The legs of these benches are set way in from the ends toward the center, and as the sailor got up to make room for me the bench tilted and the captain disappeared. A man falling is always funny, and there were belly laughs all around, all of them laughing with extremely bad teeth. The captain handed me back some of the outrageous money he had asked for this trip. He paid it back in the form of drinks of brandy, which was excellent, and, stopping at every bar on the way to the port, we eventually came to the place where the sardine boat was tied up.

The tide was low and the water still running out. The sailor leaned on the iron railing of the pier for a while and talked, looking at the sea and the sky,

Ships move slowly in and out of the harbor

and then with two bottles of brandy that they had taken along both began the perilous descent down a steep flight of slimy, green stone steps. Half the time they stood on one leg recovering their balance. In the short, wet mosses that covered the lowest steps they slid, and the captain almost fell headfirst down into the boat but, reaching as if to get at his shoelaces, succeeded in untying the boat without dropping into the water. The boat was adrift and came to a stone wall, near the *Insula Oya*—which once had brought me here and is now a rusty hull. The current turned our ship like a piece of driftwood, and she was washed out of the harbor, dancing along the piling, and finally began rocking in the open sea. The sailor took his bottle and went forward, making himself comfortable and wrapping himself in the small sail that lay there. The captain raised the mainsail, and pointed to a faraway patch of white light over the dark water. He motioned to the tiller and I held the boat in the direction he had indicated while he drank out of his bottle and then went to start the motor. He came and corrected my course

by pointing again at the patch of light, and then stood with crossed arms next to me. He came close and looked at me several times in the fashion of drunks, suddenly jerking himself away and shaking. After some time had passed, and just as the boat climbed a wave and the deck was inclined to meet his heavy body, at the right moment, he sank carefully and with much practice to the floor, rolled slowly on his back and, stretching his limbs in four directions, fell asleep. There was little wind to help the motor, and the boat went slowly. The captain got up mechanically twice in intervals of an hour. He raised himself just enough to look over the bow and check the light, and then went down again. The lighthouse rose from out of the water, and the cartwheel of its beams played silently in the darkness. As we neared the beacon the captain came to his feet and remained standing. He steered the boat away from the reefs that extend for some two hundred meters in front of the lighthouse.

"He's a good boy, gold teeth and all," he said of his sleeping sailor. "I love him like a son. Now he

174

cannot see, *il a la merde dans les yeux*, but otherwise he has eyes like a gull. He saved my life, and a German saved his, ah, the Germans, good Germans I know one. Not two, just one." He held up one finger and repeated, "Just one," then he pointed with the same finger at the sleeping sailor and said: "He saw a plane fall into the sea one day while the Germans were here, it was in flames, but we went to the rescue anyway. It sank as we got there. On our return to Les Sables there were German soldiers that took us to the Commandant. He said to me: 'I have told you before that we never go to the rescue of the enemy, you knew it was an American plane!'"

At this part of the story the captain stopped. He took hold of the cloth of his pants, and lifting one leg he said proudly: "These are American, the most wonderful trousers I have ever owned. Here everything American is appreciated. You know, when the Germans came, we looked at their equipment and said, 'Ah, that is something in the way of an army!' but when the Americans came, we really opened our eyes. But to continue with the story—the Commandant said to me, 'I will make an example of you. Take him out and shoot him.' And he nodded to an officer who was in the room with us. But my sailor here spoke: 'I am the only one to blame,' he

said to the Commandant. 'Take me, he is the father of twelve children, and it was I who spotted the plane.' '*Bon*,' said the Commandant, and motioning again to the other officer he said: 'Take *him* out and shoot him.' They were quick then with executions. The other one, however, was the good German I spoke of, and he argued the Commandant out of the sentence and promised that he would teach my sailor a lesson, so that he would not go to the rescue of any enemy planes so long as he lived. He took the boy to the door, from the side of which he took a club that hung there, and he led him downstairs. He didn't beat him, he walked him to a back door, opened it, and with a terrible kick in his backside he sent him out into the street. They took my boat away, I was forbidden to fish, and he was recruited for labor duty in Germany. The old one back there on the island approved the order, and a hundred thousand went in one shipment. I think about it sometimes and I say to myself that perhaps the Germans had asked for half a million, and the Marshal cut it down as far as he could. After all, he stayed with us when the others fled, and he said to himself: Somebody has to do it, and maybe he did the best he could.

"Anyway, that is what I prefer to think on his behalf."

Bon voyage

IT IS IMPORTANT today to have your return reservation made before you leave. It is also advisable to book your passages on trains and planes in Europe and pay for them.

To get a ticket on a good ship or train and on the airlines on the Continent is a matter of standing in line, of having a friend who knows somebody, or else of depending on the good will of the *portier* of your hotel, which means that you have to cross his palm with a few thousand-franc notes.

The trouble with a devalued currency is that after a while you attach no value at all to it and hand it out, forgetting that it is money. Five thousand francs is about twenty dollars, and the portier will not bow too deeply if that is what you hand him for getting you a ticket on, for example, the *Golden Arrow*.

In a European hotel the portier, a man in a long coat, with keys embroidered on the lapel, and a cap, is more important than the proprietor, manager, chef, and maître d'hôtel put together, and usually has more assets than they. I have never known one who wanted to own a hotel of his own, so good is his take behind the "portier's loge," a small office between the door and the stairs, which no one gets past without the portier's knowledge.

He arranges for everything, carries timetables and sailing schedules in his head, rents you cars, gets theater tickets, deals in the exchange of every country, and is remarkable for his speed at addition and subtraction.

As luxurious as it was before the war is the *Golden Arrow*, the train which runs daily from Paris to London. Sitting in individual *fauteuils* that are two to a wide window, you are taken smoothly and with the old speed to Calais. Until recently, after the austerity meal and the coffee, an old lady with a band around her arm identifying her as an agent of the Government, came to your table, held out her hand, and sweetly asked you to give her your pocketbook. "I must see how much money you have," she said. You gave it to her, and in front of you she unpacked it, searching for francs that you might want to sneak out of France. I had five hundred of them on that trip, and she gave them back to me. Half an hour after the old lady was gone a man came, in uniform and polite enough. He saluted and repeated the search, on the theory that after the first examination was over some smuggler might have transferred his hidden francs into his pocketbook from some secret hiding place.

In Calais there was a good deal of destruction, but you got from the train to the quay and onto the boat without having to climb over rubble or make any detours. The Channel steamer was crowded, and one had to wait half an hour until the baggage was taken aboard. I stood at the ship's rail for a while and saw my trunk sail up into the sky in the baggage net and then sink down in the hold of the Calais-Dover boat, and after half an hour of loading mail the Captain gave the signal and the ship backed out of the harbor.

People who go on these boats seem to get seasick easier than passengers aboard any of the big ships I have been on. The ship rolled more pleasantly than steamers do—not the slow lifting and sinking but a gay motion like that of a swing. While we were still close to the French coast, sailors appeared and handed white enameled pans around, dreadful dishes that compel the undecided to give up and lean in a corner.

There was a melodrama near the end of the boat in the third class—a scene that seemed cut from an early Chaplin film. A stout Italian mother surrounded by her five children, all wrapped in shawls, who sat on their bundles, turned green and started to moan and pray. A sailor came running with the white dishpans and the mother put hers on the floor and, kneeling down, bent over it, being joined there by all her children. She wore a beaten fur coat of red fox pelts and looked like a St. Bernard with her pups at feeding time.

"In the smoking room, sir," answered the steward when I asked him where I could change traveler's checks. The bartender there said he could not change any money, nor could the purser or anybody else. I offered them American Express traveler's checks and also dollar bills, as well as the five hundred francs, but nobody had the authority to change any of it.

The customs men in Dover are courteous and quick, and so is the passport examination. Again there was no place to get British money. Finally an official at the station, saying, "I'm not supposed to do this, but you've got to be helped," reached into his pocket and gave me the right exchange for twenty dollars.

Even more magnificent than the French edition of the *Golden Arrow* is the English, a kind of train we don't know in America—a royal train de-luxe. Every car has its own kitchen and silver such as dinner is served on in a private house, all sound is hushed with deep carpets, the train slides rather than rolls, and the first evidence of the superior man in a servile position comes to the table in the form of the steward and his aide. Such a man, you say to yourself, in America would be the manager of a good hotel, or at least at the cashier's window of a Fifth Avenue bank.

Painfully correct, with careful pronunciation and only the frayed and stained cuffs on his shirt taking from his glory, he serves you a so-so meal that ends a few miles outside of London. As he thanks you for the tip, the loud-speaker announces "The *Golden Arrow* is about to enter Victoria Station." It also says something about hoping that you have enjoyed the journey, but I did not put down the exact wording of that second announcement.

I only remember that the exquisitely tailored and very British woman who had sat opposite me on the long journey said: "What rot," as she got up.

There are the nice old cabs that are neat and polished with wear and have the feeling of worn pocketbooks. In spite of the hotel strike, the service at the Savoy was good.

The entrance to this immense hotel is badly planned. It is in a dead-end street, and one car letting off passengers blocks the approach as it maneuvers back and forth to turn and get out. In this hotel you are received by a crew of gray-clad and formidable doormen called commissaires.

The Savoy is pleasant, the corridors and rooms newly painted. There are ample bath towels, good carpets, new linen. In the bathrooms are white telephones, an arrangement that you learn to appreciate only after you benefit from it, not having to run wet into the room to answer the phone.

Another agreeable thing is that you can approach the doorknobs without hesitation. In almost every good hotel in the world, especially on cold days, after you walk over carpets and touch your doorknob you get an electric shock. Here at the Savoy

180

they are safe—dead and quiet to the touch because properly insulated.

The gentlemen of the press in England are really gentlemen. Also the photographers who come with them. They have the contemplative air of the editor-in-chief of an American literary journal, and take their hats off, cross their legs, and twist a lock of hair or fit their fingers together in a Gothic arch, looking down at them, as they put their questions. While I was being interviewed a photographer who leaned on my old trunk looked at the baggage tag attached thereon, and he straightened up and excitedly said to the reporter, "I say, Mr. Pulvermacher, come over here for a moment and have a look at this." The tag was the regular Cunard steamship line baggage tag, on which I had carefully filled out the spaces for writing in the name of the ship, the sailing date, and the number of my cabin.

"Odd, isn't it," said the photographer.

"Quite odd," said Mr. Pulvermacher.

"I say," the photographer turned to me, "would you mind awfully if I took a picture of this tag—not for publication of course, just for myself?"

"Certainly, but why?"

He then pointed out to me that where it says Name of Steamship I had put down *Elizabeth* instead of *Queen Elizabeth*. He smiled indulgently. "Now, no one in England would think of doing that, I mean calling the Queen by her first name, especially on the maiden voyage," he said, as he focused his camera on the baggage tag.

On the afternoon that the *Queen Elizabeth* started out on her maiden voyage as a passenger liner, all the humble people who had denied themselves to build her stood along the quays and in the yards in smudged clothes and with pale faces. The ship alerted the countryside with a voice that made the deck vibrate like a drumhead and sent every seagull screeching into the sky.

I put my hand on the stout railing, and felt like a blind man deciphering braille. Into the railing are carved thousands of names and initials of American soldiers and the names of the states, towns, and villages from which they came.

Exactly on time, the hawsers slackened, and the foghorn started another long blast. She sailed. That is, she suddenly stopped touching the pier. With miraculous ease she slid backward, and light came

on the dark, oily water between her and the piling. She was turned by powerful tugs, and then the pulsing of her machines started. Small ships, motorboats, sailboats, tugs, and paddle-wheelers, which were so crowded that they all swam lopsided alongside, kept pace with her on the first mile. Up above among the planes was a helicopter, in the open door of which a photographer sat, secured by a belt with his legs dangling. The Queen picked up speed on the way down the Clyde. The broad, pale green avenue of churned sea water appeared in her wake. After the bon voyage boats had whistled their last farewells and the planes turned back, one by one, everything became controlled and matter-of-fact, and as it was during the forgotten days of routine ocean travel.

As then, so now people lined up before a small table on the promenade deck and reserved their deck chairs. Pageboys with white gloves delivered cables. The first deck-walkers, in caps and leaning forward, started their runs around the ship, in the salon sat a polite string orchestra playing "Ouvre Tes Yeux Bleus, Ma Mignonne," and tea and cookies were passed around inside and outside.

I have often thought, when standing in the lobby of the Waldorf-Astoria in New York, that if it swayed a little one would have the feeling of being on board a big liner. The interiors of the *Queen Elizabeth* are such that you would think yourself in the lobby of the Waldorf-Astoria if it stopped swaying.

The Captain broadcast the progress of the ship from the bridge, and the passengers were all content—particularly the British at dinner the first night, when they broke open snowy rolls and spread butter on them with haste and swallowed them like hungry birds.

The only unhappy man aboard was an artist sent by a fashion magazine to illustrate an article about the resumption of luxury travel. In his attempts to catch the beau monde doing elegant things he wilted from day to day. He haunted smoking rooms and lounges, crept along the decks and sat in the forward bar for hours, his hand idle over his drawing pad.

The passengers were all nice people but unfashionable, in spite of the many titles on the list. They were a slurred, gray lot, moving around the deck, and in and out of the public rooms, alike as the deck chairs, and all the women looked as if they had done their own hair.

"I don't think it will ever be the same again," said the unhappy fashion artist.

"I say, that is the best thing that could ever happen," answered one of the British deck-walkers.

Upon the sundeck in the morning, Comrade Molotov took the air. He is a little man about five foot four. All the colors of his face, mustache, and eyes are faded pastel tints, and on his face is forever the expression of a disgruntled embryo. He was followed by an excessively healthy and oversized Russian, who wore a pea-soup-colored uniform, and marched usually eight feet in back of his charge, in heavy black boots.

During the war the English amused themselves about the generous display of overseas ribbons and decorations on the breasts of American soldiers. Now that it is over, there is still a large omelette of decorations on the coat of every elevator operator, steward, and engineer aboard the Queen, as it is on all porters, waiters, doormen, and bellhops in London.

For the type of ship she is, the *Queen Elizabeth* is admirably run and makes you very comfortable in the first class. As in all fast ships, the quarters of the second class are over the propellers and suffer from constant vibrations. Down there the ventilation in the inside cabins is bad. The third class is somewhat more quiet, located in the bow, but its decks are restricted.

In the time that this book was put together, I traveled on three ships. After the *Queen Elizabeth*, I took the *America* back to Europe and found her a very happy boat to be on.

The cabins were the largest I have ever seen, the beds like those you get when visiting somebody who has a nice home in the country. It's not your own

bed, but it's good; you can lie in it in every position. The comfort and décor of the cabin are such that a suburban garden with the neighbors' children belongs outside your door rather than a boat deck.

The deck is wide and ample, the public rooms are right, the food is good and properly served, and the hired help in all departments is correct. No longer does the deck steward say: "Hey, bud, got a match?" as once he did on our ships. He's been through school, and he looks as if he had graduated from West Point.

It seems, however, impossible to please all of the traveling public. A veteran commuter on the ocean, a very ancient grande dame, said to me, "You know, I love this ship, and I've been on all of them. There's no chi-chi, no ship's concert, and the Captain doesn't bother you. It runs smoothly. I love the brief and simple menu and prefer it infinitely to the lot of gick and sauces they used to offer—it's wholesome. There's only one thing I must complain about, and that's my room steward. He's a lovely, bright boy— and so nice. That's the trouble he's too nice, the dear boy. I'm used to those old broken-down room stewards, the real good old steward type, the kind that you didn't notice, who weren't there at all until the end of the voyage and they came for the tip. Now the one who takes care of me here, he's a dear boy. He looks as if he might be my grandson. It's embarrassing. He comes into my room with the breakfast tray, and here I am an old woman in bed in the morning, and not at all fit to receive anybody. You

passenger then said: "But I ordered ham and eggs —don't you know what ham and eggs are?" The young man was confused and said: "Just a moment, I'll get you the chief steward, sir." With a chestful of ribbons, the chief steward then came and said: "I beg your pardon, sir, you can 'ave bacon and haiggs and you can 'ave the 'am with the haiggs like this, but you can't 'ave the 'am and haiggs."

"But why not?" said the passenger. "Evidently you've got ham and also eggs. Why can't I have ham and eggs?"

"It's the kitchen, sir," said the head steward— "regulations." And in a fatherly voice he counseled, "Why don't you take the bacon and haiggs?"

Besides this there is a recommendation to be made to the heads of steamship corporations in general, concerning the first meal on sailing day. The passenger who boards the ship in Cherbourg has been on a train for hours, and he has eaten a poor meal on the boat train and been harassed by baggage problems. He had been standing on the windy Cherbourg·pier· and then boarded the tender. He has spent some more weary hours on the small boat, and finally around seven the liner comes in sight. It takes an additional hour until he is aboard. The passenger goes to his cabin and then heads for the dining room. The second steward is at the door of the dining room, all the tables are set up, the stewards stand waiting, but the passenger is told that he cannot be seated until he has obtained his table reservation. The passenger has to walk up two flights to the desk of the head steward, who has a plan on which all the tables are marked down, and he now gives out place cards. There are people who want to sit at small tables, others with friends, some have made advance reservations, and he has to fit all this into his plan, argue, cajole, and promise later changes. It takes time. The line of waiting passengers moves forward very slowly. The arrangement is bad for both passengers and crew. It would be much simpler, on the first day, to let people come in and sit down immediately wherever there is room and assign them to tables the next morning.

Sitting in the bar of the *Mauretania* on that crossing, I overheard this dialogue between a British Lord and a young American. And out of it we can get an idea how difficult life still is for some Englishmen.

know, I have to spend half an hour getting myself ready before I sit up and ring that bell."

A few months later, I took the *Mauretania* back to America. She is not the palatial boat that the old *Mauretania* was. She's rather what passed before the war as a good cabin-class boat. She is very steady, and generally well run. There are no telephones in the rooms. For your bath there is only sea water, hot or cold. The décor of the bar reminds you of a Santa Monica drugstore. The food, however, is excellent, and with a few adjustments the service would be perfect.

There are, for example, two small elevators that take passengers down to the dining room, and in these as in most ships' elevators only a few people have room. To run these, the two fattest men among the crew have been assigned and each of them displaces two passengers. A small briefing in the dining room concerning American eating habits would also help. A passenger asked for ham and eggs for breakfast one day, and the steward, a very nice boy, was bewildered. He moved into a corner with the menu and studied it for a while and then he spoke to another steward, who gave him advice, and after a lengthy consultation he went out into the kitchen. Eventually he came back and put two fried eggs on a plate in front of the passenger. The passenger said: "But I ordered ham and eggs." "You shall have them, sir," said the steward, and went back to the sideboard, from which he brought a silver dish with two good-sized slices of cold ham on it. The

Ile d'Yeu

Lord: "I say, are you attending the Captain's party?"

American: "I don't think so."

Lord: "Well, do as you like. I'm going—have to, since he's an Englishman and I'm one. I can't very well refuse, I'd hurt his feeling if I didn't go—and I don't like to hurt people's feelings. He's a little tin god—or rather a big tin god aboard his ship, you know. It's like Consuls. One has to be especially careful not to hurt their feelings. They're awfully class-conscious."

American: "Why?"

Lord: "Oh, I suppose it's because they're treated badly by the Embassy people. When one is asked, one must always go to their parties. But they in turn are never asked to anyone's house —just once a year, to a garden party."

Americans: "Why?"

Lord: "They're all bounders."

American: "You mean crooks?"

Lord: "No, no, dear boy—honest as the day is long."

American: "You mean heels—"

Lord: "Heavens, no—not cads—I said bounders."

American: "What's a bounder?"

Lord: "A bounder—a bounder is the son of a fish-monger—something like that. Now do you know what I mean?"

American: "What's wrong with that?"

Lord: "Of course, reahlly, these days, one shouldn't call them bounders because they're not any more bounders than anyone else is, including you or me."

American: "You mean they're common?"

Lord: "Oh no, I didn't mean that—let me explain. Now I'll go to that Captain's dinner tonight, but I won't bother changing—that's something you might copy. I'm putting on my old blue suit and a pair of black shoes, and with that I wear a black bow tie and I look dressed for dinner and no one knows the difference, but I would never do that if I were going to the Embassy. Now do you know what I mean?"

The American looked puzzled and the Lord said: "I say, come out of it," and he called the steward in a ringing voice and ordered a drink.

Toward the end of the voyage there was another such conversation piece.

Lord: "I say, dear boy, what are you giving the room steward?"

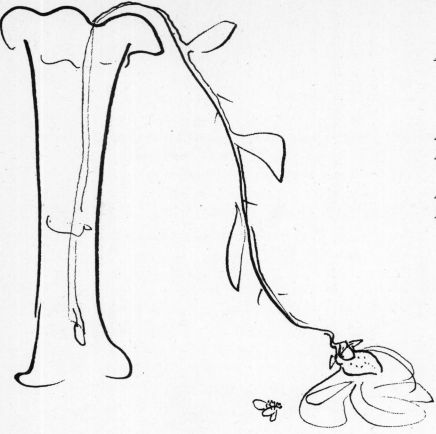

Lord: "Well, that's all right for you. You have dollars to throw away. We've got to be careful. By the way, what are you going to give the man above?"

American: "You mean the man below?"

Lord: "When I say the man above, I mean the man below—the dining room is below, isn't it?"

American: "Yes—what are you going to give him?"

Lord: "Well, as I said, you know my dollars are few. I have a villa outside of Paris, and I have an American Colonel in it who is in the Graves Registration thing—nice chap, whisky drinker, but he is not what the French call 'droll.' You know, we English say an amusing thing in an hour or two—but your people, as a rule, are just determined and unhappy drinkers. He pays me in dollars. As for the man above, two and ten, I'd say—and a dollar for *the deck stewards* each, and fifty cents apiece for the bounders in the lift."

American: "And the head steward?"

Lord: "Oh, give him a pound, and a pound for the wine steward."

American: "And the bar steward?"

Lord: "We've tipped him all along, so let's give him a dollar."

The above is about right in the way of tips for such boats as the Queens and the *Mauretania*.

In Hollywood somebody once said to me, "There was a silence so great that you could hear the buoys in Ambrose Channel ringing." I have to think of that every time I see them. They are the tacks in the green carpet that runs into New York.

American: "I wanted to ask you, what are you going to give him?"

Lord: "Two and ten—I think."

American: "What's that in American money?"

Lord: "Let's ask. I say, S T E W A R D !"

Steward: "Yes, Milord."

Lord: "What's two and ten in American money?"

Steward: "It's two dollars and eighty cents for the pound, Milord."

Lord: "Now that's disgusting, the bounder is not giving us the proper rate, it's really ten dollars."

American: "Let's give him ten dollars then."

Postscript

To check on myself and on the information I have given in this book, which was collected in the years 1946 and '47, I made a quick trip to Europe this summer.

What the Swiss passenger recommended in '45 concerning flight has been done—and more. This time I left LaGuardia on an overnight plane of Air France at seven P.M. and arrived in Paris, without stopping, the next day at noon. Dinner on board was good; I slept in a fair bed. The experience was bewildering—for me, this was no longer travel. The Place de la Concorde has moved up to Madison and Forty-sixth Street. The service is superb, and you feel secure. A captain with silver hair and a fine French face, and of the dignity and weight that you used to find on great ships before the war, comes into the cabin and wishes you bon appetit. With this Santa Claus on board, the most nervous passenger will fly in peace.

It is no longer practical to live on the Swiss exchange regulations, as I stated on page 73 of this book. The dollar has gone up. Everything else that I said about the beautiful democracy is still true. Air transport is good. The Swiss customs examination is brief and efficient. Something, however, should be done about the Zurich airport. After the examination of passports and luggage, the passengers are put into a glass-enclosed room, and though

all the other parts of the building have awnings, this room has not. It is small and, from about noon until five, like a hothouse. There is a guard outside who unlocks the door only when the plane is ready to take off. It's the most uncomfortable arrangement in this tourist-comfort-conscious country.

The Arlberg-Orient Express remains at the level of efficiency and comfort that I described last, but now you are so used to it that it would make you uncomfortable if it were faster, cleaner, or swayed and rattled less, as it clanks out of Paris to Vienna.

In Austria the people are happy that the Allies remain in occupation—or rather, that the French, the English, and the Americans remain. General Bethouart continues to do his good work. He is having French classics translated for the Austrians. The members of Tourisme et Travail, about whom I spoke on page 85, are no longer allowed in Tyrol. To be a member of Tourisme et Travail one had to be a member of the Communist party—a fact I never knew before. "Obviously," a French officer said to me, "they would make the very poorest Communists and have no idea what it means. You have seen them. You agree, no?"

I agree, yes. "But why were they members?" I asked him.

"Oh, chiefly out of protest, swindled over and over again by every other party, promises unkept, their

187

money worthless, their stomachs empty. Give them a decent life—they don't ask much—and you will have few Communists in France."

The bureaucrats of Austria continue to hinder progress. Example: In a gazette which is published for the information of innkeepers and to which I subscribe is the following regulation: "Innkeepers are warned that, if they serve Kracherln [soda pop] carelessly, they lay themselves open to punishment of prison terms of up to three months and fines of five hundred schillings. The Kracherln must be sold in the proper bottle; that is, if the man who supplies you with Kracherln in a bottle of other manufacture than his own, that is to say, with another trademark or another firm on the label or the bottle or the cap thereof than his, the manufacturer who regularly supplies you, and you as the innkeeper do not instruct your help to pick out the Kracherln that fall under this description and refuse to sell them, not only you, but the servitor, are guilty under the above decree." This is one of ten new decrees concerning only the serving of soft drinks.

The Akten, of which I wrote on page 79, are still being handed from desk to desk. De-Nazification is slow, as those in charge of the process will be without work when this business is over. The administration of the various punishments and the whole involved machinery employs thousands of Austrians who would have to look for jobs otherwise. The persecution mania became so great that one far-seeing minister, Helmer, finally decided to liquidate the political party which was made up of former inmates of concentration camps.

I am happy to report that the cured Pappelmeier Pepperl is about to be released and will return to his old home at the Golden Opportunity in Regensburg, where the work tables are already heaped with broken things for him to fix.

Arles is a good city to come back to. The Saucissons d'Arles are real again.

There is a little improvement on the Ile d'Yeu, and, so far, there has been enough rain and a good summer season. Walking out of the Street of the Sardine, I came to a shop, and in its window I found a water color which I had made of the Isle d'Yeu as it had been before the war. I now bought it for three dollars, although the proprietor said it was worth five. It is reproduced on pages 184 and 185.

In Paris on the way back I saw my underworld friend, Georges, who has decided that the good days of the black market will soon be over, and has put his savings into a clandestine bordello, where he goes over the day's take with a green eyeshade on his forehead and peculiar French cuffs made of flowered stuff with elastic sewn into the hems on both ends. These he slides over his sleeve to protect them as he audits his business. In the way of local thinking, he has become a respectable man and has une bonne affaire.

"There is a black market," he says, "and you can get about ten francs more for the dollar than at the bank, but then, who wants to soil his hands with that?" He thinks of marrying and leading an orderly life. He thinks of marrying Mademoiselle the Gouvernante of Numéro treize, combining his initiative with her great experience. "It is unmöglich," he says, "that we fail."

In Paris the black market restaurant had disappeared, and its place was taken by the chi-chi restaurants of the catégorie exceptionnelle.

In Italy I saw the elections. The statue of Garibaldi in Milano was wired for sound, and he said all day long, "I am not a Communist." The Christian Democrats showed Garbo in Ninotchka as part of their propaganda, and the Communists had Gary Cooper in For Whom the Bell Tolls.

In New York I have a small dog, and, when it is cold outside or raining, he hates to go out. When his sweater is picked up and is about to be put on him, he can make himself heavy and stiff and delay getting into it. With many maneuvers, he finally tries to rub the sweater off against the back of a chair or hides in back of pillows and drawings, and all the time he has an expression of the greatest misery on his small and old face.

I thought of him in Paris one day. In its carriage a hundred feet from the Hôtel Crillon, close to the American Embassy, sat a little baby, thin and tired and with an old face. Beside it was a woman with a face as old and tired as that of the baby. The old woman brought from her dirty bag a piece of cheese the size of a gambling dice, held it in front of the baby's face, and said, "Eat that." The baby looked at it exactly as my little dog does at the sweater when it rains. The woman then produced a tiny bit of gravel-colored bread and repeated, "Eat that." The baby now looked as if it were going to start crying, but opened its mouth and took the bread and cheese. You feel ashamed to live in a good hotel and have all you want to eat. You wonder, also, how it is possible that here, in 1948, after all the conferences and meetings, this is still possible.

August 1948   L. B.

ABOUT THE AUTHOR

BORN IN 1898 in Tyrol into a family of innkeepers, Ludwig Bemelmans spent a rebellious youth in Bavaria. He was eventually given the choice of going either to reform school or to America. He chose the latter.

He arrived here at the age of seventeen with letters of introduction to various New York innkeepers, and for a while he worked in hotels in New York, but again he followed his wanderlust.

Bemelmans knows this country better than most Americans. He is all but a born New Yorker. He lived with the Blackfeet Indians in Montana, and he is especially proud of the fact that he can steer a boat in and out of the deepest Everglades swamps. He joined the American Army in the first World War, after which he again took up his travels. He writes and paints for THE NEW YORKER, VOGUE, TOWN AND COUNTRY, and has a wide audience in England and on the Continent.

As has his friend, the playwright Ferenc Molnar, so Bemelmans has an apartment of six rooms, one of which is in New York, the second in Paris, others in London, Rome and Capri, and the last in a mountain village in Tyrol in which his family, now reconciled, still run the old inn.